℆

Islands of Eight Million Smiles

Idol Performance and Symbolic Production

in Contemporary Japan

Harvard East Asian Monographs 252

To Hitomi

In sweet and sour memories of our youth!

CR

Islands of Eight Million Smiles

Idol Performance and Symbolic Production

in Contemporary Japan

Hiroshi Aoyagi

Published by the Harvard University Asia Center
Distributed by Harvard University Press
Cambridge (Massachusetts) and London 2005

Printed in the United States of America

The Harvard University Asia Center publishes a monograph series and, in coordination with the Fairbank Center for East Asian Research, the Korea Institute, the Reischauer Institute of Japanese Studies, and other faculties and institutes, administers research projects designed to further scholarly understanding of China, Japan, Vietnam, Korea, and other Asian countries. The Center also sponsors projects addressing multidisciplinary and regional issues in Asia.

Library of Congress Cataloging-in-Publication Data

Aoyagi, Hiroshi, 1963-
    Islands of eight million smiles : idol performance and symbolic production in contemporary Japan / Hiroshi Aoyagi.
        p. cm. -- (Harvard East Asian monographs 252)
    Includes bibliographical references (p.   ) and index.
    ISBN 0-674-01773-0 (cloth : alk. paper)
    1. Popular music--Social aspects--Japan. 2. Music and youth--Japan.   I. Title.
II. Series.
    ML3918.P67A84 2005
    781.64'0835'0952--dc22

                                                        2004030643

Index by Gavin Whitelaw

 ♾ Printed on acid-free paper

Last figure below indicates year of this printing
15 14 13 12 11 10 09 08 07 06 05

The characters that stamp products as commodities, and whose establishment is a necessary preliminary to the circulation of commodities, have already acquired the stability of natural, self-understood forms of social life, before man seeks to decipher, not their historical character, for in his eyes they are immutable, but their meaning. Consequently it was the analysis of the prices of commodities that alone led to the determination of the magnitude of value, and it was the common expression of all commodities in money that alone led to the establishment of their characters as values. It is, however, just this ultimate money-form of the world of commodities that actually conceals, instead of disclosing, the social character of private labor, and the social relations between the individual producers.

—Karl Marx, "The Fetishism of
Commodities and the Secret Thereof"

Imagination envisions the reconciliation of the individual with the whole, of desire with realization, of happiness with reason. While this harmony has been removed into utopia by the established reality principle, fantasy insists that it must and can become real, that behind the illusion lies knowledge. The truths of imagination are first realized when fantasy itself takes form, when it creates a universe of perception and comprehension–a subjective and at the same time objective universe. This occurs in art. The analysis of the cognitive function of fantasy is thus led to aesthetics as the "science of beauty": behind the aesthetic form lies the repressed harmony of sensuousness and reason—the eternal protest against the organization of life by the logic of domination, the critique of the performance principle.

—Herbert Marcuse, "Fantasy and Utopia"

Construction is not opposed to agency; it is the necessary scene of agency, the very terms in which agency is articulated and becomes culturally intelligible. The critical task for feminism is not to establish a point of view outside of constructed identities; that conceit is the construction of an epistemological model that would disavow its own cultural location and, hence, promote itself as a global subject, a position that deploys precisely the imperialist strategies that feminism ought to criticize. The critical task is, rather, to locate strategies of subversive repetition enabled by those constructions, to affirm the local possibilities of intervention through participating in precisely those practices of repetition that constitute identity and, therefore, present the immanent possibility of contesting them.

—Judith Butler, "From Parody to Politics"

Acknowledgments

Michael Taussig's vivid illustration of what happened to the local ways of life in South America as the result of their collision with capitalism expanded the horizons of the critical study of commodity fetishism. It provided subsequent researchers in the social sciences and humanities with opportunities to examine local symbolism and folklore as windows into the condition of existence that is becoming ever more saturated by the principle of the market. Symbols such as the devil are stunningly apt signifiers of the alienation experienced by South American peasants and mineworkers. Only when the relationship between these symbols, the local lifeworld, and the intercultural (if not global) spread of the market system is exposed do curious nonlocals such as ourselves come to understand and appreciate these initially meaningless symbols.

My aim in this book is to expose the social meaning of a conspicuous form of symbolism in contemporary urban Japan. This form is represented by young media-promoted personalities known as *aidoru*, which is the Japanese form of the English word "idol." Idols are packaged and merchandized as adolescent role models by their promotion agencies. Although idol performances have been ridiculed by their critics as artless ever since they emerged in the late 1960s, idols continue to attract hundreds of people who consume their images in the form of various commodities. The continuing popularity of idols provides the fashion, cosmetic, and publishing industries with chances to use these idols as allegorical means to market their products, maximize profits, and gain greater public recognition.

Inspired by the fact that no thorough ethnographic study of the pop-idol phenomena exists in Japan or elsewhere, I decided to examine this curious genre of popular-cultural performance as a contemporary ritual that contributes to the habituation of capitalism, especially the fetishism of commodities. Precisely because these young personalities speak to the sexual desire of their audiences while their images are affiliated with various trendy goods, they function as "facilitators" of capitalist values in the specific social, cultural, and historical context of contemporary urban Japan. My research, based on eighteen months of ethnographic fieldwork in the Japanese entertainment industry followed by a series of surveys, analyzes idols as vehicles of cultural *qua* commercial production. I explore the criteria of idol production, the ways in which idols are produced, the perceptions of idol performances by producers, performers, and consumers, and the social consequences of idols' popularity through the examination of female idols. This study of idol production offers an empirical account of the dialogue that occurs between capitalism, a particular rhetoric of self-making, and the lifestyle of consumers—all of which are mediated by idol symbolism and the manufacturing institutions that function as the cultural apparatus. The analysis developed here hopes to provide theoretical and methodological contributions to the study of celebrities and their relationship with the expanding force of capitalism in other social, cultural, and historical settings.

A large portion of my fieldwork was assisted by Toshi Asai, a longtime acquaintance whose association with Japanese show business provided me with many insights. It was the support of my academic mentors, Professors Millie Creighton, William McKellin, and Elvi Whitaker, that allowed me to develop the blueprint of this book at the Department of Anthropology and Sociology, the University of British Columbia. I also received insightful comments from Professors Merry White and Helen Hardacre while working on the draft of this book as a postdoctoral fellow at the Reischauer Institute of Japanese Studies during the years 1999 and 2000. I also received continuous support from Mr. Akio Nakamori, a cultural critic, Mr. Masanobu Naitō, an advertising agent, and Mr. Masahisa Aizawa of Sun Music Productions, to whom I am grateful. These people were able to analyze their activities in the entertainment industry critically, and they did not hesitate to provide me with opinions when I needed them. I also want to acknowledge Tangen Harada Rōshi, Scott Hurley, David Ryniker, Naoki Tabeta, Shigeki Takeo, Gavin Whitelaw, and my significant other, Azusa Arakawa, without whose unconditional support and friendship this project would have never been completed. I would also like to send my gratitude to Ann Klefstad for her assistance in editing the original draft of this book.

Finally, I thank the Faculty of Graduate Studies at the University of British Columbia and the Reischauer Institute of Japanese Studies at Harvard University for their funding of this research project.

H.A.

Contents

Figures   xv

Introduction   1

1   The Ethnography of Idol Production: An Overview   25

2   The Making of Japanese Adolescent Role Models   56

3   Idol Performances and Gender Identities   86

4   Explorations in the Field of Competing Styles   126

5   Following the Trajectory of an Idol Superstar   166

6   Idol Fans and the Adoration Cult   204

7   The Spread of Idol Performances in New
    Industrial Economies   232

    Conclusion   259

Reference Matter

Works Cited   269

Index   285

Figures

I.1   Crowd of young people around a kiosk
where idol goods are sold   5

I.2   Scenes from an audition in Tokyo   8

1.1   A sample column by the author   53

1.2   The author at work with idol informants   54

2.1   Idol fans gathering around their object of worship   71

2.2   A cute personality represented on a postcard   75

2.3   An idol autograph accompanied by a
cute animated character   77

2.4   Scenes from a walkway in Shinjuku station, Tokyo   79

3.1   Sample images of *kogal*   103

3.2   Idol candidates undergoing a choreography lesson   110

3.3   A scene from dance practice at the
Body-Wave Agency   115

4.1   The cover of a Noriko Sakai fan club newsletter
called *Nori-P Times*   143

4.2   A scene from *SPA!* photography session   152

4.3   The first cover page of the November 15, 1995,
issue of *SPA!*   153

4.4 The second cover page of the November 15, 1995, issue of *SPA!*   155

4.5 The third cover page of the November 15, 1995, issue of *SPA*   156

5.1 Seiko Matsuda with her typical cute, naïve look.   173

5.2 Seiko Matsuda as a well-established pop diva   174

6.1 Enthusiastic students interact with their idol of the year   205

6.2 Miyuki Asano chatting with fans online   213

6.3 An editor in chief organizes the layout of an upcoming issue   223

6.4 Enthusiastic fans cheer their idol in a concert   226

7.1 The cover of the 1996 issue of Japan's *Asian Travellers Journal*   233

☙

Islands of Eight Million Smiles

Introduction

In the spring of 1996, Nippon Telegraph and Telephone Corporation (NTT) posted a large billboard on a busy street in the Shibuya district of Tokyo. On it was the image of Ryōko Hirosue, a slender sixteen-year-old girl who had made her way into the Tokyo-based entertainment world from the rural prefecture of Kōchi to join approximately 1,100 female idol talents (*josei aidoru tarento*).[1] Hirosue acquired her chance to pursue a career in Japanese show business by entering an audition, the Clearasil Shiny Face Contest, and winning its grand prize.

On the billboard, Hirosue appeared in short black hair, a clean white shirt, and short brown skirt. She was standing with her legs apart, making direct eye contact with the viewer. On her side were two small paging machines that NTT had invented, called DoCoMo. Toward her right was a catch phrase, "[I] will start improving. Ryōko Hirosue" (*Yoku naru, o hajimemasu. Hirosue Ryōko*), which complemented another statement on her left, "Improving. DoCoMo" (*Yoku naru. DoCoMo*). Identical billboards and posters appeared throughout Japan, along with television commercials that advertised DoCoMo and featured Hirosue in action.

It did not take long for Hirosue to attract public attention and become one of the most celebrated public personalities of the year. Considered by the public to be cute-looking, bright, and healthy, Hirosue appeared in magazines, television shows, and radio pro-

---

1. In Japan, the family name is written before the given name; Ryōko Hirosue, for example, is written Hirosue Ryōko. In this book, however, I apply the English name order to all Japanese names.

grams. Many teenagers and young adults talked about her, followed her to concerts, and screamed in joy when encountering her at public events. Her photo album was published in September 1996, followed by the release of her debut single in April 1997. Her debut song was composed by Maria Takeuchi, a well-known singer and songwriter. More than 360,000 copies of the photo album (according to the October 23, 1996, issue of *SPA!*), and 600,000 copies of the CD (according to the June 17, 1997, issue of *Josei jishin*) were sold. These numbers signify smash hits according to Japanese standards.

In spite of this growing popularity, Hirosue downplayed her celebrity status. In a column, "People This Week," that appeared in one of Japan's most widely read weekly magazines, *SPA!*, the editor characterized Hirosue's talent as marvelous, to which Hirosue responded that she was "just ordinary." Hirosue argued:

It's amazing for me to receive such a comment, but there is nothing extraordinary about me. I am told that to be "not extraordinary" is my charm. . . . I mean I am just an average person. I get many fan letters from young women these days, and they say they want to enter show business, too. When I told the members of my staff about it, they teased me and said: "Doesn't this mean that if Ryōko can do it, I can do it, too?" I wonder whether or not this was a compliment. (*SPA!*, October 23, 1996: 11)

Rather than confirming her uniqueness and accepting her celebrity status as many Hollywood personalities might do (as can be seen in programs aired in the United States such as *Entertainment Tonight*), Hirosue presented herself as a humble person who wished to be "remarkably ordinary," leading the editor to comment that her "unaffected purity is the source of her adorable personal quality and her popularity."

The point here is not so much whether an idol talent like Hirosue is actually pure (the truth of which we do not really know) or ordinary (if she were truly ordinary, she would not be considered a star). Rather, it is the fact that she is presented this way. Hirosue's case demonstrates the way marketing corporations package adolescent female personalities. It also shows what it means to be adorable in Japan today. At the level of public performance, idolization of Hirosue represents a symbolic process whereby Hirosue framed her personality in a publicly adorable way and transformed herself from an ordinary young local girl to a renowned public figure in Japanese popular culture and consumer society. This packaging of self, in which an adolescent persona is signified as "cute," "pure," "modest," and "full of promise," is a cultural practice that aims to collectivize public imagination.

This book will focus on the symbolic qualities of idols, and how these qualities relate to the conceptualization of adolescent selfhood in Japan as well as other developing Asian countries into which Japanese popular cultural forms are disseminated. The understanding of idol qualities and their instrumentality in the organization of youthful lifestyles adds a new dimension to the growing body of anthropological literature on public socialization. I will use Japanese idols as windows to examine how the self is capitalized. Ethnographic descriptions in this book concentrate on how the idol-manufacturing industry absorbs young people into its system of production, molds their selves into marketable personalities, commercializes their images for the masses, and contributes to the ongoing construction of ideal images of adolescent selfhood. This capitalization process is commercial, social, and cultural at the same time.

THE WORLD OF
JAPANESE POP IDOLS

Idols are designed to contribute to the industry's establishment in the market by virtue of their abilities to attract people and perform as lifestyle role models. Whether they are loved or disliked, widely admired or ridiculed, idols inform their viewers about appearances and personal qualities that are considered socially appropriate and trendy. As such, idols constitute a showcase of selfhood in reference to which consumers, especially young people, can construct their own self-images. In the subsequent chapters I will attempt to capture the different aspects of this commercial *qua* symbolic configuration.

Idols perform as all-around popular talents (*tarento*) who appear mainly on television. They sing melodramatic love songs, dance to peppy electronic tunes, act in dramas, and strike poses in commercials that advertise certain products. Images of idols also appear on the covers of popular journals, most notably fashion magazines. Their shapely poses can also be found on billboards, many of which garnish the streets of Tokyo as well as other towns in Japan. There is a wide variety of idol memorabilia or "idol goods" (*aidoru guzzu*), including compact discs, photo albums, calendars, telephone cards, T-shirts, key chains, breast pins, as well as all sorts of stationery goods: notebooks, note pads, pencil cases, and bookmarks on which idol images are printed. One can observe crowds of young people and their parents in retail outlets where these goods are sold (Fig. I.1). Thousands of these commodities are sold each year, allowing their producers to develop a multimillion yen industry.

Idol performances, known collectively as "the idol-pop," emerged in Japan in the late 1960s in the general category of popular music, or *kayōkyoku*. Unlike the singers of many earlier forms of pop music, which touched on more mature subjects and were targeted mainly at adults, idols came to represent adolescence. They are roughly equivalent to young idols and idol groups in the United States and Western Europe such as Frank Sinatra in the 1930s, Paul Anka and Tony Bennett in the 1950s, Silvie Vartan, the Shirelles, and Shangri-Las in the 1960s; Shawn Cassidy and the Bay City Rollers in the 1970s; Debbie Gibson, Menudo, Candi, and New Kids on the Block in the 1980s; the Beastie Boys, Shampoo, Back Street Boys, Hanson, and Spice Girls in the 1990s; and Britney Spears and Christina Aguilera in the first decade of the 2000s.

During my fieldwork in Tokyo, a record company employee told me that the creation of idol-pop as a commercial genre in Japan was influenced by a 1963 French movie called *Cherchez L'idole*, which dramatized a couple's search for a stolen diamond. In the story, a young man steals a diamond for his girlfriend and places it in an electric guitar as he enters a music shop while running from the police. He and his girlfriend are subsequently drawn into frustrating interactions with clerks and acquaintances as they return to the shop and try to regain the diamond. It turns out that there are five identical guitars, and they are reserved for popular bands. The

Fig. I.1 Crowd of young people around a kiosk where idol goods
are sold (photo by the author, February 1995).

story takes a complicated turn. This movie featured French pop
stars of that time including Silvie Vartan, Charles Aznavour, and
Johnny Hallyday, and there are scenes in which these personalities
appear on stage and sing their songs. When the movie was released
in Japan, its title was translated as *Aidoru o sagase*, or "In Search of
an Idol." The movie was a hit, and one of the featured teen idols,
Silvie Vartan, was invited to Japan and became a celebrity. According to my informant, an employee of a record company that handled the release of Vartan's song in Japan, this led a producer to
create "idol-pop" as a new genre of pop music in Japan, one that
emphasized the promotion of adolescent personalities.

Adult critics ridiculed the apparent crudeness of idol performances as "artless," "fluffy," or "bubble-gum," but this did not dis-
courage young people from taking active parts in idol production
and consumption. In the 1970s and throughout the 1980s, idol performances generated a whole new domain of popular culture that
was happily sponsored by the media as well as retail corporations
specializing in the construction of profit-generating teen-oriented

trends. Contests were held each year in which hundreds of young women and men participated, each hoping to become the next new star. Some of these contests took the form of local auditions, while others such as the television program *Star tanjō* (Star search) were broadcast nationally as the gateway to the "dream factory." Support groups and fan clubs sprang up to bolster the efforts of idol wannabes, the most successful of whom made it onto the record charts and into the national consciousness via appearances on popular television shows such as *Best Ten*.

Promotion agencies orchestrated the marketing of idols and idol groups. One of the most successful was and is Johnny's, which focused exclusively on the promotion of young male talent. In 1967, Johnny's debuted its first official idol group, the Four Leaves, whose popularity lasted through the next decade. Ever since, Johnny's has dominated the male side of the Japanese idol market, producing a stream of big names over the years, including individual stars such as Hiromi Gō, Toshihiko Tahara, and Masahiko Kondō, as well as groups like Hikaru Genji, Shōnentai, SMAP, Kinki Kids, Tokio, and V6. On the women's side, Hori Agency and Sun Music Productions have been the dominant producers.

In 1971, three female idols, Mari Amachi, Saori Minami, and Rumiko Koyanagi banded together to form a popular trio known as San-Nin Musume (Three Young Girls). This was followed in 1973 by the appearance of another female idol trio, Chūsan Trio, or the "trio of ninth-grade schoolgirls," which included Momoe Yamaguchi, Masako Mori, and Junko Sakurada. All these female idols went on to be solo megastars. Countless subsequent female idols and groups have followed these pioneers into stardom, including Candies and Pink Ladies in the 1970s; Seiko Matsuda, Onyanko Club (Kitten Club), Noriko Sakai, and Wink during the 1980s; and Rie Miyazawa, Yumiko Takahashi, Yuki Uchida, Ryōko Hirosue, Rie Tomosaka, and Morning Musume (Morning Girls) in the 1990s.

Idol performances continue to attract "wannabes" today, and the number of applicants for the nearly twenty contests I observed during my fieldwork in 1996 ranged anywhere between 100 and 10,000, depending on the size and reputation of promotion agencies that held them (Fig. I.2). Hundreds of books and magazines are written about pop idols each year, in popular, semi-academic, and academic genres. Journalists write some of these texts, while researchers and cultural critics produce the others. Many essays, purportedly written by idols and presented as first-person accounts, are likewise published and bought yearly. Fan clubs and support groups develop as idol candidates make their debut. Some of these voluntary support groups produce their own events and publications that are intended to contribute to the celebration of their adolescent stars. Some enthusiastic idol-fans are referred to as *aidoru otaku* or "hardcore idol aficionados" for their cultlike devotion. They follow their favorite idols to various events, collect idol goods, and embellish their living space with idol-related materials—often to the extent that nothing else really matters to them. Together, these events, materials, and expressive behaviors constitute the "idol fad" (*aidoru boom*).

New commercial technologies advance the idol fad. An example of this is the emergence of the sound system called *karaoke* (empty orchestra) in the 1980s. The *karaoke* system uses prerecorded musical accompaniments on laser discs. This technological dissemination created amusement plazas where people could get together to enjoy singing along with video-monitor displays of lyrics. Socialization in *karaoke* bars has become an essential part of leisure-time activities in Japan, especially among young people, thereby contributing to the transmission and thus popularization of idol songs. Songs that are requested in *karaoke* plazas throughout Japan are carefully monitored and rated, and talent promotion agencies and media institutions use this rating as a way of evaluating whether their talents may or may not be further promoted.

Advances in internet technology in the 1990s facilitated the idol fad. There are hundreds of websites on idols, some of which are officially owned and managed by promotion agencies while others are constructed unofficially by fans and voluntary support groups. Common features of idol homepages include biography, discography, and photographs. Some sites offer message boards where idol fans can post supportive comments. Other sites offer discussion

Fig. I.2 Scenes from an audition contest in Tokyo
(photo by the author, June 1995).

forums where fans can exchange their opinions. Some promotion agencies and media networks establish cyberspace communication programs for which fans can register and occasionally participate in real-time e-mail exchanges with their favorite idols.

Japanese idols are becoming global icons in the sense that the popularity of these adolescent personalities has recently extended far beyond the Japanese archipelago. Idol groupies are emerging in other Asian countries, and Japanese idols make frequent trips to these countries to give concerts or to participate in media events. Their images frequently appear in local newspapers and popular journals. Homegrown idols are emerging in these countries, and the stamp of the Japanese idol styles on many of these new stars is unmistakable. Idol enthusiast groups are growing in Europe and North America as well, as can be evidenced from an increasing number of internet homepages and idol conventions held in these areas.

Idol performances are by no means the main genre of Japanese pop culture, and the entertainment industry offers a wide variety of performing arts to satisfy the demands of different taste groups. In pop music, for example, there are folk, rock, hip-hop, and country-like *enka* alongside idol-pop. In my view, however, idol performances offer important anthropological insights regarding the ways in which the ideal images of adolescent selfhood are socially constructed. The gist of idol performances, then, is to socialize young personalities.

My objective in writing this book on idols is to demonstrate the significance of symbolism based on what David Harvey (1985) has called "studies on the urbanization of capital," which are primarily concerned with the process in which labor, working under the control of capitalism, creates environments with specific kinds of spatial configurations. In this process, capitalist institutions try to shape in their image physical landscapes and, by extension, social relations according to their commercial interests. Idols are personified symbols, their performances contemporary rituals in a form of popular art, and their manufacturing industry is a culture industry. I will show how the network of commercial institutions in contemporary urban Japan produces and uses idols as allegorical means to cultivate its territory and habituate its corporate ideology.

Roy Rappaport (1999) defines ritual as the performance of more or less invariant sequences of formal acts and utterances that generate collective consciousness by constructing meaningful orders in a society. Ritual appropriates knowledge and encodes morality through the representation of the sacred or through the shared awareness of the divine (1999: 27). According to Rappaport, rituals are observed in religious practices of traditional societies, and they are important for the continuation of human life, but they tend to get lost with the rise of scientific authority in modern societies. In contrast, the Japanese ethnologist Eiji Ōtsuka (1989) contends that rituals continue to exist in contemporary urban societies, manifested in popular arts and media events, in reference to which individuals organize their lifeworld.[2] In agreement with Ōtsuka, I will describe how the idol industry develops socializing rituals that provide Japanese adolescents with a passage that links the self with society in accordance with what their producers perceive as appropriate personal appearances and qualities.

While the practitioners of traditional rituals follow the prescribed set of behavioral rules in order to bring about the desired transformations in participants, those who compete for survival in the contemporary market develop through trial and error their own set of rules that could be characterized as contemporary popular rituals. Producers try hard to symbolize marketable personalities, while performers struggle to mold themselves into symbolic images, in order to establish their positions in the market economy that conditions contemporary urban society. A study on the meaningful construction of contemporary rituals would contribute to the understanding of how certain values, behaviors, and attitudes

---

2. This view bears a similarity to that of William Noonan (1996), which perceives hospitalization in contemporary urban societies as a set of contemporary rites of passage: that is, hospitals are shown to serve as a liminal space in which the medical staff develops a series of rituals that transform the patients' selves from diseased to healthy states. For the use of popular culture and the mass media by the spiritualists to develop a new form of commercialized religious ritual around the problem of abortion, see Hardacre 1997.

are customized in a present-day consumer society by a group of people who control the modes and means of production.

In the world of consumer capitalism in which symbolic competition over stylistic details of goods sold in the market becomes an important cultural logic, the popularity of idols is measured in reference to how much and in what ways their images appeal to their buyers.[3] Thus, the analysis of idol symbolism must take into account the dynamic relationship between trendsetters and the consumers of these trends—particularly the relationship between the ideal images of adolescent selfhood that are represented by idols on the one hand, and the buyers of these images on the other. Which personalities and styles become popular, how they become popular, and why, are the questions with which idol producers, journalists, fans, and researchers all cope. Although my intention here is not to provide journalistic accounts of idol performances or critiques of particular idols in Japan, I will consider cases that demonstrate how certain personalities, their promoters, and their critics deal with styles in the public arena. I do this in order to provide points of entry into a critique of late capitalism. Such a critique considers how the system of symbolic production furnishes a corporate ideology to a contemporary urban setting, and it illustrates how the participants in such a symbolic system, including the trendsetters and the trend-buyers, are assimilated into this system.

SYMBOLS OF COMMODITY FETISHISM: THE DEVIL

In his groundbreaking work, *Devil and Commodity Fetishism in South America* (1980), Michael Taussig provides an insightful ethnographic study of commodity fetishism that shows how the principles of market economy reshape local ways of life. Taussig uncovers the social meaning of the devil used as a symbol in the rural communities of Columbia and Bolivia. He demonstrates how this symbol, contrasted against the symbol of the saint, relates to

---

3. See, for example, Bourdieu 1984, 1993; Jameson 1984; Ewen 1988; and Clammer 1997.

commodity fetishism, a concept that Karl Marx elaborated in *Das Kapital* (vol. 1, 1867).

Commodity fetishism represents the historical condition of the people who incorporate it as a cultural practice: in the cases of the Columbian and Bolivian communities that Taussig emphasizes, it signifies an intensive capitalist development to which the members of these communities were exposed after the Spanish conquest. Local peasants and tin-mine workers used the image of the devil as a symbolic instrument that mediated the tension between two otherwise incompatible ways of objectifying human conditions: the pre-capitalist mode of production that arose from the sense that organic unity is maintained between people and things that they produce; and the capitalized mode of production in which the economics of commodity marketing subordinated people to things that they produce. The devil signified the evils of capitalism, and folktales about devils were developed as a way for plantation workers and tin miners to make sense of the harsh realities of their everyday lives as subjugated to the market economy (Taussig 1980: 26–38).

Taussig's aim in his study is to guide readers from the industrialized world to think critically about the exotic ideas and customs that are associated with the market organization of human affairs, especially the socioeconomic system that regards the essential qualities of human beings, their labor, and their products as commodities. Taussig argues that these ideas and customs illustrate how the relations of production and exchange, which most of us who live in consumer societies have come to accept as natural, are represented as vividly unnatural, even as evil, from the perspective of other cultures (1980: 2,4).

Although Taussig's point—that one should reflect on how white-collar lifestyles at home may be perceived from an exotic cultural perspective (that is, from a more proletarian point of view)—is telling, I do not think that everyone in capitalist societies necessarily accepts the human condition under capitalism as natural. Taussig speaks as if there is only one form of capitalism, or one mode of production in the capitalist world. Yet I believe that there are many cultures within the capitalist world, and many modes of production within one and the same consumer society. What, then, can one say about the different ways in which the residents of urban consumer societies consider the lifeworld around them? Are there symbols that these urban residents develop and use to keep their market-saturated lives going? In the present case study, I wish to use Japanese idols and their promotion agencies as tools to examine some of the specific ways in which capitalist values are promoted in the urban consumer society of contemporary Japan. I consider that this urban segment of the present Japanese society stands miles away from the harsh social reality of South America, to which the Marxist view of exploitation is more directly applicable.

SYMBOLS OF COMMODITY FETISHISM 2: THE MENACING FETUS

In conducting the present study, I am particularly inspired by Helen Hardacre's case study, which examines how religious institutions develop abortion rituals in contemporary urban Japan. Known commonly as *mizuko kuyō* ("commemorating the flushed-away child"), these rituals for aborted fetuses have been developed and commercialized in Japan since the 1970s. *Mizuko kuyō* is a trans-sectarian ritual style that draws selectively upon such historical religious traditions as *shintō* and Buddhism, but it departs from historical traditions of ritualizing reproductive life—especially from the ideas about the unity of mother and child (1997: 3).

The absence of any textual "anchor" in the past allows spiritualists to symbolize aborted fetuses (*mizuko*) as the cause of spiritual attacks (*tatari*), including sickness and misfortune for would-be parents, especially the mother. The spiritualists avert the gaze from men's role in women's unwillingly pregnancies and target women in their ideology of motherhood: the view that all women have a duty to become mothers. *Mizuko kuyō* develops as the major form of ritual to commemorate abortion by filling the space created by the de-ritualization of reproductive life. The spiritualists offer a fetocentric discourse as their regimen for clients. They argue that the fetus has the same moral value as a human being, and their clients, otherwise regarded as "foolish" or "irresponsible" women, must perform commemoration rituals in order to demonstrate that they can act responsibly in a society that stresses social responsibility (1997: 3, 14).

Hardacre demonstrates how abortion rituals have been developed as an invented custom; her treatment depicts contemporary religious institutions in Japan as active adopters and transformers of religious traditions. Moreover, she points out that the rhetoric of *mizuko kuyō*, which draws on the emotionalism aroused by worshiped images of the fetus, has been immersed in vast industries of popular culture, including print and broadcast media, popular literature, and film, in order to maximize the social and commercial effect of the rite of abortion. Hardacre's findings provide the present study of idol performances with a framework with which to understand the institutional organization of fetishism, which serves spiritual, social, cultural, historical, and commercial purposes in a context of contemporary urban society.

While Hardacre's work concentrates on a specific style of religious ritual, my study will explore how this religious logic applies to the construction of idolatry by the entertainment industry in present-day Japanese consumer society. While abortion rituals aim to rescue women from the sense of guilt associated with abortion, idol performances are designed to salvage young worshippers from the spiritual, emotional, and social struggles that characterize youth in contemporary urban settings. While abortion rituals develop out of the spiritual ground that has been prepared by traditional religions, the worshipping of young media-promoted personalities is invented by the promoters, actors, and consumers of these young celebrities in a form of secular religious praxis.

IDOLATRY IN THE HISTORY OF JAPAN'S INDUSTRIAL DEVELOPMENT

Japan has its own history of industrialization. The country transformed itself from an agrarian society into an industrial nation-state in a matter of forty years after its importation of modern sciences and technologies from Europe and North America in the latter half of the nineteenth century. Japan's current international reputation as an economically developed nation comes to a large extent from the nation's will and effort to look up to, and master, what was regarded as "the civilization of the West" (*seiyō bunmei*) (see, for example, Ohnuki-Tierney 1990). Unlike rural workers of Columbia and Bolivia who saw an essential conflict between capitalism and their local ways of life, Japanese people, especially city dwellers, most typically found themselves to be positive recipients of capitalism for over a century. This does not obviate a series of labor movements in which workers organized unions and fought against the exploitative practices of various industries. In my view, however, these movements were aimed at the improvement of working conditions, rather than the elimination of industrial practices altogether. Against this backdrop, Japanese consumer culture emerged as the fruit of national labor, facilitating the construction by capitalists of an urban space that could be compared to the consumer cultures of America and Western Europe. At the same time, the Japanese have repeatedly emphasized the national identity at the core of their capitalist habituation—as in the configuration of homogeneity as the strong cultural drive that lies at the center of consumerism (Clammer 1997; see also Rohlen 1974; Tobin et al. 1992).

With this cultural specificity in mind, I wish to expose the mechanism of commodity fetishism that revolves around commercialized personalities to illuminate the role of invented symbolism in the manifestation of consumer capitalism. I regard idol performances as public rituals that substantiate capitalist values, and idols as personified symbols in this terrain who help to establish the entertainment industry as an agent of public initiation. Subsequent chapters will map out the personal and institutional aspects of this industrial mechanism, which drives public desires toward the consumption of commodified fantasies.

FRAMING IDOLOGY, OR
THE CULTURAL STUDY OF IDOLS

The idol phenomenon encompasses a complex set of practices and relationships that involve producers, performers, and fans, as well as the members of the general audience. The study of such a complex field requires an analytical focus; my focus in this study will be on the capitalist production of personal images through idol performances. I consider these personal images to be more than random projections of different individuals as such: these images constitute "selfhood," which I define here as collective representations of self that signify ideal personal qualities in a culture or society at a moment of history. My discussions in subsequent chapters are attempts to demonstrate this point through concrete instances and empirically grounded case studies.

All too often, studies of the culture industry tend to treat production as an entity that stands in contrast to consumption, but I will treat production as intimately related to consumption—to such a degree that these two aspects cannot be separated analytically or in practice.[4] The consumption of idol images by fans will be considered an integral part of the process of constructing and distributing idols as cultural commodities. Idol fans, especially those who are enthusiastic, function as connoisseurs of idols and the system of their promotion. As such, they contribute to the popular digestions and significations of images and messages that are launched by idols and their promoters. The opinions and activities of the people who participate in the social production of idol performances will be illustrated in order to reveal what cultural meanings these individuals use in framing the images they try to produce, and how they manipulate and are manipulated by the system of commercial production as well as the ideology that reinforces this system.

Idols include young female and male personalities who are considered "girls and boys next door." These personalities reflect adolescent femaleness and adolescent maleness. There are also some individuals and groups whose performances represent androgyny by challenging the stability of gender representation premised on a female versus male dichotomy.[5] I will examine the cultural meaning

---

4. See, for instance, Suzuki 2000, especially her critique of Karl Marx and Theodore Adorno on p. 204.

5. One good example is Izamu, a male rock singer who is known for his cross-dressing and feminine gestures. When he married a cute idol, Hinano Yoshikawa, media reporters and fans wondered which one of them looked more feminine.

of idols in contemporary urban Japan through the venue in which female idols are produced for public consumption. I have two reasons for this. First, I became aware of how women are the focus of representation in popular culture in Japan, a society that has been characterized as male-dominated until very recently (and in many respects still today). As I stepped into the Japanese entertainment industry, I immediately became aware that idol producers and corporate decisionmakers were nearly exclusively men, although female idols were more numerous than male. Images of adolescent femaleness became the subject of constant debate, differentiation, and reformulation among these male producers. Thus, I wanted to examine the ideological implications of femininity represented by female idols in the Japanese commercial industry. I had limited access to the small number of producers and performers who controlled the production of masculinity or androgyny. In the end, I could not gather sufficient data for analyses from these people.

In light of these limits and opportunities, I will consider the production of female idols as a point of ethnographic reference for investigating how idol performances manifest gender ideology in contemporary urban Japan. This does not imply that I will not take other aspects of gendered representations and practices into account. I will make inferences about heterosocial and homosocial relationships that revolve around the production of adolescent female personalities. The former relationship of production encompasses the marketing of female idols for male audiences and/or the consumption of female idols by male audiences; and the latter relationship consists of the marketing of female idols for female consumers and/or the consumption of female idols by female consumers. I will also make inferences about the ideal images of adolescent maleness by examining the ideal images of adolescent femaleness as represented in female idol performances as far as idol performances fantasize romantic ties between young girls and boys. In sum, I will use heterosocial interactions that are implied in the promotion of female idols as the basis for understanding other gender-oriented interactions.

The study of the idol phenomena is anthropologically significant because it demonstrates how the commercial industry operates as an institution that develops substantiating symbols and rituals in a form of popular art. This system of production utilizes its human resources as capital, packaging young performers as commodities that urge people to consume by virtue of their sexual appeal. Packaging involves stylizing performers into personalities who can represent both prominent cultural values as well as innovative trends. To be an adorable idol is to become a role model for contemporary Japanese youth. Thus, idol production, the goal of which is to influence the public, is situated in the Japanese cultural landscape. That is, the idol industry can be perceived as a terrain in which cultural symbols and their images are constantly generated, contested, and refined. In this sense, the idol industry is attributed to what Pierre Bourdieu (1993) calls "the field of cultural production," or an arena in which symbolic artforms are produced, differentiated, and mutated through the interactions of individuals who hold different tastes and occupy different positions in a capitalist society. Investing one's mind, energy, time, and money on these different forms of art as well as the symbolic competition between these forms constitute the core of meaningful existence in such a social arena.

The "field of cultural production" bears similarity to Jennifer Robertson's (1998) concept of "encompassing cultural matrix," which focuses on popular culture as a site in which certain artforms are selected and culturally appropriated by actors who make various assumptions about their world and their lives. By observing popular culture, one can determine particular configurations of these assumptions at particular times and in specific places. As Robertson elaborates:

I locate popular culture in an encompassing cultural matrix . . . in which sociohistorical forces and relations are generated and reproduced, stimulated by encounters with ideas, things, and peoples both within and outside the matrix as a whole or any area in particular. . . . The figure-ground relationship between popular culture and culture emerges and develops continuously as a complex series of communications technologies, increased literacy, a market economy (nominally) premised on choice and competition, and other factors; these factors, moreover, appear in different combinations at different historical moments. (Robertson 1998: 35)

Thus, studies of popular culture themselves contribute to the understanding of a process in which the ideas and practices of a segment of society are framed to become part of cultural competence. This is the basis on which I would like to build my discussion of Japanese idols.

Robertson's comments were made in reference to a specific genre of all-female popular theater, the Takarazuka Revue, which has existed in Japan since 1914. This genre of theatrical performance tends to distinguish itself from other, more typical genres of popular cultural performances in Japan today such as pop and rock music, or television drama.[6] In contrast, I will investigate the more recent and widespread genre of entertainment that constitutes Japan's popular cultural scene—so as to see how ideal images of adolescent femaleness are mass-produced, distributed, and consumed, to become a prominent part of cultural competence in contemporary Japanese society.

My ambition in writing this book is to conduct a case study of young Japanese entertainers as a first step in the development of what I would like to call "idology," or the ethnographic study of idolatry. Yet, when I explain to people that I am an "idologist," one common reaction I get is ridicule. It would have been different if I chose historically acclaimed stage performers, but trying to justify the value of objectifying childlike female personalities to academic audiences has been very difficult. Oftentimes, I have been characterized as a sex maniac with whom one does not want to associate. On several occasions, my acquaintances have implied that my study is "interesting but bizarre" and "quite unsuitable for my age and my status." Perhaps it is difficult for well-educated audiences to accept the fact that the study of young pop stars can be a legitimate subject of inquiry in the current academic climate.

What these audiences do not initially recognize (and I am pretty sure that some may never will) is my intention to exemplify how idolatry—as trivial and mysterious as it may seem—works as an organizing force in our taken-for-granted lifeworld. Just as ancient

---

6. Most of my informants in the Japanese entertainment industry argued that the Takarazuka Revue served the specific interests of relatively high-class, elite women who wished to distinguish themselves from the masses.

cities were so often built around religious institutions such as shrines, temples, and churches that idolized divine personalities and sacred characters, social ties—especially adolescent social bonds—in contemporary urban societies are often developed around popular engendered-personalities. Just as traditional religious institutions sanctified people's customs and lifestyles, contemporary pop stars that are often regarded as sex symbols of our time consecrate the living environment of their fans. Why are certain personalities objectified and attended with certain emotions—whether adored or ridiculed—in social, cultural, and historical settings? How do these personalities become desirable objects? Above all, how could social institutions revolve around these personalities? These are predictable questions, but I do not see any insightful explanations for them. My aim in developing this project is to use Japanese female idols as accessible and familiar but never before thoroughly investigated instruments for making inferences that may contribute to the understanding of the symbolic aspect of contemporary commercial institutions and their practices. Insights that are obtained in this book may be applied to the study of other personified symbols, including politicians and cult leaders, in various sociocultural and historical settings.

IN SEARCH OF POP
IDOLS: CHAPTER OUTLINE

Chapter 1 provides the theoretical and empirical orientations of my study. I will discuss the recent anthropological discourse on selfhood, followed by a discussion of the religiosity of idol performances that highlights purification as an important aspect. In this chapter, I will also outline my fieldwork, demonstrating my approach to the idol phenomena.

Chapter 2 introduces readers to the basic features that characterize idol performances and how these features contribute to the formation of adolescent identities. Of particular interest is the fact that idol performances function in contemporary urban Japan as rites of passage for adolescents. The conceptualization of adolescence in contemporary Japan will also be elaborated here. Chapter

3 will focus on sex, gender, and sexuality, showing how these are manifested in the process of idol production. The way young girls are packaged into desirable female personalities will be specified, along with the mixed feelings that young women have about subjecting themselves to the overt forms of male discipline. Here, I will also consider the relationship between the production of female idols and the construction of gender in a wider context of Japanese society in order to reveal what counts as acceptable and unacceptable images for female idols in Japan today.

Chapters 4 and 5 are intended to unfold how performers and their promotion agencies use idol images as symbolic capital in order to establish their place in Japanese popular culture and consumer society. Chapter 4 focuses on the institutional side of this practice, while Chapter 5 will consider the personal aspect of it. Chapter 4 delves into the arena of symbolic competition in which idols are stylized, differentiated, and contested. My discussion in this chapter focuses on strategies that promotion agencies use to build social bonds, expand their territories using idols as an identity marker, and position themselves in the arena. From the standpoint of outsiders, this symbolic competition over individualized idol styles appears to be a differentiation within an actually homogeneous class of commercialized performance.

In Chapter 5, I trace the trajectory of Seiko Matsuda, one of the best-selling idol singers in the history of Japanese pop music, delineating how she constructed and utilized her public image as an instrument for personal growth. Matsuda's footsteps in show business since her debut in 1980 reveal how a performer stylizes the self through the process that can be characterized as social drama (Turner 1982). This process includes a set of conventionally structured stages of personal development in which a person is expected to accomplish public recognition by overcoming a series of struggles. In the case of Matsuda, this is acted out as an interplay between the will of the performer to establish the self in the society and the evaluation of her attitudes and behaviors by the public. The media, especially tabloids, acts as a stand-in in this process that shapes as well as reflects public opinion. Matsuda's model role is signified by her ability to gain agency in a culturally appropriate manner: her ability to transform herself from an immature girl to a mature woman as she endures public criticism, overcomes challenges, and accomplishes her goals without losing self-control. In effect, Matsuda, like other pop divas in Japan, has become a legend—an important figure in public folklore.

Chapter 6 examines the practices of idol fans in order to demonstrate how idol symbolism is manifested in the domain of consumption. Of specific interest in this chapter is the manner in which fans organize their activities around their objects of worship. Enthusiastic idol followers, otherwise called idol *otaku*, generate rituals of worship, which includes decorating their living quarters with idol goods (considered sacred objects for these idol fanatics), setting up alcoves devoted to their favorite idols, developing communal ties with other idol enthusiasts, publishing their own versions of idol magazines as a form of hagiography, and attending idol concerts regularly as a place of collective worship. My ethnographic observations will try to expose the religiosity of idol performances as manifested in the activities of adolescents and young adults who use idols as instruments for heightening their spiritual well-being in their urban lifeworld. I will develop the concept of "idol cult" in order to make better sense of the activities that characterize idol fetishism as a secular religious phenomenon.

As emergent studies of cultural globalization show, consumption in its context is an act that contributes to the construction of class identity beyond the boundary of one industrialized culture or society (Friedman 1990; Appadurai 1991; Miller 1997). With this in mind, Chapter 7 looks at the spread of Japanese and Japanese-style idols in other parts of Asia as a phenomenon that symbolizes the cross-cultural development of a white-collar lifestyle in the Asia-Pacific region. Consumerism is encouraged in many rapidly developing Asian countries, known as New Industrial Economies (NIEs) such as Taiwan, China (including Hong Kong), and South Korea. The growing popularity of idols in these countries is evocative of socioeconomic progress for an emerging middle-class identity, which is meaningfully associated with youth, the future labor force of national, regional, and international development. The analysis in this chapter demonstrates two perspectives that are inherent in the cultural hegemony of idol production: from the standpoint of Japanese promotion agencies, the emergent popularity of Japanese-style idols in Asia reflects the expansion of the idol market overseas, suggesting Japan's leading symbolic role in the international economy; from the perspectives of non-Japanese Asians, this process implies the local formation of modern identities as signified by homegrown idols representing socioeconomic affluence.

Finally, the Conclusion summarizes the implications of the idol-pop phenomena in understanding the relationship between popular performance, commodity fetishism, and the capitalization of selves.

I

The Ethnography of Idol Production:
An Overview

This study of idol production attempts to understand how capitalist institutions shape adolescent selfhood in a contemporary social setting; the study must thus take into account existing anthropological discourse on selfhood and identity. "Performance" and "self-framing" will be guiding concepts, as will the analogy between idol performances and religious rituals. I will work with the notion of "idol" in light of studies on religious rituals, especially in reference to the theory of charisma and institution building.

IDOLIZED SELF
IN JAPANESE SOCIETY

In recent anthropological discourse the self is regarded as nonexistent apart from the collaborative practice of its figuration. The self is continually reified by its entanglements with other subjects' actions, experiences, and histories; with ideological forces and collective representations (Battaglia 1995: 1, 2; see also Merleau-Ponty 1960; Mead 1962 [1934]). Japanese people are familiar with such a notion of selfhood as multifaceted, constantly changing with respect to social conditions. The cultural emphasis on interpersonal relationships (*aidagara*) accustoms Japanese individuals to enmesh themselves in interpersonal relationships such that personal intentions and opinions become transparent—at least in the long run (Watsuji 1935; Hamaguchi 1977; Kondo 1990).

There are two noteworthy implications to this view as far as this study is concerned. First, the idea that individuals are socially involved invokes within each individual a strong sense of "indulgence" (*amae*) that encourages empathetic ties between the one who seeks indulgence (*amaeru*) and the one who provides that indulgence (*amayakasu*). The most fundamental form of this mutual commitment could be found in the relationship between Japanese children and their mothers.[1] Second, developing an indulgent relationship also means that social interactions are expected to protect the face of each agent of interaction. Research has shown that Japanese distinguish between what ought to be presented up front (*omote*) and what should be kept unseen (*ura*), or between their outward expressions (*tatemae*) and their hidden personal intentions (*honne*). They tend to surrender, or at least tone down, their individual qualities to the conventional images of collaborative selfhood in order to avoid face-threatening actions (Lebra 1976; Bachnik 1994).[2] Combine these psychological and attitudinal aspects and one can infer the effectiveness of idol performances—that is, the virtue of presenting oneself as a publicly adorable figure who can invoke the sense of indulgence.

---

1. Some of these concepts are part of a whole literature known as *Nihonjinron*, or "theory on Japanese," that is concerned with differentiating Japanese national identity from other nationalities by pointing out aspects of cultural uniqueness. What one sees in these theories is an effort to withstand reification of person, self, and identity as concepts rooted in egocentrism by developing folk models of self as embedded in interpersonal relationships—albeit the potential devotion of these alternative models of selfhood to reinforcing, in academic language, ideological, and even racist, cultural discourse.

2. In a relevant case study, Brian Moeran (1986) analyzes Japanese advertising and indicates that the strong cultural emphasis on the group prevents the idea of individualism as we understand it in the United States and Europe from developing in Japan, despite the increased pervasiveness of American and European fashions in Japanese life. The extreme suspicion of individualism, considered as "negatively egocentric" by the Japanese people, led advertisers to invent *kosei* or "individuality," which implies personal creativity that does not lack the actor's concern for the good of the group, as a term that neatly adopts the advantages of individualism without disrupting the spiritual unity felt by the Japanese public (1986: 75). This word is frequently used in recent Japanese commercials as a point of mediation between Western fashion and Japanese identity.

In such a setting, performances become behavioral foci. Within the field of anthropology, the idea of performance is theoretically oriented toward the problem of identity and representation, and this certainly applies here. Goffman's classic study (1959) indicates that every individual is dialectically poised in a world of others, where self-presentation becomes the single most important reason to exist. In such a context, every individual is a performer who is motivated by impression management. Goffman's notion of self as existing alone in this social world, however, still echoes the North American individualist notion of selfhood (cf. Whittaker 1992: 200).

Suggestive recent theories on "performing identities" point out that the constituents of identity such as gender, class, and ethnicity are less a function of knowledge than performance, or less a matter of final discovery than perpetual reinvention (Fuss 1991: 7). For instance, Epstein (1987) argues that identity is neither a determinative characteristic of a person that unwinds from within nor a serial enactment of socially imposed roles that could vary considerably over the course of one's life, but an intermediate position between these two extremes.

For Epstein, performing identities signify performance as an act of identity formation. He notes: "People make their own identities, but they do not make them just as they please. Identities are phenomena that permit people to become acting "subjects" who define who they are in the world, but at the same time identities "subject" those people to the controlling power of external categorization" (1987: 30). In a similar vein, Judith Butler observes in reference to gender identity:

There is no volitional subject behind the mime who decides, as it were, which gender it will be today. On the contrary, the very possibility of becoming a viable subject requires that a certain gender mime be already underway. The "being" of the subject is no more self-identical than the "being" of any gender; in fact, coherent gender, achieved through an apparent repetition of the same, produces as its *effect* the illusion of a prior and volitional subject. In this sense, gender is not a performance that a prior subject elects to do, but gender is *performative* in the sense that it constitutes as an effect the very subject it appears to express. (Butler 1991: 24, emphasis original)

These comments indicate how members of a society incessantly shape and reshape their subjectivities (who they are and what they would be) by acting and being acted upon by others. They demonstrate that the self (and its image thereof) is molded through interactions that are rooted in performance.

In concurrence with these theorists, Bethe and Brazell's (1990) discussion of Japan's six-century-old *noh* theater provides insightful observations of how identity is manifested in the process of becoming in the domain of performing arts. This study shows how actors acquire their skills in performance through a long-term process that consists of the constant repetition of set exercises. As Bethe and Brazell contend: "The knowledge of *noh* is only possible through somatic, oral, and psychic immersion in the art. To practice *noh*, to know *noh*, is to have it ingrained in body and psyche. . . . Mind and body function as one [in such a state]; intellectual understanding is fused with visceral knowledge" (Bethe and Brazell 1990: 186, brackets mine). Thus, *noh* actors could attain the essential skills of acting only by devoting their total being to the performance. The processes by which these established styles of performance are acquired become consistent with a way of life that strives for the perfection of selfhood.[3] Such a manner of apprenticeship is by no means limited to *noh*, and one could more or less find it in almost every genre of Japanese art and performance—from *kabuki*, *sumō*, and *karate* to all sorts of craftsmanship. Stylized promotion is a common feature of idol performances, and devotion of the self to the stylized figure is expected here as well. Idol candidates, like students of traditional performing arts, are encouraged to transform themselves from raw, inexperienced, unskilled novices to seasoned, experienced, and highly skilled actors as they become idolized characters by mastering the art of self-presentation—that is, the art of presenting oneself as a publicly adorable figure.

Of particular interest for the purpose of this research is the idea of *kata*, a term in Japanese that could be translated as "form," "style," or "module." Zarrili (1990) introduces this concept in his

-----

3. Singleton (1989) also discusses how parents demand this kind of disciplined concentration from their children in Japanese folkcraft pottery apprenticeships.

study of Indian *kathakali* acting to refer to the set form whose constant repetition "leads to a level of ability beyond empty, vacuous, presence-less, and powerless mimicry" (Zarrilli 1990: 133; see also Goffman 1974; Hendry 1993). Although Bethe and Brazell do not explicate this Japanese concept, they imply the significance of this idea in the apprenticeship of *noh* theatre:

At every level of training, teaching concentrates on form, even though the art of a performer is judged by his [*sic*] expressive intensity. While learning the form, the young performer is expected to make it his own and fill it with meaning. This process is regarded as too personal, too individualized to teach overtly. Yet it is exactly this which constitutes the secret art and which the observant student hopes to gain from a master. (Bethe and Brazell 1990: 174)

Mastery of performance could thus be understood as a process in which actors meaningfully embody a convention of style and make their performances a part of their identities.[4] It is the process of becoming a character by unifying the dichotomy between the internal self and the external structure, or mind and body, through the integration of meaning and form (see also Yasuda 1984). In idol performances, ideal images of adolescent selfhood are considered *kata* into which young performers mold themselves through repeated practices of enactment. Ways in which idol-forms are created, and ways in which adolescent selves are molded into these forms, condition and are conditioned by labor relations between young performers, their producers, and contemporary Japanese culture and society. To understand what sorts of images are conventionalized through these relationships will be the focus of my ethnographic undertaking in this book.

In sum, the perspectives presented above demonstrate how performance could function as a behavioral strategy to establish linkages between the self and society. Performance could be used as a formal means to present the selves publicly, to manage impressions,

---

4. A similar argument is given by Scott (1955: Chap. 8) in reference to kabuki. *Kata*, in his view, is specified as the actor's speech and movements on the stage, although the term's meaning extends to stage properties, costumes, and make-up, which are not simply decorative accessories but are also necessary aids to the technique of the actor. These ornaments frame the actor into an established style (1955: 105).

and to take up positions within the society. In accord with this, the term "idol performances" will be used in subsequent chapters of this book to signify a form of symbolic self-presentation that encompasses the packaging, characterizing, stylizing, or modeling of self as practiced by adolescent personalities in the domain of popular culture and mass society in contemporary urban Japan. What makes the idol style distinct from other styles of performance is its position in the youth market. In a society where a significant portion of the consumer market consists of children and young adults, becoming a popular adolescent role model means making a considerable amount of profit. This is the single most important motivator for idols and their promotion agencies to produce idols as symbols.[5]

RELIGIOSITY IN
IDOL PERFORMANCES

What, then, is an idol? What does it mean to stylize oneself as an idol personality and to be worshipped in Japan today? The study of idol performances as a symbolic phenomenon calls into question the religiosity of idol performances. In saying this, however, I do not mean to treat idol performances as a religious praxis. I intend to consider idol performances as secular religion by highlighting analogies between idol performances and religious rituals using concepts such as "charisma." Doing so unfolds the mechanism of idolatry: that is, the way in which social relationships, networks, and institutions are built around objects of popular worship. I will keep intact the distinction between religion, which consists of community rituals that are performed to influence the nonhuman realm, and popular culture, which consists of commercial events and representations, even though I will discuss the *religious aspect of popular culture.*

Idols, referred to in Japan as *aidoru* (from the English "idols"), is a derivation of a term that originally referred to an image of a per-

---

5. Yoshida's (1984) study, for example, reports that Japan's children's market constituted a gross product of 10 trillion yen (estimate) in the fiscal year of 1983. According to one of my informants, an advertising agent, this particular article inspired many people in the trend industry.

son or thing used as an object of worship, or something visible but without substance. The Japanese equivalent of the original meaning of "idol" in English is *gūzō*, which is a combination of two words: *gū*, which means "fabrication," and *zō*, which means "image" or "statue." This implies that *aidoru* is an arbitrary concept that could be defined in many ways.

In discussing the fluidity of idols as a philosophical concept, Francis Bacon once said:

> The idols imposed by words on the understanding are of two kinds. They are either names of things which do not exist . . . , or they are names of things which exist, but yet confused and ill-defined, and hastily and irregularly derived from realities. . . . The [latter] class, which springs out of a faulty and unskillful abstraction, is intricate and deeply rooted. . . . For it both signifies that which easily spreads itself round any other body; and that which in itself is indeterminate and cannot solidify; and that which readily yields in every direction; and that which easily divides and scatters itself; and that which easily unites and collects itself; and that which readily flows and is put in motion; and that which readily clings to another body and wets it; and that which is easily reduced to a liquid, or being solid easily melts.   (Bacon 1985 [1625]: 284; brackets mine)

This statement shows that idols are semantically unstable, and idolized objects are subject to changes in meaning. For Bacon, idols basically referred to preconceptions or misconceptions. Reflecting his iconoclastic Puritan background, Bacon treated idolatry as philosophical obstruction, or a force that prevents us from attaining truthful understanding about the nature of the world. As a remedy to such an intellectual disorder, he proposed empirical analyses in which objects of our thought are critically examined and evaluated. Any truthful understanding of the world could be generated through thorough analysis of gathered data. Bacon called this method of investigation "induction."

For young boards of directors, stockholders, advertisers, and distributors who wish to assure their place in contemporary Japanese popular culture and consumer society, the semantic ambiguity of idols is an instrument rather than an obstacle in conceptualizing their world. Their activities are oriented to the commercial mystification of desirable objects rather than the scholarly analyses of their essential qualities. Precisely because idols have fluid meanings, idol producers can mold idols in many publicly adorable ways, create various catchy phrases to signify their symbolic values, and develop a showcase in which differentiated images of idealized personalities are displayed to be contested. The stylization of young idolized personalities in multiple ways that shape and reshape the representational contents of these personalities in accordance with changes in the public taste is what the idol industry in contemporary Japan has been doing over a period of almost four decades. My task as an "idologist" is to uncover through the inductive method of analysis how actors, producers, and audiences incorporate specific social, cultural, and historical aspects into the making of idol imagery.

In religious practices, worshippers construct and construe their icons as the symbolic centers of their communities through ritualized permances and folkloric narrations. Ritualized performances that revolve around icons could frame distinctions between sacred and profane, the special and the routine, or transcendental and concrete realities. Of analytical importance here is the effect of framing rather than what is being framed: through rituals, people set themselves, their places, and their activities off from the rest of their society and remove physical and psychological impediments to their relationships with the divine (see Bell 1997: 160). Such a function of ritual is apparent in Japan where, as Nelson (1996) observes with fascination, ritual practices that resemble those dating to centuries ago in structure and expression can be found today.

In Japan's indigenous religion, *shintō*, rituals serve purposes such as thanking the divine beings for plentiful food supply; beseeching protection for local communities by these divine beings, known as *kami*; and honoring the departed souls of clan members. Purification for removal of physical and psychological impediments to one's relationship with *kami* constitutes a significant aspect of *shintō* rites, and this is expressed in behaviors such as rinsing the hands and mouth with water upon entering a shrine, which is considered the home of the *kami*, waving a wand of white paper streamers in the air over the heads of priests and trays of offerings before important events take place, or taking babies to local shrines for their lifetime blessing. More important, purification rituals are communal practices: *shintō* rites consist of public expressions of worship that involve a group rather than a solitary person, and purification rituals help reinforce community boundaries, asking the divine to cleanse a localized segment of humanity such as the clan, tribe, or village. In Nelson's view, *shintō* orientations permeate everything from day-to-day life to major rituals and ceremonial observances (1996: 38, 39, Chap. 12).[6]

In idol performances, idols are typically presented to the public as "pure" personalities, and this reflects the relation of idol performances to the Shintoesque idea of purity. The "pure" image of an idol encompasses "innocent," "childlike," "cute," "tomboy" appearances and personal qualities, all of which signify the naïve and thus charming performances of young celebrities that are supposedly untainted by commercial professionalism. The pure image of idols often accompanies a consecrating catchphrase "*Kiyoku, tadashiku, utsukushiku!*" or "Pure, honest, and beautiful," and for idol fans especially this means that idols are distant from scandalous romances and acts that are considered immoral—although in fact idols, like performers of other entertainment genres, often become the subjects of scandals. Thus, the purity of idols could be regarded as pretense, an aspect of deliberate style, rather than an essential quality.

One notable aspect of the *shintō* view of purity is that defilements and pollutions are not necessarily thought of as "sins," even though these transgressions violate a divine state of harmony. Nelson observes that while "sins," according to American and European religious sensibilities, directly affect the individual's soul like a filthy cloak that only the direct forgiveness of God can remove, defilements are thought of in *shintō* as temporary separations from the harmonious interaction of body, soul, and the lifeworld. Thus Judeo-Christian preoccupations with virtue do not apply to the Japanese conceptions of impurity and purity. Purity and impurity are not antithetical to virtue or harmony. They are simply a fact of existence afflicting all of us, including divine beings; with no lin-

---

6. Elsewhere, Goulding (2001) observes that popular cultural forms of contemporary Japan such as animation tend to project old religious themes—directly or indirectly. One example is a recently popular animation movie called *Princess Mononoke*, which reflects the Japanese worship of forest spirits.

gering guilt complexes, defilements can be obliterated by purification rituals (Nelson 1996: 104). Such a perspective applies to idol performances, wherein idols that have been involved in scandals can be and often are reintegrated into the public scene after a period of dismissal from the entertainment world, accompanied by the demonstration of apologetic attitudes before audiences. As we shall see in the chapter on Seiko Matsuda, some idols use scandals and their noncontagious characterizations to stir public consciousness, give voice to their challenging spirit, and establish their unique positions in the mass society of present-day Japan.

Media institutions operate in this context both as developers of idol mythology and as "demonizers." They watch the growth of idols and invent stories that shape and reshape the images of idolized subjects. Some of these stories glorify their subjects, while others (such as those in tabloids) create scandals. Communities of worshippers—support groups and fan clubs—develop their own fetishistic rituals, including choreographed cheers and special handshakes. From the perspective of those who worship idols, these figures purify their hearts and provide them with peace of mind, if not satisfaction of desire per se. Promotion agencies tied up with the media enhance rites of worship with concerts, conventions, essays, and magazine articles. Enmeshed in these networks, the positions of young hopeful personalities are gradually transformed into those of the stars. The symbolic values of these personalities are incessantly translated into monetary values along the way, and the processes of idols' personal development are marketed.

THE CHARISMATIC
QUALITY OF IDOLS

Because they can become the objects of public adoration, idols are charismatic personalities (Weber 1968; Shils 1965). One crucial aspect of charisma lies in the power of these personalities to transform themselves and the society in which they are positioned meaningfully. Charismatic individuals and groups can reorganize existing institutional and social orders through their extraordinary, exhilarating qualities (Eisenstadt, quoted in Weber 1968: xl, xlv).

Weber's classic work (1958) exploring the relationship between the Protestant ethic and the building of capitalist institutions shows, for instance, that the structural transformation of the European economy from precapitalist to capitalist modes of production was dependent not only on changes in the objective conditions of the market (the development of automation, mass production, surplus value, an exploitative system, and so on) but on a charismatic reformulation of the meaning of economic activities in which Protestants, especially Calvinists, and their work ethic played a major role (Eisenstadt, quoted in Weber 1968: xxxii). Weber illustrates how charismatic forces could reshape the centers of a society by altering the meaning of these central social orders and the ways people participate in these orders.[7]

In contemporary Japanese popular culture and mass society, successful idols such as Seiko Matsuda, whose story will be told in a subsequent chapter, are considered charismatic because they demonstrate the transformation from an ordinary young person to an extraordinary figure that influences the public. In Japan, charisma encompasses a person's abilities to face challenges, overcome struggles, and accomplish dreams against all odds. It also includes the person's ability to surpass the limits of tradition and attain a new meaning in life that can inspire other members of the society. In the case of Matsuda, old expectations about Japanese femininity have been vastly modified as more and more women in Japanese society have been influenced by her will to sacrifice romance, marriage, and family for her career. Matsuda's will to stand out in the Japanese entertainment world and contest the traditional view of women as mothers rather than artists or workers captured public attention. The trajectory of her transformation from an object of

---

7. There is a problem inherent in the initial assumption of any sociological analysis of charisma: such an analysis may stress its disruptive effects. While charismatic forces could be seen as a focus of social conflict, cultural dissension, or the destruction of existing social order, I adopt Eisenstadt's insight that this does not negate the idea that these forces could also become a part of the institutional framework. The perspective that charismatic forces can be both destructive and constructive at the same time enables one to see that the very quest for participation in a meaningful order may be related to processes of sociocultural transformation (see Eisenstadt, quoted in Weber 1968: xlii).

adolescent male romance to a creative and confident performer provoked the Japanese masses to reconsider the meaning of womanhood in their society.

PLACING IDOLOGY IN THE
FIELD OF CELEBRITY STUDIES

There is a great deal of discussion in the social sciences about the charismatic quality of celebrities, especially regarding the ways in which popular personalities represent social values and affect the way people view their world. C. Wright Mills (1956), for example, looked at personalities of the so-called Café Society, which developed in the United States in the early twentieth century along with the elaboration of the national means of mass communication. Mills showed how nationwide hierarchies of power and wealth supported this organization. Eckert's (1991) case study of Shirley Temple demonstrated the mechanism of popularity that produced "America's little darling" in an era of economic depression. He uncovered how Temple presented herself in many films as a poor but optimistic, or rich but sympathetic, young girl. Whichever was the case, Temple was presented as a lovable personality that became an ideological lens through which American government officials and middle-class industries mitigated the reality of the poor through the charity of fantasy.

Many studies on the American pop singer Madonna have broached the mechanism of popularity that characterizes this world-renowned figure. One good example is a collection of essays edited by Schwichtenberg (1993) that illuminates how Madonna skillfully deployed themes such as gender, sexuality, class, generation, and race to insinuate herself into various aspects of people's everyday lives. These studies show how Madonna gained fame by providing connections between people's lived experiences and the various discourses in circulation (Schwichtenberg 1993: 10; see also Hooks 1992; Frank and Smith 1993). In a similar vein, Simpson (1993) examined the popularity of Brazil's pop star Xuxa and the cultural strategy of mega-marketing that promoted her public image. Simpson demonstrated how Xuxa's child-friendly image on television told her viewers, especially young audiences, about the meaning of beauty, power, success, and happiness that privileges white middle-class and submissive femininity in a society structured on ethnic and gender inequalities.

Materials in English on the study of Japanese pop stars have been scarce until recently. Judith Herd's introductory article on pop singers (1984) was the only one of its kind. Although pop stars appear as examples in sections of Japanese studies literature, ethnographic case studies on the subject are virtually nonexistent. Yano's study on Japanese fandom (1997) was the first to provide an empirically grounded account of the symbolic qualities of Japanese celebrities. She focused on the emotional ties between male *enka* stars and their middle-aged female fans. In recent years, more works have been done in English on Japanese celebrities, some of which include studies of idol phenomena as part of the analysis of popular expressions of gender, class, and ethnic identities (Kinsella 1995; Allison 1996; Aoyagi 2000). Yet the system of idol production and its sociocultural basis have not been investigated.

Provocative but somewhat underdeveloped discussions of idols by Japanese scholars include Ogawa (1988) from the standpoint of musicology (i.e., pop idols as personal constituents of urban sound production), Inamasu (1989) using media and communication theories (idols as signifiers of young people's modes of communication in the age of television), and Ogura (1989, 1990) taking a feminist perspective (idols as objects of sexual fantasies and gender identities). Arguments presented in these works, however, are often anecdotal, and analyses rarely extend beyond the authors' own interpretations of selective idol texts.

To repair the shortcomings of these studies, I will provide an ethnographic study of the field of idol production—a "thick description" of the idol industry, to borrow Geertz's expression (1973). In this field, ordinary young people in the idol industry construct their identities as they act out adolescent role models and commercialize themselves in the consumer society of modern Japan. These people and their promotion agencies attempt to secure their positions in the market as well as society at large, and thereby maximize their commercial profit. The ways in which this is negotiated between performers and their promotion agencies make up the core of idol-based transactions and the resultant social organization, which will be the emphasis of the present case study.

CONDUCTING
IDOLOGICAL FIELDWORK

My approach to the phenomena in question is primarily ethnographic, and this means that I consider idol performances as a site where interactions take place between involved individuals and institutions, including myself as a researcher, rather than as a showcase of idol-texts per se. Participant observation, as canonized in the early part of the twentieth century by Bronislaw Malinowski through his pioneering works in the Trobriand Islands, is the predominant means by which anthropologists acquire knowledge about people and their cultures, or "insiders' views" as Malinowski would put it (1922: 29). Observation grounded in participation allows researchers to rise out of their armchairs, experience the social world, and investigate why and how members of a society construct certain social realities. There is more to the practice of fieldwork, however, than taking part in what people do. Given the critical eye of a researcher, ethnographic field research could reveal certain aspects of culture that might not be recognizable to the participants.

To analyze social relationships and cultural institutions that develop around the symbolic practices of idol production, my fieldwork subsumed three major approaches: observation, conversation, and participation. Although the distinction between these is mostly technical, it helped me differentiate the kinds of information I could generate in the field. I used observation as a primary means to acquire knowledge about the people being studied. Observation is a subjective endeavor that depends on the researcher's impressions and perspectives about observed phenomena, as well as the researcher's own way of approaching the phenomena. By conversation, I mean a dialogue between the researcher and the informants that generates information beyond the limits of subjectivity.

Through a series of conversations, the researcher could clarify problems that emerge in the field and develop further observational possibilities in light of various points made by the informants. Participation has many dimensions other than simply taking part in the "native world." Participation allows the researcher to enrich ethnographic experience about the local way of life, determine one's distance from the people being studied, and evaluate the significance of activities and relationships on the basis of information that can and cannot be acquired. In the field, I amalgamated these three approaches into a dynamic, mutually interactive approach to the phenomena in question.

By my count in the spring of 1995, Tokyo had over 1,600 promotion agencies, 860 publishers, 380 broadcasting corporations, and 36 record companies, along with hundreds of large and small sponsoring corporations, which together made up the idol industry. Here, I contacted over 300 informants, including 68 idol producers and promoters, 49 performers, eight writers, three graphic designers, and 47 idol fans as well as general members of the audience. I built rapport with these people, conducted interviews, participated in idol production, and collected ethnographic data that elicited how idols served as trendsetters for adolescent consumers.

Conversations with my informants ranged from a 30-minute, one-time interview to repeated get-togethers that lasted many hours. I tape-recorded 172 hours of interviews with 84 people. I attended idol concerts and visited backstage scenes. I also observed public events and media programs featuring idolized personalities, as well as informal get-togethers. I used these places as primary sites to examine how my informants acted or to confirm (or contradict) what my informants told me during our conversations.

With my native competence in Japanese language and my experience growing up in Japan, I had no problem hearing and speaking Japanese on day-to-day basis. Yet there were several problems with communicating on a cultural level. A typical Japanese attitude, taken by the majority of my informants, was for one to act with ambiguity, reservation, indifference, or what Japanese would more precisely call "professed intention" (*tate-*

mae), which cloaked one's "true intention" or "real feeling" (*honne*). Personal reservation was often due to a strong cultural emphasis on protecting everyone's face in public interactions. In such a social environment, it was difficult for me to develop conversations with many of my informants. Even if a conversation was manageable, I could not confirm whether my informants meant what they said unless I became close enough for them to eventually reveal their feelings. To compensate for this problem, I often contacted the same informant more than once, and I repeatedly checked the points that were previously made. I also raised the same question in different conversational settings so that I could compare the information between these cases. I tried to build as much rapport as I could with each informant that I met, allowing them to express their opinions and reveal their true feelings more by the end of my fieldwork.

To get a better sense of what it is like to work in the idol industry, I adopted existing native roles including that of a judge, an adviser, a commentator, a writer, and an idol-like personality. In doing so, I had to consider whether I should hide my identity as a researcher or be honest, because these alternatives had different implications and outcomes for the overall orientation of my research. The more I managed to participate, the more I was able to adopt the insiders' points of view. Still, there was a danger of developing a bias and sacrificing critical analysis. After having had a chance to experience media attention, and as my identity as an outsider became more and more blurred, it was difficult for me to determine how much participation was enough. To deal with these problems, I deliberately kept myself away from my informants for several hours every day (usually at the end of the day) to reflect upon my experiences, analyze the data I collected, and organize my field notes. I also explained my objectives for participation to my informants whenever I adopted the insider's role. My right to participate was questioned by those who could not accept me as one of them, or who could not accept any participation by an outsider. When this happened, I did not hesitate to investigate their motives.

My fieldwork also included archival research. I spent many hours reading through idol-related materials in places such as Ōya Sōichi Bunko, a library in Tokyo that holds one of the largest collections of popular magazines and periodicals in the nation. Other sources included the archives of promotion agencies and media institutions. Some fans turned out to be the collectors of valuable idol texts, and I asked for their help from time to time. Since one of my research goals was to understand the relationship between the production of idols and the wider context of Japanese society, I had to obtain materials that included demographic information and socioeconomic analyses. The National Diet Library of Japan (Kokkai Toshokan) offered a large inventory of these materials. Various bookstores in Tokyo carried books and magazines that were useful as well.

I recorded television shows and radio programs and live events on topics that were relevant to my research. I also collected promotional videos that included a series of 15- to 30-minute clips featuring idol profiles, songs, and advertisements. These recordings amounted to approximately 400 hours. Other data sources included national and local newspapers. Some of these, such as *Asahi shinbun*, *Mainichi shinbun*, and *Yomiuri shinbun*, provided me with more general views about Japanese culture and society, while others, such as *Hōchi shinbun*, *Sankei shinbun*, *Nikkan Sports*, and *Tokyo Chūnichi Sports*, allowed me to collect tabloid materials on idols. I obtained fan club newsletters from three promotion agencies periodically, which helped me keep track of idol careers and activities as well as fan reactions to them.

All these approaches contributed to the overall aim of my fieldwork: to immerse myself in the field of idol production, and gather as much spoken and written data as possible on the subject of idolatry as a commercial practice. I have subsequently kept in touch with some of my informants, who continue to enrich me with information, ideas, and materials that they think will advance my research. The analysis presented in this study testifies to a collaborative effort made between my informants and myself to explain idol performances and the culture in which they are developed.

RESEARCH SETTING:

CONTEMPORARY URBAN JAPAN

Any visitor to Japan can see that its crowded city streets are filled with billboards representing young personalities that either smile coquettishly or strike shapely poses. Identical images appear on the covers of popular magazines at which many businessmen gaze intently on their way to work, or on the covers of comic books that children read on their way to school. Television shows are full of similar adolescent personalities. At public events, one finds many of these performers on stage trying to attract the adoring fans that scream and cheer them—however "without art" these performers may appear to act.

My first glimpse of these scenes as a fieldworker in Tokyo led me to feel that this youthful liveliness counterbalanced my general impression of urban Japan: a highly digitalized and impersonal space where workaholic clones run around like ants, or function as cogs in an economic machine that led the nation to earn the reputation of Asian economic superpower. Japanese people are often characterized as economic animals, but observing these personal images of adolescents in Tokyo and other towns in Japan led me to believe that there is a very human orientation to this socioeconomic environment. One of my first journal entries reads:

The whole city is lit up by countless numbers of young celebrities whose images emerge everywhere—smiling at times, crying at other times, and showing anger at yet other times. However artificial they seem, these media-crafted images of young idolized personalities supplement the impersonal atmosphere created by busy people rushing on the street. Each of these idols has a name recognized by many people whether or not they are willing to adore them. The city itself becomes a festival ground where life is being celebrated, but celebrated through commercially produced images, fantasies, and products.   (October 28, 1994)

Idols seemed to have created a symbolic landscape that functioned as an antistructure to the existing social structure—a liminal space to which workers could escape and forget about the harsh realities of everyday life in the city. Workers who entered this space were to be entertained by young, refreshing personalities. Yet I was also aware that this fantasy world was built on a realistic principle of its own: the commercial logic that allowed idol producers to capitalize on fantasies that idolized personalities offered to the viewers. The images of idols generated commodity fetishism, and the liminal space was commercial territory for entertainers and their producers.

This scene was part of a larger urban topography that characterized Tokyo. Like other cities in Japan, Tokyo was a vast array of concrete houses, office blocks, small shops, restaurants, and supermarkets, traversed by streets crowded with busy people and roads filled with traffic. The frantic rhythms of the latest consumer culture mingled with the tranquil scenes of the traditional past, such as shrines, temples, and local shops that had operated for hundreds of years, creating an enigma. Business districts stand side by side with leisure spots such as game parlors, nightclubs, dance halls, and cinemas, which are ready to provide workers with exhilarating escapes from the twelve-hour workday.

Tokyo is where most image-related commodities are made, sold, and dispersed. Most performers, producers, writers, and copywriters seek their jobs in this capital city, contributing to the city's reputation as the powerhouse of the modern economy and popular culture. I was informed by an editor of a popular journal who came to Tokyo from a rural prefecture to work over two decades ago, "New trends, new brands, and new customs all flow out of Tokyo, and they never end. Everyone everywhere tries to follow up on what goes on in this city. Even if anything new and exciting originates elsewhere, it is only when it goes through Tokyo does it become magnified as a nationwide phenomenon." This confirmed the fact that Tokyo is the center of Japan's trend creation and thus consumer culture.

One may characterize consumer society as a society in which the consumption of commodities, rather than their production, is the basis of social order. Or one may call it a world imbued with a system of codes in which the functional values of material objects are lost to their symbolic exchange values (e.g., Baudrillard 1981, 1988 [1968]). I find neither of these characterizations satisfying, because they overlook cultural variations within the consumer world. They also fail to specify the distinction between the consumer cultures of the industrialized world and the consumer cultures of the "traditional," "nonindustrial," or "premodern" setting where the exchange of symbolic goods (or the exchange of goods based on their symbolic values) is also present (cf. Adshead 1997). I also believe that production is as important as consumption in any modern society, and to characterize the society as a whole using one analytical perspective does not provide an accurate view.

In this study, I treat "consumer society" as a society in which the consumption of materials is equated with the consumption of fictions about one's socioeconomic well-being. Such a society is identical to what Wolfgang Haug (1986) calls a "commodity world of attractive and seductive illusion." In such a world, images and illusions are designed, produced, and marketed in order to shackle the human desire for satisfaction, enjoyment, and happiness to a drive toward certain styles of conformity. Haug writes:

An innumerable series of images are forced upon the individual, like mirrors, seemingly empathetic and totally credible, which bring their secrets to the surface and display them there. In these images, people are continually shown the unfulfilled aspects of their existence. The illusion integrates itself, promising satisfaction: it reads desires in one's eyes, and brings them to the surface of the commodity. While the illusion with which commodities present themselves to the gaze gives people a sense of meaningfulness, it provides them with a language to interpret their existence and the world. Any other world, different from that provided by the commodities, is almost no longer accessible to them.   (1986: 52)

This indicates how images and fictitious stories become important aspects of human life in present-day consumer societies. Fictions that are produced by trend industries become so much a part of our everyday life that they saturate our consciousness and become determinants of our social well-being. Shinji Miyadai offers a similar point in reference to contemporary urban Japan. He argues:

The contemporary urban Japan is a fictitious society. . . . By fiction, it is not meant a "falsehood that does not match the fact." Regardless of its consistency with the fact, it makes possible for one to feel "Oh, my household is as good as everyone else's." The reality of fiction is not a matter of whether or not this fiction matches the fact, but rather the fact that everyone who shares it believes in what it stands for. In this sense, a fiction accompanying the consumption of commodities is a story lived by the contemporaries [who consume these commodities]. (Miyadai 1994: 143; brackets mine)

Through the consumption of fictions imbued in commodities, Japanese consumers link themselves to other members of the society, creating personal linkages or a network of solidarity.

From the perspective of the Japanese trend industry, the urban consumer society of contemporary Japan consists of the masses (*taishū*), or the aggregate of consuming individuals to which their marketing strategies are targeted. Some of my informants in the industry referred to their marketing activities as "mass control" (*taishū sōsa*), the goal of which is to standardize consumer tastes and lifestyles through fictitious narratives and image-making processes. In Tokyo and other Japanese urban centers, business corporations and media institutions focus on offering, along with commodities, interesting stories that provide consumers with a meaningful repertoire of characters, relationships, and outcomes that represent their socioeconomic well-being.

Certainly, fictitious narratives may garnish the social life of the public in any consumer society. Perhaps what distinguishes contemporary urban Japan from other consumer societies is the way the consumers perceive stories offered by the industries. As Yano indicates, the molding of desire by the mass media is more easily accepted in Japan than elsewhere; in the United States, for instance, media stories tend to be received with greater skepticism. Just as shaping a tree by pruning is a traditional practice considered to produce greater harmony with one's natural surrounding, the molding of desire by the mass media is regarded by the majority of consumers in contemporary Japan to be the way by which one acquires information about the needs, wants, and pleasures of the other members of the society. Thus the media tends to promote a greater harmony between people and their surroundings in Japan than in other places. The acceptance of this molding is "a matter of course and even part of a cultural definition of maturity" (Yano 1997: 337). This is especially true for young consumers who are eager to embrace what is learned in the media and popular culture as part of their everyday lives. I will return to this point in the next chapter of this book.

In such an environment, idol performances could be perceived as ways of appropriating the system of idol production by connecting consumers and media-promoted personalities through the act of consuming.[8] More generally, idol performances could be seen as ways of generating spaces of socialization wherein idol producers interact with each other in their attempts to influence consumers by offering a series of potentially adorable personalities, while consumers interact with each other and influence producers by making consumption choices about fantasized images of selfhood. Thus, idolatry as a form of commodity fetishism reflects both the constraints of cultural values and codes on the one hand, and the pragmatics of cooperation and competition on the other.

IDOL INDUSTRY

The entertainment industry, or *geinōkai* ("entertainment world") as Japanese would generally call it, consists of large and small promotion agencies, media institutions, and a corporate network of manufacturers, distributors, and retailers. Like other commercial organizations in Japan, some of these firms consolidate into large industrial families, known as *keiretsu*, while others remain relatively small and independent ventures. *Keiretsu* usually include one large manufacturing company and a constellation of its subsidiaries, affiliates, and subcontractors.

The human resources in each of these institutions are divided into separate departments or sections whose roles include planning, production, marketing, management, and advertising. Positions within each of these areas are hierarchically arranged. Various marketing programs and public events are proposed by producers, authorized by administrators, and put into practice by directors, performers, and members. Promotion agencies specialize in nurturing the careers of potential stars. These agencies hold auditions

---

8. The view that consumption is a means for consumers to appropriate the production system is developed by Certeau (1984) and Jenkins (1992). Suzuki (2000) develops a cultural analysis based on this view, showing how changes in the consumer lifestyle in urbanizing Japan transformed the way funeral rites are commercialized in Japan over time.

every year through which prospective individuals are scouted, trained, and crafted into marketable commodities. Some lucky candidates are personally recruited into the manufacturing system, while hundreds of other candidates struggle through a series of contests.[9]

Idol promotion agencies institute fan clubs, publish newsletters, and produce a wide variety of idol goods. Personal image is the single most important commodity of performers, which is translated into a fee known as "guarantees" (*gyara*), and the marketing of this image is the *raison d'être* of promotion agencies. Performers' images are subject to copyright, otherwise known as *shōzō-ken* ("portrait rights"), the misuse of which can lead to lawsuits by the protecting agencies. Unlike Hollywood, where performers in show business act individually and establish contracts via agents on a one-to-one basis, the majority of Japanese performers are employed by promotion agencies and become part of the company.

Contracts between Japanese performers and promotion agencies are called "talent contracts" (*tarento keiyaku*). These include two categories: part-time contracts (*teiki keiyaku*) that normally cover a period of two years, subject to renewal; and full-time contracts (*senzoku keiyaku*) that guarantee the performers' permanent employment status. The latter are usually not signed unless the agency and the performer are confident of each other's abilities. While the performers' abilities are measured on the basis of how well they please the public and attract viewers, agencies' abilities are demonstrated in terms of how well they can nurture their performers and acquire quality jobs for them.

Unsatisfied performers may transfer from one agency to another as long as they are marketable. In such a case, performers tend to adopt a new name. A version of headhunting is a common practice for prospective performers, although restrictions and penalties, such as suspension and compensation, apply to headhunters. All these aspects contribute to the development of the idol industry as a highly competitive field of symbolic production in which pro-

---

9. In 1995, I counted over 1,600 promotion agencies that were striving to promote approximately 6,800 young and old personalities of both sexes, in addition to 300 duet and group performers.

moters and performers use a genre of popular performance as an instrument for establishing their social positions as well as maximizing their commercial profit.

Media institutions create a social space for participants to interact with a shared interest. As one advertising agent told me in an interview, these institutions provide a frame (*ba*) for performers and their agencies to advertise themselves, sponsors to advertise their products, and members of the audience to gather information about the latest trends. Given the function of the mass media to provide the public with fictions that cultivate conventional themes and perspectives, pop idols strive to become the topic (*wadai*) of media-constructed narratives. In such a context, performers and their promotion agencies may have a love-hate relationship with media, especially tabloid publishers. The sole interest of tabloids is to cover any story there is about the lives and activities of the famous people that may interest the audience—whether the story praises or blames the famous. For well-known performers and promotion agencies, tabloid reporters are sometimes strong allies who cement their prestige, and at other times unpleasant abusers of public images. For unknown performers and agencies that are struggling to become popular, these reporters are attractive promoters who hold the keys to their success, but they are also difficult to convince.

Corporate institutions, which include manufacturers, wholesalers, and retailers of material products, sponsor public events and media programs such as advertising campaigns, television shows, and commercials. In exchange, they use these events and programs for their advertising campaigns. In these settings, idols are hired as campaign personalities in order to attract a greater number of people, impress the public, and thereby magnify commercial impact. The willingness of corporate institutions to sponsor an event or program is measured in terms of audience rating (or turnout), which motivates media institutions to produce publicly appealing programs. It also motivates promotion agencies to produce popular talents.

In producing idols, corporate institutions ask advertisers to call for applications from promotion agencies. Then, an audition, or *konpe* (an abbreviation of the English word "competition"), is held. The most suitable applicant is chosen, and the guarantee is negotiated. The campaign period for a specific new product is usually anywhere between three months to one year. The guarantee paid to a promotion agency for hiring its performer during this period can range from three to ten million yen, depending on the potential of the performer. The rule holds that more than one company in the same industrial classification cannot hire the same performer during that campaign period. Whether or not corporate institutions will continue to campaign for the same product, using the same performer, will depend on the product's sales.

Although it is generally agreed that a currently popular performer could influence productivity through advertisement, this does not always turn out to be the case. There are cases in which unknown performers become suddenly well known through advertising campaigns—which make campaign events and programs an incalculable but attractive arena for promotion agencies. Lucky breaks fuel competition. Idol promotion agencies try their best to produce young personalities who could win corporate sponsorships with good images.

Among hundreds of companies that offer sponsorships, manufacturers of confectionery, toiletries, and electronic products are the foremost employers of young idols. In a roundtable conversation with agents from a large confectionery company and a vice-president of a large promotion agency, I was told that this was the case because "these products and personalities commonly appeal to young consumers." Indeed, eating candy (and fast food), keeping oneself clean and beautiful, and possessing all sorts of digitized machines are the preoccupation of young people in Japan as well as any other urban (or urbanizing) bourgeois societies, and the vice-president's statement confirmed that agencies are using idols to target children and adolescents in their marketing.

What I will discuss in the subsequent chapters of this book is the product of my entry into this commercial *qua* sociocultural institution that capitalizes on youth culture. A Japanese graduate student who has been educated in American universities, I first became interested in studying the idol industry in 1988. The idol boom was at its peak, and I wanted to investigate the phenomenon by writing a term paper on this subject for a class I took on symbolic anthropology. I was especially concerned with issues such as why premature, apparently amateurish personalities attracted the minds of so many people, and what preserved this enigmatic genre of popular cultural performance in present-day Japan ever since its emergence in the late 1960s. Over the next few years, I also became interested in using the idol phenomenon as a window to investigate the applied significance of anthropological theories and ethnographic methods in the study of contemporary culture.

My entry into the entertainment world was not easy. Having no initial relationship with anyone who worked there, I had to develop contacts from scratch. Between 1988 and 1992, I made frequent trips to Tokyo to observe idol-related events. In the summer of 1992, contacts were made with two individuals who worked in promotion agencies. I proposed the possibility of conducting field research on idols to these people. I was generally met with indifference, if not active discouragement. One of them said that such research would be difficult because everyone in show business is extremely busy, and nobody would give a free interview to some student who wanted to reveal the inside story. I was also warned that some agencies might be acquainted with the underworld, and that it was best to stay out of trouble—as it is said in a Japanese proverb, "If you don't lay your hands on gods, there will be no curse" (*Sawaranu kami ni tatari nashi*).

In 1994, after passing to doctoral candidacy and becoming better equipped with ethnographic techniques, I established a research base in Tokyo. I wrote a project profile that explained my research rationale and faxed copies to two dozen promotion agencies that were listed in a phone book. None of these agencies replied. I then decided to telephone these agencies to find out if they received my fax and if I could somehow get in touch with them. Some admitted that they received my fax and others did not, but all rejected my request on the basis that they did not wish to reveal any information related to their business to outsiders. Neither were my previous contacts helpful at all. Those whom I contacted told me that they would get back to me, but they never did. Seeing me grow increasingly frustrated, one of my research assistants, a Japanese university student, suggested that I get hold of someone who could appreciate my work and who would be willing to introduce me to people in the industry. He said that getting such a middle person is the most appropriate way of developing business relationships in Japan.

One person I failed to contact while doing my earlier surveys was Toshio Fujiwara (a pseudonym), another university student in Tokyo who chaired a pop-music research club. This research club was one of many informal groups of friends that develop in Japanese universities, otherwise known as "circles" (*saakuru*). After spending three months in the field without any contact, I pulled his phone number out of a file in my dusty notebook and made a call. His mother answered the phone and instructed me to call back on Sunday when he was usually at home. I also learned from her that this key informant-to-be had become a marketing agent who worked at a large advertising company. His primary job was to hire suitable personalities for television commercials that his company produced.

After a brief introduction over the phone, an appointment was set on the first day of February 1995 at Fujiwara's office. After learning that I was conducting serious research that would introduce Japanese idols to the academic community of North America, Fujiwara indicated that he would help me in any way he could. He made a copy of his notebook where he kept the cards of his acquaintances in the industry. He circled the names of seven individuals whom he would be able to contact without difficulty, and handed me the copy, promising that he would try to contact these people and inform them about me as soon as he could. Accepting his offer, I spoke to three of these individuals during the following week. Two were freelance writers on idols, and one was a sociologist who is also a pioneer in the study of Japanese idols. Further contacts with people in the industry were subsequently developed through these individuals. In the end, my informants gave me a weighty introduction to what it is like to work with or around idols in the world of Japanese show business.

When I was not seeking interviews, I attended concerts and public events, the schedule of which could be acquired from monthly magazines such as Gakken's *Bomb!* and Ticket Saison's *Ticket Jack* (more popularly known as *tj*). I also visited stores where idol goods were being sold and kept track of television and radio programs in which idols performed. Whenever there was a chance, I developed spontaneous conversations with people in the audience, staff members, and clerks. All of this helped me reconfirm many of the things that I was told by my informants during interviews. As my relationship with people in the industry evolved dramatically from April 1995, many of them provided me with materials they thought would be helpful for my research. They also invited me to concerts and gave me access to backstage areas. Some producers and managers took me to their meetings and get-togethers to show me what went on in these settings, while others took me to restaurants, bars, and coffee-shops for informal conversations.

On one privileged occasion in August 1995, I met Akio Nakamori, a distinguished columnist and a critic of popular culture who promoted idol candidates. After two months of occasional conversations and rapport-building, Nakamori offered me his media backup, which changed the nature of my interaction with informants substantially: producing me as an idol-like personality in his magazine columns. In October 1995, I struck a pose with idols, and this appeared on the front page of a widely distributed culture, business, and entertainment magazine called *SPA!*. After this, I was no longer regarded as a curious researcher from abroad, but as an expert on Japanese idols. First, I received calls from publishers who wanted me to write articles for their books and magazines. One of these articles, "Aidoru o tōshite miru Nihon no shin-jidai" (A look into Japan's new era through idols), appeared in the 1996 issue of *Chūmoku Aidoru Kanzen Data Book* (*The Dictionary of IDOL '96*), an annual publication of Tokyo's Scholar Press (Fig. 1.1). Here, I described the recent transformation of idol images from cute, innocent personalities to more sensual and mature-looking personalities and argued: "This transformation seems to represent a wider social change, namely, from a communal society, in which individuals were concerned about the way they appeared in public, to a more individualistic one, in which people need to be more self-

Fig. 1.1   A sample column by the author (© 1996, Scholar Press).

expressive and opinionated." This particular article created a sensation, and I began receiving frequent invitations to audition contests
and stage performances, where I was requested to participate as a
commentator. Some agencies sought my advice on the strategies of
idol production (Fig. 1.2).

While these privileged occasions provided me with opportunities to experience insiders' roles and get a good sense of ways in
which idols are produced as a cultural phenomenon, they also led
me to question my own authority. Did I know enough to proclaim
my expertise? People in the industry did not seem to mind as long
as they could use me as part of their stories. Yet some idol fans

Fig. 1.2   The author at work with idol informants (February 1996).

began to indicate problems they had with what they considered to be my authority. These fans questioned what qualification I had to comment on idols without a long-term commitment and real-time experience in the Japanese entertainment industry. In response, I wrote an article, "Bunka-genshō to shite no aidoru-hiiringu: jinrui-gaku wa aidoru ni tsuite nani o shirieru ka" (Idol healing as a cultural phenomenon: what anthropologists can learn about idols), in a book called *Aidoru tanteidan* (Idol detectives) (Tokyo: Takara-jima Press, pp. 156, 157) and explained the difference between the emotional involvement of idol fans with a particular idol who they admired and my research in the cultural aspects of the idol phenomenon.

My primary concern in the field was the possibility that my informants would consider me a spy who wanted to reveal their secrets to a curious crowd. I traveled freely across the boundaries of mutually competing institutions as I collected a variety of data that no journalist or consumer had ever collected before. Indeed, I was boldly traveling across the commercial universe to reach the stars in the name of social scientific discovery! To avoid an accusation that I was a spy, I presented a copy of my research proposal to all corporate representatives I contacted. In this I explained that my interest was academic, not commercial, and that my research would not jeopardize any agency or its members in particular. I also indicated that the study of idols would benefit the industry by providing a critical understanding of the symbolic significance of celebrities, or the cultural function of idol production.

In the end, the majority of people with whom I interacted accepted me as a researcher who had a genuine interest in the study of Japanese popular culture. Many of them gave their precious time on behalf of my research. For my part, trying to win understanding, trust, and support from my informants was a nonstop effort. The tension of maintaining a good image contributed to my daily exhaustion, along with the need to catch up with events in a highly competitive and unpredictable environment where things come and go very quickly and often without notice.

2

The Making of Japanese
Adolescent Role Models

How do the symbolic qualities of idols relate to the conceptualization of adolescence in Japan? The understanding of how idol images play a part in the organization of adolescent lifestyles adds a new dimension to the growing body of anthropological literature on adolescence and socialization. Discussions in this chapter will emphasize youth culture as a collection of processes in which values related to gender, class, and nationality are developed, contested, negotiated, and transmitted between adults and young people, as well as among young peers. Youth as a subject of anthropological inquiry will occupy the first sections of the chapter; this will address the question of how youth is perceived in Japanese society. This perception, given its anthropological context, informs aspects of idol imagery. These discussions will provide the basis for subsequent ethnographic analyses of the role played by idol-promotion agencies as the agents of public socialization.

ADOLESCENCE: BETWEEN
CHILDHOOD AND ADULTHOOD

Adolescence, the period of transition between childhood and adulthood, has been widely studied in the social sciences. In anthropology, studies on the conditions and experiences of youth in different cultural contexts followed Margaret Mead's pioneering work, *Coming of Age in Samoa* (1928).[1] These studies focused on social and cultural reactions to physiological changes that occur in individuals at the onset of puberty. Of special interest to researchers was how adolescents acquire social behaviors through parent-child interactions, peer group relations, schools, and other institutional means as they are initiated into adult society (e.g., Leemon 1972; Schlegel 1973; Condon 1987; Davis and Davis 1989; Hollos and Leis 1989).[2]

Researchers such as Wulff (1995) recently began to focus more on youth culture in its own right by asserting the need to reconsider adolescents as creative agents. In this view, adolescents are "producing something on their own which might not last in the long run but could still be significant for them at the time" (Wulff 1995: 1, 3). While this may free adolescents from being seen merely as the institutional objects of adult society, other studies warn against overemphasizing adolescent subjectivity. Any youth culture that may appear to emerge in and of itself often tends to be largely manipulated by adults who provide what they believe would appeal to adolescents (Schlegel and Barry 1991: 202). Following Jourdan (1995), I will analyze idol symbolism using the view that the adolescent lifeworld is best perceived as situated within the dialogue between adolescent subjects and the social structure. Influencing and influenced by the instrumental forces of adult society, adolescents establish their positions, enact their roles, and

----

1. Mead suggested that adolescence is subject to cultural conditioning, and different cultures condition youth in different ways. Based on her fieldwork in Tau Island of Samoa between 1925 and 1926, Mead demonstrated that the transition of Samoan girls into adult women occurred without emotional crises because the local society placed no stress on these girls. She indicated that this transition contrasted with that found in the United States. Derek Freeman (1983) challenges Mead, claiming that she ignored biological factors in favor of the cultural determination of sex roles. My proposition in this chapter is to investigate how each culture shapes the selfhood of adolescents who undergo physiological changes.

2. The study of adolescence and youth culture is abundant elsewhere. For detailed sociological studies, see Hall and Jefferson 1976, Willis 1977, Hebdige 1979, Brake 1980 and Van der Linden 1991, among others. In history, Ben-Amos 1994 offers an exquisite case study of the adolescent lifeworld in early Modern England.

fulfill their lives by "putting new meanings into the old shells" (Jourdan 1995: 205).

According to research in the field of European and North American developmental psychology, adolescence is a time during which children experience hormonal changes and corresponding adjustments to self-image. The ability to objectify oneself intensifies during youth, and this facilitates self-reflection, self-criticism, cognitive discrepancies, emotional discomforts, and behavioral disorders (e.g., Leahy 1985; Higgins 1987; Damon and Hart 1988). In anthropology, Schlegel and Barry (1991) adopt this characterization of adolescence as a "dis-eased" state of being, due to its ambivalent positioning between autonomous childhood and responsible adulthood. Comparing data from 186 societies of nonindustrial origin, the two scholars of youth conclude that stressful experiences are common to adolescents everywhere. They argue:

Although adolescence worldwide might not have the *Sturm und Drang* quality attributed to it in some of the more florid nineteenth and twentieth century literature, adolescence . . . displays points of stress that may be widely characteristic of this stage. . . . In small closed societies, adolescence is not just a period of training for adult life; it is the time during which the ground is prepared for adult social relations with the same people who are currently one's peers. . . . It is likely that adolescents are aware of this as they struggle to cope with the social pressures to conform and often to excel.   (1991: 43)

Thus adolescence is defined as a cross-cultural concept that represents an ambiguously situated age group that provides guidance for becoming an adult.

However, gross generalizations about youth using psychological concepts developed in the modern industrial societies of nineteenth- and twentieth-century Europe and North America, much of which owes to Hall's (1904) idea of "emotional turbulence" and Erikson's (1968) "identity crisis," are made untenable by ethnographic studies. Such a characterization is debated within the context of Euro-American psychology itself. For instance, Maslow (1962) considers the process of adolescent maturation as self-exploration rather than crisis. Moreover, others have argued that life itself might be regarded as stressful regardless of its stage, and identifying one particular stage with stress is questionable (see Marcia 1966, 1967; Bocknek 1980).

An essential task for the ethnographer of youth, then, is to examine how adolescents organize their world as they interact with one another as well as with adults in a local context. Such an examination operates in terms of a culturally defined concept of adolescence. To this end, I will examine how adolescence is conceptualized in Japanese society, and what role idol perfor-mances play in affecting the world organized around young people.

ADOLESCENCE IN JAPAN

A variety of traditional rituals associated with the life cycle are practiced in Japan, and some of these rituals derive from *shintō*—the most ancient and pervasive religious influence in this country. A set of rituals related to a child's birth, for example, includes a naming ceremony in which the child's name will be written out and hung up in a prominent place in the house. The child's separation from the pre-birth state is marked by the careful preservation of the child's umbilical cord when it drops off (it will be kept in a box by the mother). Some families may take a child to a local shrine to commemorate the child's incorporation into community life, while others may hold a family gathering to celebrate the safe arrival of their new member (Hendry 1995: 134, 135).

There are rites that formally mark the progress of a child through various stages of maturation. On Girls' Day (March 3) and Boys' Day (May 5), families set up tiers of shelves with various symbolic ornaments. These ornaments include for girls splendid representations of figures from the ancient imperial court, accom-panied by small but elaborate accessories including palanquins and tableware. For boys, there are miniature suits of warrior armor and helmets, as well as dolls depicting fierce heroes. By setting up these ornaments, the families pray for the child's protection and good fortune. For approximately one month before Boys' Day arrives, huge carp made of cloth are set up over households with young sons. Even though Girls' Day and Boys' Day are currently being collapsed into Children's Day (May 5), the use of gender-specific ornaments remains the same in most Japanese households.

On November 15 each year, children of three, five, and seven dress up in traditional garments and visit local shrines to pray for further protection and good fortune: this is a ritual called "Seven, five, and three" (*shichi-go-san*) (1995: 135, 136). Those who have reached the age of twenty participate in a public event known as the "coming of age ceremony" (*seijinshiki*) in January. They visit a local community center to attend the ceremony, which includes listening to speeches made by officials about how upright citizens are expected to behave. From this ceremony, they obtain legal rights and responsibilities as adults (1995: 138).

Other occasions at which rituals take place include marriage, the years of calamity (the major ages of which are 33 for women and 41 and 42 for men), retirement, and old age, as well as death and memorial celebrations. Hendry (1995: 145, 146) points out that these rites demarcate the life cycle into a set of intervals. Each of these rites marks the transition of the participants from one stage of life to another within this socially recognized system (see also Sofue 1965). Adolescence, however, has not been a part of this traditionally marked life cycle.

Adolescence, although a recognized stage of life, was substantially reshaped in Japan during the country's rapid transition from an agrarian society to the industrial nation-state in the late nineteenth century. Ōtsuka (1989) shows, for example, that this stage was reconstructed under the government's intention to modernize, which in Japan at the time meant "Westernize." According to Ōtsuka's analysis, the Ministry of Education categorized adolescents as such in the late nineteenth century in order to institutionalize the system of universal education. In premodern times, coming of age was a simple and quick process of transition from childhood to adulthood as signified by rituals such as *genpuku*, which recognized a boy's transition into an adult man by shaving off part of his hair, or by the practice of serving sticky rice with red beans, called *sekihan*, at a girl's first menstruation. Under the Japanese government's modernization program, this process of transition from childhood to adulthood was reformed into a rather lengthy period in which children were prepared for adult social relations through formal schooling.

In Japan today, the mixture of premodern and modern concepts of youth marks adolescence as the period in which individuals become socially and sexually "awakened" (*mezameru*) to the adult social reality. It is regarded as relational and emotional reorganization—an idea similar to what Coleman (1980) describes as severance of early emotional ties to parents and experimentation with adult social (and sexual) roles. The Japanese word for adolescence, *seishun*, is literally translated as "green spring"—a plant metaphor that signifies the beginning of maturation into a full-grown adult in terms of the "sprouting" of adult consciousness. Studies show how this stage is understood by both contemporary Japanese adults and adolescents as a life stage in which children are expected to progress into responsible adult social life through self-explorations: explorations that often take the form of chasing and accomplishing one's dreams (White 1993; Kawai 1994).

There are downsides to such a prospective view of the modern Japanese youth, especially since the 1980s when Japan became recognized as a rich industrialized nation. The youth of this era have been referred to as *shinjinrui* or "new humankind," which implies that their lifestyle is distinct from that of previous generations, who were preoccupied with the resurrection of Japan from the devastation of World War II. There has been much concern by adults in general about the recent inadequacy of traditional Japanese traits in the *shinjinrui*: that is, the lack of prominent cultural values such as loyalty, self-sacrifice, diligence, and patience. Social discourse about the new generation laments the loss of *seishin* or the Japanese spirit, even though elements such as *dōtoku kyōiku* (moral education) continue to be part of schooling. Catering to this discourse, some Japanese psychologists characterize adolescents as those who are in a state of "limbo": that is, those who cannot grow up to be adults (Okonogi 1981, 1985). Some Japanese entertainers and producers share this image of adolescence. Kōichi Morita, for example, projects it in a 1977 hit song called *Seishun jidai* (Youthful period). Part of its lyric reads, "Adolescence appears to be full of dreams only when one fondly looks back to it. Adolescence is full of delusions for those who are going through it." This supports the Anglo-American view of youth as being caught between childhood and adulthood, not knowing where exactly to situate oneself.

These rather negative images of contemporary Japanese youth coexist with a more positive characterization of *seishun* and its derivative term *seishun-jidai* ("youthful period"), which represents a romanticized community of high-spirited young people who share similar emotional experiences while undergoing physiological changes and a corresponding development of self-awareness. In such a community, personal stresses resulting from the need to manage one's relationship with the self and the world are overcome by mutual support among friends. One undergoes interpersonal conflicts and faces challenges from peers in such a community, thereby acquiring interactive skills. A statement made by one of my informants, a university student in his mid-twenties, reflected this view. He argued:

Youth symbolizes a contemporary rite of passage in which one forms solidarity with peers and shares various wonders, dreams, and tragedies of life with them. One also overcomes emotional difficulties that we all experience as underdeveloped adults and appreciates what it means to coexist with other people in this inevitable, otherwise ruthless world we call society, which is full of hardship and loneliness.

This indicates the importance of peer solidarity, or having a fraternity of belonging, as part of an adolescent's initiation into adulthood.[3] *Seishun-jidai* is also known as *shishunki*, or the period in which young individuals become aware of their gender roles and sexual expectations. Exploring sexual relationships through love affairs with one's peers becomes one of the main themes of this life stage.

Part of becoming an adult in Japan is to acquire the distinction between prominent cultural categories, such as professed intention (*tatemae*) and true intention (*honne*), front (*omote*) and back (*ura*), or outside (*soto*) and inside (*uchi*). This allows the actor to adjust her or his behavior differently between the outward-public and inward-private realms of life. Both Japanese adolescents and adults

---

3. Though there is significant variation in their duration and elaboration, fraternities exist as important aspects of initiation rites in other cultures including Africa, Melanesia, and Papua New Guinea (Young 1965; Paige and Paige 1981).

share an understanding that the gap between these two realms of life is an acceptable area of freedom for adolescents to explore themselves.

Maturation in Japan means becoming publicly more responsible, but as long as one performs social duties well, private activities and dreams (such as engaging in hobbies and sexual pleasures) can deviate from the norm to some extent (White 1993: 20). White refers to this ambivalence as "complementary conflict," distinguishing it from the American perception of personal development during adolescence, which stresses consistent behavior, or assumes a single, integrated personality as the ultimate positive goal. Thus, behaving differently in different situations may be considered a kind of hypocrisy for Americans, and many adolescents who tend to demonstrate this trait in the United States are treated as deviant. Yet such behavior has been more easily accepted in Japan (1993: 20, 21).

Set in such a cultural environment, idol-pop is thought to have become the basis for symbolic interactions: that is, a space of socialization in which young performers and their fans get involved in all sorts of activities that contribute to their development of a sense of self. How to acquire a publicly adorable appearance becomes an important issue for idols as they undergo the process of self-formation, while how one is to demonstrate one's devoted support may become an issue for fans. The task of the idol industry, then, is to maximize its profit by coordinating the public relationship between these two groups of self-presenting and self-acquiring agents.

For most adolescents, family and classroom contexts are considered sites where social skills are taught. Japanese parents and teachers place strong emphasis on group conformity to reinforce a sense of self-discipline. Adolescents are required to undergo intense competition in which their paths of life are determined on the basis of how well they perform overall on exams. The conditions of the formal education system supported by family and school beset adolescents with constant pressures (Lanham 1979; Rohlen 1988; Dore and Sako 1989). In contrast, friendship provides a context where adolescents can seek refuge from the shared pressures of the education system, engage in private noninstitutionalized togetherness, and freely acquire skills to negotiate the hierarchical necessities of society (White 1993: 17). Friendship, in this sense, becomes a significant training ground for adolescents to learn how to socialize informally. In friendship grounded in mass culture, the generation of *shinjinrui* (new humankind) are referred to as "info-maniacs" (*infomaniakku*), which implies that an intense focus is placed on adolescents to negotiate appropriate lifestyles through mutual interaction. As White writes:

Young teens in Japan are *infomaniakku*, "informaniacs." When they get together, it is to share the latest on their favorite pop-music stars, news on where to buy that great shirt, or what CD rental shop has a special offer this week. The young teen is intensely focused on being appropriate, and she negotiates the path by testing on friends what's learned in the media—discovering who she is by what her friends like—to wear, to hear, to buy. (1993: 14)

Adolescence encompasses peer communities in which members conventionalize consumer choices through social interactions. Else-where, White (1995) indicates that the trend industry is well aware of this adolescent tendency to share information between peers and is prepared to manipulate it:

[Adolescence in Japan] implies style, aspirations, a way of thinking and behaving. To some it may imply the older notion of "neither here nor there," the *chūto hanpa* limbo of "betweenness," but the consumer industries have targeted these young people in a more specific way. The "naming" of this "stage" has thus outlined a category permitting, and indeed demanding, diversity and slippage. Because of the speed of marketing, the case of Japan reveals the market-driven aspects of coming of age as well as the active involvement of teens themselves in creating new cultures and practices that then feed back into market definition of adolescence. (1995: 255, 256; brackets mine)

Teens have become an important consumer category in contem-porary Japanese society, for whom corporate institutions can create commercial narratives and organize marketing practices.

I could see the outcomes of this commercial conceptualization of youth culture clearly during my fieldwork in Tokyo. Taking public transportation with groups of high-school students, for example, I noticed that information acquired in the media about "what's trendy these days" was one of the three most frequently discussed issues in their conversations.[4] Simply walking down the street revealed that the vast majority of young people dress in a similar fashion. Most of the garment designs and hair styles resembled those appearing in some of the latest issues of widely distributed fashion magazines, such as *Non-No, An-An, Junon, Popolo, Can Cam, McSister*, and *Cutie* for young women, or *Men's Non-No* and *Popeye* for young men.

A survey conducted among a group of ten informants between the ages of 18 and 25 confirmed that they use magazines and television programs as their primary sources of information. It was also revealed that these informants often discussed the details of what they learned in these media sources with close friends. All ten indicated that they frequently passed on to others the latest fashion magazines and pop-music CDs as part of their information exchange. When asked why they were so concerned about media-created trends, their answers included the following replies: "Good fashion develops one's individuality out of a conventional style!" (25-year-old female); "Good lifestyle is socially appropriate" (22-year-old male); "I wanted to do things right" (24-year-old female); "I want to make sure that I'm not sticking out, even though I want to look cool" (22-year-old male); "It's embarrassing to stay behind other people" (18-year-old female). These answers indicated that propriety and conventionality were important reasons for adolescent consumers to socialize, even to discuss such informal concerns as personal lifestyle. They demonstrate that Japanese adolescents are delicately situated between how they want to present themselves to the world personally and how they are expected by others to present themselves in the world.

All in all, the introduction of adolescence as a life stage in modern Japan provided grounds for new institutions (such as the family, school, and the media) to codify norms that become part of the system of cultural classification.[5] It is in this spectrum that the

---

4. The other two topics included: descriptions of what had happened around them recently; and gossip about someone that they knew in real life.

5. Ōtsuka (1989: 105), for example, writes about the development of high schools for young women, known as *jogakkō*, or "girls' schools," in early modern Japan,

idol industry can be grasped—as another socializing apparatus that constructs adolescent symbols and rituals. Idol promotion agencies deploy various aspects of youth to create marketable role models that suit the tastes of young people in present-day Japan.

POP IDOLS: MARKETING
ADOLESCENT COMPANIONS

In North America, high self-esteem is strongly emphasized through notions such as individualism and self-reliance (Hsu 1953). "The squeaky wheel," as the English saying goes, "gets the grease." In contrast, Japanese expect their members to tone down their individual opinions in deference to those of the group or social norm. The practice of thinking too highly of oneself is discouraged, as in the saying, "The nail that sticks out gets hammered down" (*Deru kugi wa utareru*). Of course, characterizing these cultural propensities as national character dangerously misrepresents the diversities within each culture.[6] Yet studies in cross-cultural communications show that different social groups develop different communicative protocols that reinforce these behavioral tendencies (Kondo 1990; Yamada 1990).[7]

---

arguing that modern Japanese society created girls' schools in order to isolate female adolescents from the rest of the society. This prevented the sexually maturing bodies of young women from freely contacting the opposite sex. It also prepared these young women for the matrimony to come with appropriate husbands by improving their skills in accordance with guidelines set by the nation's administrative body. Middle schools are shown here as a kind of institution established to control teenagers via curriculum programs and activities.

6. See, for example, Mourer and Sugimoto's (1986) critique of Japanese group models.

7. Yamada's comparative study of conversational styles between American and Japanese businessmen shows that the different cultural expectations that Japanese and American businessmen develop in regard to verbal communication influences the way they actually talk: On the one hand, the Japanese—for whom talk is considered to lead to unreliable or mistrustful interactions that jeopardize collectivity—employ nonconfrontational strategies in conversation that use the mistrusted medium of talk in a way that still allows for speakers and listeners to reach collective goals. On the other hand, Americans—who try to express themselves and relate to one another through talk—use conversational strategies that can enhance both individuality and collectivity (Yamada 1990: 253).

Popular celebrities embody this cross-cultural difference. In her study of Japanese pop music, Herd (1984) points out that most stars in Western countries are popular because of their outstanding personal attributes. Japanese idols, on the other hand, typically depict images that are fairly standard: appearance, ability, and charm that are above average, but not so much as to alienate or offend the audience. Prototypical idols are "just enough to provide their fans with the sense that they too could be stars if they try hard enough" (Herd 1984: 77, 78). Japanese allude to this characteristic as *tōshindai*, or "life-sized." Life-sized idols keep pace with their audiences: they perform as familiar personalities rather than outstanding stars. My interview with Hideyoshi Aizawa, the president of Sun Music Productions, which is known for its promotion of big adolescent pop stars like Kensaku Morita (debut 1969), Junko Sakurada (debut 1973), Seiko Matsuda (debut 1980), Yū Hayami (debut 1982), and Noriko Sakai (debut 1987), revealed that the life-sized image of idols helps produce feelings of solidarity and reciprocity:

By being life-sized, idols can harmonize with the audience, especially young fans. Also, to be life-sized is to publicly confirm that idols are not living in this world on their own, but together with people who are there to support them and whom they are expected to support. I mean . . . everyone who is interested. Human relationships are what hold idols in their place and enable idol businesses to function. Although idols are expected to become role models of some kind and to represent the public in certain ways, this role cannot be accomplished unless they keep pace with the people all around them. . . . To be life-sized, that is. They cannot run ahead too fast or lag too far behind.

This comment indicates that idols function as companions for adolescent fans by emphasizing the importance of interpersonal ties over personal achievements. Through entertainment offerings, idols continuously invoke in the minds of young audiences the sense of being together, doing things together, and growing up together.

Playing on the needs of young people to socialize, life-sized idols are marketed as the "personifiers" (so to speak) of an ideal girl or boy next door (*tonari no onna no ko* or *tonari no otoko no ko*), who are chosen for their potential to become stars representing their generation. Sociologist Hiroshi Ogawa (1988) calls them "quasi companions" (*gijiteki nakama*) who provide their teenage followers with an imagined sense of intimacy—the feeling that affirms cultural emphasis on interconnectedness in Japan. Ogawa contends that although the companionship that Japanese idols emphasize is understood as artificial, impervious, and thereby realized only in fantasy, the intimacy it evokes can be as strong as, or even stronger than, that shared among school friends (1988: 122, 123). This is due to the fact that unlike real-life companions, with whom there is always the potential for conflict and loss of friendship, idols smile and appear to be friendly all the time. Unlike real people, idols never reject those who wish to approach them—provided, of course, that the relationship is professional in nature (1988: 123).

The performer's own inclination to sustain the image of the life-sized adolescent companion is revealed in an essay by Rie Tomosaka, an idol who debuted in 1992. Tomosaka has been characterized in the media as a "genius" (*tensai*), but she downplayed her celebrity status in the essay and proclaimed that she was, before anything else, an ordinary teenage girl.[8]

I am ordinary. I may be much plainer than ordinary people. I am a high-school student who goes to classes when I don't have any work to do. . . . I also shop and play with my friends. . . . I am not so much aware of the fact that I am an entertainer or an idol. . . . I simply have many friends who work in show business. . . . Perhaps the sad thing is that the ordinary people do not treat us in an ordinary way. We, too, want an ordinary life and an ordinary romance, but we are not considered ordinary by other people. . . . That's about all, I think, that is not ordinary. (Tomosaka 1997: 118, 119)

Like Ryōko Hirosue, whose comments were introduced in the beginning of this book, Tomosaka modified the fame that puts her in an uncomfortably "higher" position by attaching herself to peer-solidarity. As a typical Japanese idol, Tomosaka projected herself publicly as modest and thus audience-friendly.

According to Hideyoshi Aizawa of Sun Music, the image of the life-sized adolescent companion allows idols and their manufactu-

---

8. The characterization of Rie Tomosaka as an "ingenious" idol talent is found, for instance, in the June 10, 1997, issue of *Weekly Playboy* (p. 61).

rers to "create and maintain an interactive space." Within this social space, adolescent consumers can "continuously connect the context of their own maturation with that of idols undergoing growth from inexperienced debutantes to experienced actors." Makoto Yasui, a former editor in chief of Gakken's monthly idol magazines, *Bomb!* (1979–present) and *Momoco* (1983–94), elaborated on this point and said that one of the primary functions of idols is to sympathize with experiences and emotions of those who undergo youth, or *seishun no mon* ("gateway to youth"), by means of encouraging messages and performances:

Idols enact the role of compassionate partners who are capable of comforting that particular age-group of adolescents who become sensitive about their life and their world. Wonders, tensions, emotional ambiguities, curiosity about the opposite sex, a sense of conflict with society, the search for the meaning of existence, and problems associated with romance: idols could share these issues with their teen audiences by expressing their own ideas about youthful experiences, thus providing their fans with a sense of communal ties, or . . . "skinships" if you will. In the process of growing up with these fans, idol talents themselves could attain skills and confidence in performance.

Yasui demonstrates the connection between idols' self-preserved images and the cultural emphasis on social ties in Japanese society. "Skinship" is a clever combination of "closeness" (symbolized by skin) and "kinship" that does not simply mean intimate contact, but also involves a sense of family connection. By using this term directly from English, Yasui tries to indicate how intimate the relationship between idols and their fans can ideally be.

The following excerpt from an essay written by Seiko Matsuda provides an example of the empathetic message offered by an idol to her fans: "Seiko is so happy to meet you!! As a singer and an eighteen-year-old girl, I feel for the first time that I am able to become independent. Please watch over me warmly forever!!" (Matsuda 1980: cover page). Similarly, Atsuhiro Satō, a former member of a popular male idol group, Hikaru Genji (1987–94), wrote in a published essay: "I want to establish my personal position as a singer, actor and all else put together! Yet, this may still be too vague to be called a dream . . . . Although I am still at a stage where I am working hard, please keep watch over me. Let's continue spending time together" (Satō 1991: 215). Both Matsuda and Satō build on their companion status and call upon readers to empathize with their "will to mature." These statements explicate the intention of performers to share their youthful visions and efforts with the audience, and thereby grow up together. Statements such as these that collectivize the individual's maturation process can be observed in many comments made by idols, contributing to the production of peer solidarity that can facilitate communal progress.

Activities that build and maintain "intimacy" between idols and their audiences are carried out to a degree and with a uniformity that has no apparent equivalent in the American pop star scene. Japanese idol duties include handshaking ceremonies (*akushu kai*) that accompany stage performances, get-togethers with fans (*fan no tsudoi*) where fans can talk and play games with their favorite idol, public photo shoots (*satsuei kai*) where idols strike poses for amateur photographers, known as "camera kids" (*kamera kozō*), and periodic correspondences with fans by letter. When idols release CDs and promotional videos or publish photo albums or essays, autograph ceremonies (*sign kai*) are held for buyers at retail outlets. There are also idol hotlines for fans wishing to hear recorded idol messages or learn about upcoming idol events, as well as web pages where one can read an idol's personal profile, including place and date of birth, blood type, hobbies, and prospects in life. Promotion agencies organize some of these profiles, while fans and support groups construct others (Fig. 2.1).

During my fieldwork, I occasionally visited the homes of idol fans to observe their communications with idols on the internet. Each of these fans paid the annual registration fee of about 3,000 yen to join the program, which was provided by a media agency. For this one received one to three monthly sessions on line that depended on the availability of idol guests. During each session, which lasted for approximately one hour, fans could freely correspond with their idols as well as each other in cyberspace. Each session ended with a quiz that tested the fans' knowledge about the idol, and the winner of this quiz received memorabilia

Fig. 2.1   Idol fans gathering around their object of worship
(photo by the author, March 1995).

that was subsequently delivered to his/her home. Sessions typically
began with a brief introduction by the server that welcomed
participants and introduced the guests. The guests usually began by
greeting their fans, and then the fans replied by sending their
greetings, asking questions, and writing supportive comments.
Messages are posted on a first-come first-serve basis, but lengthier
messages tended to be interrupted by other messages.

For every fan I talked to, the goal of these real-time communications with their idols on the internet was twofold: to enhance
the sense of intimacy between themselves and their idols; and to
strengthen the sense of interconnectedness between fans. One of
these fans, a male university student, told me that it was always
nice to examine how close one could approach an idol, seeing how
far he could go in terms of dedicating his affection to her. He
explained that a truly adorable idol would not betray his expec-

tations, the foremost of which was that she be friendly and thus approachable. Events such as real-time chatting on the internet provided an opportunity to examine how much the idol could live up to his expectations—a point confirmed by most of the other fans I interviewed. The website becomes a socializing space in which the intimacy between idols and their fans is realized in a way impossible elsewhere.

Popular idol magazines, such as Gakken's *Bomb!* and *Momoco*, contain idol photos, featured interviews, and commentaries. The readers' columns, which consist of letters and homemade idol cartoons, often follow these. These sections together constitute a two-way communication between idols and their fans, in which the editors act as a stand-in for the readers. In her observation of idols that appear in Japanese fashion magazines for adolescents, Merry White points out that these young talents "speak" to the readers with solidly predictable advice about being loyal in friendships, working hard at school, and holding on to a dream about a special someone (1995: 266, see also 1993: 123). My observation confirms this point: magazines that feature idols are expected to generate an interactive space wherein idols function as spokespersons for adolescent lifestyles.

Enthusiastic fans, known as "idol chasers" (*aidoru okkake*), follow their idols almost everywhere, awaiting the chance to have a close encounter. Those who prefer to be more organized team up as "cheering squads" (*ouen-dan*) in order to encourage their idol on the stage with choreographed cheers, while others create voluntary support groups, known as "supporting squads" (*shin-eitai*), in the spirit of what one former member described as demonstrating the members' dedication to their idol and protecting her from possible dangers.[9] All these practices are part of producing an interactive space-time that materializes the imagined companionship and thereby facilitates a sense of collec-

---

9. According to this informant, the number of *shin'eitai* reached its peak in the mid-1980s, paralleling the popularity of idol-pop singers. Though no longer active today, many of these groups were hierarchically organized with their own ranking of "senior and junior officers." Some of these members were employed part-time by promotion agencies as bodyguards and for other supportive activities.

tivity between idols and their audience within a controlled environment.

Not only are idol images used by private corporations to empower their advertisements, but the images of "the adolescent companion" are also manipulated by the state in order to attract public attention. One example of this is a campaign by the Ministry of Health to deal with drug-related problems. The members of the organizing committee apparently perceive that drug abuse is on the rise and poses a serious threat to the well-being of the nation, especially young people. Each year, the committee asks a popular, healthy-looking idol to become the "young citizen's representative" (*wakamono shimin daihyō*) for that year. Public events are held on a monthly basis, and the chosen idol appears with committee representatives and local politicians to address the public about the devastating effects of drug use. From season to season, some selected idols perform as "one-day police officers" in public safety campaigns organized by the National Police Agency, calling on the public, particularly young people, to follow traffic rules. Others participate in campaigns designed to promote public transportation. Still others participate in baseball games by throwing the first pitch. The list of such campaign rituals is endless. All this points to the fact that life-sized public images of idols are used as a symbolic means to direct the public consciousness toward certain socioeconomic and political goals.

THE FANTASTIC
WORLD OF CUTE IDOLS

Often accompanying "life-sized" images of idols is another fundamental idol characteristic: "cutesy." The "cute style," as it is called, encompasses pretty looks, heartwarming verbal expressions, and singing, dancing, acting, and speaking in a sweet, meek, and adorable way. A form of handwriting that consists of chubby rounded characters also expresses cutesy. Written laterally and in contrast to normal Japanese script, which is written vertically using strokes, these characters, generally considered by adults as lacking discipline, appear in many texts with cartoon figures such as hearts, flowers, stars, animals, and faces that resemble childish drawings (e.g., Yamane 1986; Ōtsuka 1989; Kinsella 1995: 222). *Kawaiko-chan*, or "cute girls and boys," has become a synonym for idols in Japanese, representing carefully crafted public personae that try to appeal to viewers' compassion. According to Tetsuko Kuroyanagi, the former host of the prestigious Japanese music countdown program *The Best Ten*, people adore cute idols for their sweetness and purity—characteristics that evoke the feeling that idols should be "protected carefully" (quoted in Herd 1984: 77, 78). Cutesy can be overdone, however, even in Japan. Young women who carry the cute style too far are called *burikko* (a "pretentiously cute girl"), a mildly derogatory term that was first used to describe the idol Seiko Matsuda for overdoing cutesy. Since Matsuda, *burikko* can also refer to an attitude often adopted strategically by young women to attract personal attention.

The cute style has clear historical roots. The Japanese word for cute, *kawaii*, can be traced back to notions such as *kawayushi* and *kawayurashi* from the premodern era. *Kawaii* is also a derivation of *kawaisō* or "pitiable," a term that implies the vulnerability of the subject. The "cutesy" observed today in idols closely resembles "sweet little girls" (*otome*) or "cute Japanese women" (*yamato nadeshiko*) images found in books, magazines, advertising, and motion pictures from the late nineteenth and early twentieth centuries (Fig. 2.2).[10] The young Shirley Temple and Annette Funiciello may provide American examples of the "cute style." Temple was nicknamed "America's little darling," while Funiciello was considered "that sweet girl from Walt Disney's Mickey Mouse Club"—except that they were also recognized from the outset as talented personalities who could sing, dance, and project their personae in work. According to some of my American informants, by the time that these child stars reached their late teens, their "cute" features no longer worked for them since these features were considered inappropriate for people above the age of fifteen or so. The

---

10. Detailed historical studies on the image of "cutesy" in Japan have been conducted, for instance, by Ōtsuka (1989), Akiyama (1992), and Karasawa (1995).

Fig. 2.2 A cute personality represented on a postcard
from the turn of the twentieth century.

difference in Japan is that "cute" is considered acceptable and even
attractive in older teens and young adults as well as in children.[11]

To express cutesy, idols generally smile with bared teeth and
clear, sparkling eyes. Female idols tend to strike "coy" poses, while
male idols adopt a more "stylish" or "cool" appearance. All fifteen
female fans of male idols with whom I spoke during my fieldwork
stated that to appear "stylish" is what makes male idols cute.

---

11. Walt Disney discovered Funiciello at the age of thirteen and made her a
member of the so-called Mouseketeers, a group of regular personalities that
appeared on *The Mickey Mouse Club Show*. This children's television show aired
between 1955 and 1959.

Among these informants, one female university student remarked that "the earnest attempts of young and innocent-looking bodies to act stylish make them somewhat pitiful and therefore very sweet." The autographs and handwritten letters of female idols are often accompanied by cute animated characters, including kittens and bunnies (Fig. 2.3). In the past, cute female idols dressed up in frilled dresses, otherwise known as "fake-child costumes" (*buri-buri ishō*), which resemble the clothes of fancy dolls. Although this fashion is considered to be outdated, and idol fashion now tends to focus more on the "classy," this sense of fanciness remains as an important factor in idol-image representations. On the other hand, male idols have always appeared in a "dandyish" style. Nevertheless, all these styles have a common goal: "to heighten their attraction," according to one idol costume designer.

Idol cutesy encompasses other personal qualities that together generate a sense of empathy in the minds of viewers. These qualities include purity and liveliness. Most idols are represented as "pure-hearted and pretty" (*junjō-karen*), and their sweet, meek performances enhance this image. Purity entails a lack of ego, and pure personalities are, ideally speaking, moderate, open-minded, and accepting. Purity is a prominent value in Japan, and it has a strong association with *shintō* rites of ablution (*misogi*): the ritual cleansing of body and spirit, or the ritual removal of physical and spiritual pollution.[12] Idol producers and fans frequently compare idols with *shintō* goddesses or *miko*, a group of maidens who provide services to shrines, claiming that a cute, innocent idol can comfort her viewers by cleansing their hearts.

Purity can have implications for sexual politics. For a female subject to be pure-hearted implies that she is meek enough to subordinate herself to any form of male sexual domination. The

---

12. One of the most familiar examples of purification rituals is rinsing one's hands and mouth in a shrine before worshipping. Another example is an assembly of company managers on New Year's Day (or on other important occasions) before an altar to pray for the safety of the employees and the well-being of the firm. For the latter, a priest is invited from a local shrine to officiate over the rites of purification (e.g., Lewis 1993; Nelson 1996).

Fig. 2.3 An idol autograph accompanied
by a cute animated character.

stance taken by innocent-looking female idols before their male
fans implies a double objectification: as objects to be viewed and as
objects to be desired. This explains the tendency for male idol fans
to consider themselves as being more comfortable with adoring
cute-idols than with real-life women, thinking that idols are less
resistant (therefore more accommodating) to these fans' libidinous
demands. It also explains why some regard these cute-idol fans as
disturbed individuals who derive joy from sexually objectifying
young and innocent female personalities—a point to which I will
return in a subsequent chapter.

Another subtype of cute is liveliness. "Youthfulness that bursts
open" (*hajikeru wakasa*), as it is called, encompasses singing,
dancing, and acting in animated, high-spirited, and tomboyish
ways. This saucy image of an idol, as represented by Ikue Sakaki-
bara (debut 1977), Noriko Sakai (debut 1987), Kyōko Koizumi
(1982), Yoshie Hayasaka (debut 1990), Yuki Uchida (debut 1994),
and Tomoe Shinohara (debut 1995) at the time of their debut, is
replaced by a more temperate, adult image as she matures. Such an
image is successful if it can stir the viewer into a frenzy. All of
these images embellish idols with youthfulness, the purpose of

which is to comfort those who wish to grow up together with them or build their lives around them (Fig. 2.4).

Song lyrics also enable empathetic communication between idols and young followers. Idol songs are typically romantic fantasies of having a "crush" on someone. Thus, in a song titled *Yoroshiku ai-shuu* (Sorrow, with regards; CBS/Sony, 1974), a male idol, Hiromi Go, sings, "I want you to believe in my love more tamely, I want to live with you, if I could. . . . You are always there when I close my eyes!" and idealizes the typical mentality of an adolescent boy who desires to cherish his lover. And Seiko Matsuda, a well-known female idol, sings "Oh my milky smile, I want to take a journey in(to) your arms. . . . Hold me tight with your tender love!" in a song called *Kaze wa aki-iro* (The wind is autumn-colored; CBS/Sony, 1980), expressing a young girl's desire to fall into the arms of a nice man. Songs such as these address the relationship between a young couple who experience adultlike romance for the first time in their lives.

Other songs illustrate the adolescent struggle with sexual feelings—as in *Hitonatsu no keiken* (One summer experience; CBS/Sony, 1974), in which a female idol singer, Momoe Yamaguchi, sings, "I will give you the most important thing that a girl treasures in her little heart. . . . Love is so precious. . . . It's a sweet bewitching trap!" A group interview I conducted with four female listeners of this song indicated that virginity was the first thing that came to mind when they heard the word "a girl's most important thing." The loss of virginity is contextualized as a rite of passage for girls who are on their way to becoming adult women. It is an event that is supposed to invoke, in every adolescent girl who experiences it, a mixture of excitement and fear. Lyrics of idol songs thus often portray romance as an index of emotional in-stability. A male idol, Toshihiko Harada, signals the adolescent's desire to experience sexual intercourse in his song titled *Koi = do!*

Fig. 2.4 Scenes from a walkway in Shinjuku station, Tokyo.
Cute, saucy images of idols appear on walls (top) and
poles (bottom; photos by the author, June 1995).

(Love = do!; Canyon Records, 1981), part of which reads "I wanna do! I wanna do! I want your shy heart. Isn't it okay to love you more? Let's dance, it's a party for the two of us!" Having a sexual affair is a central topic for adolescents, and idol songs tend to magnify this theme, albeit in euphemistic ways. According to the four female listeners who participated in the group interview I conducted, this song represented the idea that adolescent boys just want to get laid.

Because adolescents are considered to be in a state of emotional instability, they are considered incapable of rightly expressing their feelings. Ballads sung by idols are emblematic of such a perception, and these songs express sorrows and frustrations that may be felt by adolescents when relationships fail as the result of their lack of communicative skills. In a song entitled *Haru nanoni* (Even though it's spring; Nippon Phonogram, 1983), for example, the female idol Yoshie Kashiwabara sings, "Even though it is spring, we will have to separate. . . . Even though it's spring, tears flow out of my eyes. I am only drawing a sigh," representing how fragile adolescent love affairs can be. Building on the notion that youth is a transient life stage, this song exposes the sadness of youthful romance: an affair that is destined to be short-lived—not unlike spring, which in Japan is regarded as a precious moment in which the sprouting of life on earth is appreciated.

In another ballad called *Seishun no ijiwaru* (Malicious youth; Bermuda Records, 1984), the female idol Momoko Kikuchi sings, "You were sitting on a guardrail, somewhat away from me. You seem to be angry, and you won't say anything to me. . . . The youth that prevents us from being honest provokes pain," describing how two friends who care about each other find it difficult to reveal their feelings toward one another. One appears to be frustrated, but does not know how to express it. The other, the subject of this song, quietly observes the situation, and the lyric offers a description of the subject's feelings. It poses youth as a state of emotional unrest: the state in which adolescent lovers are too hesitant to reveal their feelings or incapable of communicating with each other like grownups. In these ways, ballads operate as corollary expressions of emotional instability built around love affairs that contribute to the social characterization of youth.

While songs such as these signify the betwixt and between "limbo of youth" (so to speak), other songs represent the will of adolescents to overcome youthful hardships through peer solidarity. The song *Dream* (Pony Canyon, 1988) by Hikaru Genji provides a case in point. Part of the lyric of this song reads, "My love, let's get together with our usual friends. My love, we are all concerned about you! I am also lost in a labyrinth, dashing with my anxious heart!" Even though this represents anxieties and incoherent selves as adolescent themes, it signifies friendship as a means to overcome these psychological frustrations. The song shows that young people tend to get lost in their own lives and their own feelings, but that friends are there to share in that sense of being lost. Friendships can help one overcome this feeling through peer solidarity.

These lyrical excerpts from smash hits are a small portion of a great many narratives epitomized by idols, who provide pathways that allow young listeners to develop as social beings. While some of these hit songs are ballads that adhere to the pessimism of youthful immaturity, others generate optimistic attitudes toward living; and both of these traits are developed within the grand scheme of romance. If, as Lindholm (1995: 57) contends in his discourse on romantic passion, romance can be understood as a "creative act of human imagination" and more specifically a "cultural expression of deep existential longings for an escape from the prison of the self," then we can understand these idol narratives as using romance to cultivate the exotic world of imagination to which Japanese consumers who fantasize about romance can escape through idol consumption. It should be mentioned that it is not only to love-struck adolescents that these singers appeal. Interviews I conducted have shown that many older Japanese favor young cute-idols due to their fascination with youth, and because idols bring back nostalgic memories of their own younger days when their lives were still full of wonder and possibility. Although these people may become constituents of idol audiences, they are onlookers rather than enthusiastic participating consumers. Participants in the idol cult are adolescents and young adults whose ages range, in my observation, between early teens and mid-twenties—mostly those to whom romantic (or sexual) fantasies have a maximum appeal because they are not married.

IDOLS, FEMALE-LED YOUTH CULTURE, AND THE POSTWAR SOCIOECONOMY

In her extensive study of women, media, and consumption in Japan, Kinsella (1995) shows that what the "cute style" idols embody is part of a broader popular-cultural movement that emerged in Japan in the mid-1960s, expanded over the subsequent two decades, and reached a peak of "saccharine intensity" in the early 1980s. This movement coincided with an era in which Japan celebrated the birth of a new consumer culture at the height of its postwar economic growth. With this culture emerged a female-led youth culture that refused to cooperate with the established social norms or values of adult society.

To be cute in this socioeconomic setting was to celebrate appearances and attitudes that are "infantile and delicate at the same time as being pretty" (Yamane 1990: 35, quoted in Kinsella 1995: 220), and thereby participate in the creation of a utopia in an affluent environment where people could remain forever "young," "playful," "childlike," and thus "liberated from the filthy world of adult politics." According to Kinsella, the cute style also generated a sense of nostalgia in urban dwellers, which harkens back to an imagined rural past associated with childish simplicity and spiritual unity, in opposition to the alienating forces of city life: "As [Walt] Disney romanticized nature in relation to industrial society, so Japanese cuteness romanticized childhood in relation to adulthood. By idolizing their childhoods and remnant childishness, young Japanese people implicitly damned their individual futures as adults in society. Condemning adulthood was an individualized and limited way of condemning society generally" (Kinsella 1995: 241, brackets mine). Young people in Japan use the cute style to signal their resistance to adult society. Although I am not sure how many of the young Japanese are clearly conscious of the resistant aspect of their embodiments of the cute style, I see from my observations that the act of embodying the cute style provides its young enactors with a refuge from the stressful adult lifestyle typical of industrialized society.

It may not be coincidental, then, that youth-oriented movements like the "idol boom" appeared when it did in Japan—at the height of Japan's postwar "economic miracle." This was a time of rapid economic growth, as marked by the rise of the gross national product to the second highest in the world after the United States. The work and sacrifice that contributed to that growth were giving birth to a new consumer culture fed by rising incomes and enjoyed by a new generation intent on differentiating themselves from their elders not only by not working hard but also by enjoying the fruits of their labor.[13]

This was also a period of rapid social change, with people moving from the countryside to the cities in search of jobs and excitement, and the nuclear family replacing a tradition of "three generations under one roof." Add to this the stress and fast pace that accompany modern industrial life, and one has an adjustment period not unlike the growth years of adolescence, or what may be called the "youth of a nation." Many Japanese people, not just teenagers, were required to make the transition from older social boundaries and ways of life to an increasingly dynamic, complex, and cosmopolitan world of contemporary urban life. Idols, themselves struggling to find their feet on the escalator of show business that packages their "images of becoming," served as "guiding angels" for a population making a similar journey.

By the mid-1990s, or the era of the post-bubble recession, the star of the cute idols was burning less brightly than it had at any time over the three previous decades. In October 1994, the leading daily newspaper, *Asahi Shinbun*, announced that "idols have been in the so-called 'winter period' for some time now," and many producers and magazine editors, including those I interviewed, were saying that idols were "becoming passé." One explanation for this decline of cute idols is found in the increasingly blurred boundaries between different genres of performance.

While the first generation of idols generally stuck to singing, from around the late 1980s it has become common for idol singers to act, for actors to sing, and for both to do comedy and talk-show hosting. Adding to this was the appearance of a large number of idol-like personalities that transformed the term "idols" into a rhetorical resource that could be applied to almost any genre or style of performance—professional and amateur alike—as long as performers seemed cute. In the eyes of many, all this has diminished both the commercial value and the level of expertise among pop singers, leading to an increased demand for, and supply of, more "powerful" and "unique" performers, including "new music" artists

---

13. For statistics regarding Japan's socioeconomic growth, I found, for example, PHP Kenkyūjo 1995 helpful.

and rock stars. Many of these new young performers fall into a new and emerging category, the "post-idol." Cute seems to be on the wane as well, as performers projecting a more mature and sensual image come to the foreground.

Many young performers themselves began to lose interest in the "idol" label, as one informant, a sixteen-year-old female actor, told me in an interview: "People can call me an 'idol' if they wish, but I don't want to project myself in such a 'childish' fashion. My goal is to become a 'professional' singer like Mariah Carey or Janet Jackson." This young talent rejected the cutesy style, contrasting the style with that of young American singers who are viewed as more hip, classy, and professional. Elsewhere, a president from an idol promotion agency evaluated the status of cute idols over the past three decades and indicated how this type of personality no longer possesses the symbolic power that it used to have:

Idols were supposed to be professional debutantes, but now they seem to be a synonym for "immature" talents who lack performance skills. I feel sad to see such a transition. From another standpoint, however, one can say that the level of Japanese idol-pop has improved, and no longer can idols sell themselves by being simply cute. This might be good. Whatever is the case, the fate of "idols" will depend partly upon how we the suppliers will present them to the public, and partly upon whether the people will continue to buy these cute, fantastic image characters. It all comes down to the simple business law of supply and demand as applied to the young people of contemporary Japan.

His comment implies the need for idol suppliers to reform idols in accordance with shifting consumer tastes. What was popular in the past may very well become a point of ridicule once it becomes passé. Idol performances, in this regard, are grounded on an ongoing, dynamic process of symbolic production.

COLLECTIVE SYMBOLS OF JAPANESE MASS CULTURE

Scholars such as Barnouw and Kirkland (1992) argue that pop culture personalities and performances serve not merely to provide entertainment and earn money but also to develop a repertoire of themes, perspectives, characters, relationships, and outcomes that can be used by the public to make sense of the world. Japanese idols certainly perform this function. This relevance to the lives of their audience, particularly those of young fans, is surely a key to their success.

Pop idols may not be the most talented actors on earth, but their images continue to reflect and contextualize the concerns of their audience, offer models of attractive lifestyles, and substantiate adolescent identity as a socialization project to make some sense out of how to bring together separate life forces such as age, class, gender, and sexuality. As long as idols and their manufacturing industries do that, they will be a strong and profitable symbolic presence in Japanese popular culture and mass society.

3

Idol Performances and
Gender Identities

One of my informants, an editor of an idol magazine, commented that the term "idol" could be interpreted as a combination of two English words, "I" and "doll." There are even idol groups that incorporate the word "doll" in their names, such as "Performance Doll" and "En-Doll." This, according to the magazine editor, implies that the subject "I" becomes a doll-like object to be adored by the viewer. Another informant created a pun by associating the word "I" with *ai*, which in Japanese means "love," thus equating idols with "love-dolls." Female idols, in these senses, are treated as motifs with which viewers identify themselves: either as types of adolescent females that young boys wish to possess or as types that young girls want to emulate. Another informant thought, however, that the "-dol" part of the word could be interpreted commercially, as *doru* from the English "dollars," thus "I-dollars" or "love-dollars." This reflects the producer's perspective that idols can be sources of profit. These cases together indicate that becoming a female idol is to be wrapped up in a package of toylike femininity designed by idol-manufacturing agencies to attract consumers and enlarge profits.

In light of these possible interpretations, the discussion presented in this chapter investigates female idol performances within a wider context of gender construction in modern Japan in order to understand how the idol industry sets up interplays between the existing roles of Japanese women and constructed stereotypes of adolescent femaleness. How the shaping of young performers into models of adolescent femaleness is actually done, and how idol promoters try to legitimate their molding practices as contributing to the socialization of youth, are the questions addressed in this chapter. I will use as a frame of reference the compulsory male discipline that young female performers are subjected to as they become marketable personalities representing ideal types of adolescent femaleness.[1] The idea underlying the discussion presented in this chapter is that gender is crafted: an enactment of received norms, which surface as physical style. Disciplinary practices produce a body that in gesture and appearance is recognizably feminine or masculine (Bartky 1990: 65).[2]

Jennifer Robertson (1998) offers a clearer definition of gender as distinguished from sex and sexuality. While sex denotes both a physical act and the physical body differentiated by either female or male genitalia, and by their usual capabilities (e.g., menstruation, seminal ejaculation, and orgasm), gender refers to social, cultural, historical, and political conventions of deportment, costume, voice, gesture, and other styles of embodiment. Sexuality may overlap with sex and gender, but it pertains specifically to a domain of desire and erotic pleasure (Robertson 1998: 17). The following discussion will apply these concepts to the understanding of how the images of adolescent femaleness are negotiated in the name of producing adorable—thus marketable—female personalities.

Becoming an idol involves winning public recognition in a commercial world where "winner takes all" (*ureta mono no kachi*) is the basic principle. One could say (to be Marxist about it) that the system of idol production, operating on this principle, exploits the labor of wannabe girls in the process of appropriating contemporary gender ideals. For someone from the puritan tradition of Anglo-America, the idol industry's subjugation of adolescent per-

---

1. I use the term "femaleness," as distinguished from "womanhood," to suggest a stage in which female sexuality is emerging but not fully developed as in the case of an adult woman.

2. Gender is also realized through creative cultural practices. See, for example, Babcock 1986. I believe that there is a fine line between discipline and creativity in artistic activities. See also, for example, Bethe and Brazell 1990.

sonalities to Japanese gender ideals may appear unhealthy, alienating, and annoying. This impression is due at least in part to the different cultural assumptions that Anglo-Americans and Japanese have about gender and sexuality. Concentrating on how cultural institutions shape female idols can uncover how young Japanese women transform their selves as they are enmeshed in the ideological discourses on gender and sexuality in each culture.

EXPLORING THE SHOWCASE
OF GENDER STEREOTYPES

The study of idol engineering from the perspective of gender analysis would not be complete without mentioning how the "cute style" is constructed, embodied, and popularized. As previously demonstrated, the cute style made idols the representatives of female-led youth culture. However, I question how female-led the culture represented by cute idols truly is, because the representations of cute idols are overwhelmingly framed by men and imposed upon performers to please the male audience. Moreover, the current shift in the public preference from cute idols to sensual post-idols is happening when the male-dominated socioeconomic system seems on the verge of a breakdown and restructuring. This is a phenomenon known in Japanese as *risutora*, from the English "restoration." This is also the era in which women are becoming considerably more powerful and outspoken in the public sphere than ever before: the *onna no jidai*, or "the age of women." I wish to investigate how these social changes and their perceptions are shown in the way female idols are packaged and sexualized as commodities that serve patriarchal interests.

My investigation also attempts to reveal the parameters of acceptable and unacceptable imagery for adolescents in Japanese society. These manifestations of gender are different from those in North America. Content analyses of media texts show not only that femaleness is portrayed differently across cultures but also that each culture has its own set of standards in portraying sexual images. For example, Japanese are shown to focus on "cutesy," as opposed to a North American emphasis on a more mature image of female sexuality, represented as "sexy" (Takayanagi 1995). But "cutesy" and "sexy" are arbitrary concepts (some may find a cute person to be sexy and vice versa), and any generalization about culture based on these two simplistic criteria is problematic. There is a need to focus more on the ways in which sexualized performances are perceived and enacted by their actors in specific contexts.

A focus on female idols offers insight into the difficulties encountered by young Japanese women as they grow up in a society where male and female gender roles are traditionally strongly differentiated and where women's key role has been biological and social reproduction (see Ochiai 1989, 1997). With this in mind, the subsequent analysis will emphasize the perceptions and expectations that male producers have of adolescent femaleness; how their perceptions and expectations influence the ways female idols are crafted; how female performers feel about enacting female role models; and how these emotions influence the way they perform.

Another relevant issue to be investigated here is the dialogue between the idol industry and female-led youth culture. Even though heterosexual men may have dominated the realm of capitalist production in Japan, there are sets of cultural configurations that serve the interests of young women. "Gal culture" (*gyaru bunka*) is one such configuration relevant to idol engineering. While the formal organs of capitalism are built around a masculine mode of production, Japanese girls develop informal arenas of production by and for themselves. These arenas do not stand by themselves, but are constantly exposed to institutional forces that try to erode, manipulate, and appropriate them into the heterosexual, masculine system of production. Given these social conditions, the current chapter will investigate some of the ways in which the idol industry operates as a hegemonic force as participants situate themselves in the ongoing dialogue with female-led youth subcultures and use these subcultures as sources for symbolic production.

The emphasis on how female idols are produced may not provide sufficient understanding of gender reproduction in idol performances because there is also a construction of masculinity as manifested in the performances of *male* idols. I planned to investigate how male performers understood the relationship between themselves as idols and the Japanese concept of masculinity, but lack of time and contact prevented me from investigating these research areas systematically. In what follows, I will include the discussion of masculinity to the extent that the construction of female idols involves the production of both female and male gender ideals: the projection of a female image encompasses visions of the relationship between women and men, or statements about maleness in terms of what kind of women men like and why. Working in reference to the available data, I will uncover the ways female idol performances project female adolescents, rather than scattering my perspectives by trying to expand on both male and female idols.

The first section of this chapter looks at the positioning of women in Japanese society, exposing some of the social and historical aspects of male domination alongside the corresponding downgrading of women apparent in the public sphere. My point here is to elaborate on the recent development of female-led youth subcultures as a form of rebellion against the existing ideological force that tends to conform adolescent femaleness to the traditional image of Japanese femininity. The second section will detail how the idol industry adjusts to, and encourages, the ongoing struggle between conservative and innovative aspects of womanhood in contemporary Japanese society through its construction of an arena in which gender role models are contested. I compare two cases in which I followed idol candidates to training sessions and observed how they embodied two mutually distinct images of adolescent femaleness. Conversations that illuminate producers and performers' thoughts on these distinct role models and their embodiments are included in this section.

JAPANESE WOMANHOOD AS
AN IDEOLOGICAL FORCE

Japan can be seen as a male-dominated society largely because of the conventional downgrading of women. Two key features play out here: a traditional emphasis on male chauvinism or *danson-johi* (respect men and downgrade women), and a corresponding idealization of "womanliness," or *onnarashisa*, as "good wife, wise mother" (*ryōsai kenbo*). Officials in the Ministry of Education differentiated women from men in the 1890s and universalized the image of women as homebound agents of biological and social reproduction. Ever since, women have been simultaneously typified as "protectorates" (so to speak) of the patriarchal rule—a characterization that continues to influence the public imagination of womanhood in Japan today.

Womanliness in the traditional sense is achieved through enacting a feminine *kata* (form). It is to stylize oneself in a womanly fashion, which involves a distinct speech style, body posture, and attitude. The feminine speech style involves speaking in *onna-kotoba* (women's language), which differs from men's language in vocabulary, intonation, and the use of "gentle-sounding" particles at the end of an utterance. Bodily postures and carriages include scurrying about in a head-down position, feet shuffling in small skittish steps, and sitting with tightly closed legs. Women are prepared to accommodate themselves to the needs and interests of others, and they are ready to subordinate themselves to their superiors, especially those who are elder men.[3]

Starting from birth, girls are treated differently from boys: they are nurtured to be gentle, quiet, meek, accommodating, and self-sacrificing. *Onnarashisa* consists of physical manipulation, sexual disposition, and communication limitation as well as attitudinal compliance. The training to become a woman in Japan has focused on the enhancement of these qualities to the extent that they can be manifested in the form of a perfected public appearance. These gendered personal qualities are to be completed and enacted effortlessly in order to become a culturally appropriate woman in Japanese society (e.g., Ohinata 1995; Creighton 1996).

Ideologues and bureaucrats developed "good wife, wise mother" as the ideal image of a woman in order to help transform Japan from a feudal state to the modern nation-state. This was part of the effort to create a polity strong enough to stand up against the Western imperialist superpowers of that time. The Japanese government planned to institute a "family-state" (*kazoku kokka*) in

---

3. See, for example, Shibamoto 1985 and Endō 1995, 1997, for details regarding Japanese women's speech-acts and related expressive behaviors.

which the emperor played the role of father. Under this policy, women were expected to contribute to the nation's welfare by serving the male family head at home and devoting themselves to the upbringing of children—the nation's future work force (Ohinata 1995: 200).

With such a definition of woman's place in modern Japan, women were at the margins of the public domain and absent from the political arena. Prewar laws prohibited women from participating in voting, organizing political associations, and, before 1925, attending political meetings (Sievers 1983: 52, 53; Uno 1993: 299). The 1898 Civil Code placed women under the authority of the patriarchal head. The head could choose the family domicile, manage his wife's property, and make decisions on legal issues involving his family members (e.g., marriage and divorce) (Uno 1993: 299; Kaneko 1995: 4, 5). Many women entered the job market from time to time, but their occupations were low-wage industrial workers, clerical attendants, teachers, nurses, domestic servants, and home-based workers doing piecework. These occupational types were considered supplemental to those occupied by men (Kawashima 1995: 272–75). In education, the 1899 Girls' High School Law stated that the aim of secondary education for girls was to provide women with the training to become good wives and wise mothers (Kaneko 1995: 5). All these laws during the early modern era helped to construct and support an ideology that regarded the home as the primary place for women.

The 1947 democratic constitution forbade discrimination based on sex in political, economic, and social domains. Yet, evidence suggests that throughout the postwar period, Japanese bureaucrats and politicians, most of whom belonged to the ruling Liberal Democratic Party (LDP), continued to form their policies in accord with the vision of women as domestic agents. Many other formal and informal institutions followed their lead. For instance, the provisions of the 1948 Eugenic Protection Law aimed at preserving the prewar role of women as mothers, rather than protecting their health as individuals. Abortion and contraception were forbidden. As Uno (1993: 306) points out, reproductive policies served national needs rather than women's needs. This suggests that the postwar state still considered women to be bearers of the nation's work force—except that this time, their wombs were borrowed largely to meet the labor needs of industry rather than the needs of households for successors or the state's need for colonists and military conscripts.

The Ministry of Education continued to issue guidelines recommending that primary and secondary coeducational schools organize different course orientations for men and women. Homemaking courses were often mandatory for high-school girls (true of most high schools between 1969 and 1989), and female and male students were on separate teams for sport-oriented activities (Hara 1995: 104). In many primary and secondary schools, female and male students continue to wear differently designed uniforms, carry different-colored school bags (red for girls and black for boys), and have separate classroom rollcalls in which boys' roll is consistently called first (Kameda 1995: 114).

Restrictions were imposed upon women's qualifications to work in companies, whereas men's pursuit of a career path was taken for granted. The 1986 Equal Employment Opportunity Law (EEOL) was implemented to enable Japanese ratification of the International Convention, the goal of which was to eliminate all forms of discrimination against women. However, gender bias continued to exist in many Japanese companies and was reflected in salaries and occupational types.[4] In large companies especially, female employees, or office ladies, were regarded as the "flowers of the workplace" (*shokuba no hana*). Their function was little more than decorative: that is, to please the eyes of the male employers and employees, or to "brighten up" (*hanayaka ni suru*) the company atmosphere as assistants and extras.[5] Women did not get the respect, or the money, that men did.

---

4. For instance, as late as 1991, women's monthly contractual salary was, on average, 60.7 percent of that of men; and 50.8 percent on the basis of total monthly earnings, which included overtime and bonuses. The data from the same year shows that nearly half of the 5.5 million women in the labor force were part-time, temporary, or exempt from the benefits of full-time employment (Kawashima 1995: 278).

5. One in-company newsletter, published in 1977, that I found during my fieldwork had a column in which female employees were compared with flowers, and its title included the phrase "Blossoms of Maidens."

The typical career path of a permanent female employee, as envisioned by Japanese firms, was to be hired for a relatively low-skill or low-responsibility job out of high school. She would work until she got married, retreat to her motherly duties, and, if possible, return to work after her children were grown (Ōuchi 1981). This scenario was part of the labor policy created to cope with a growing shortage of workers during the period of Japan's economic growth (during 1960s and 1970s). It encouraged women to enter the labor force without reducing their responsibilities for household management and childcare (Uno 1993: 305). In reality, opportunities for married women to re-enter the labor market on a full-time basis are limited even today. Most large companies are still reluctant to hire women with outstanding skills or good educational backgrounds (Rohlen 1974; Lebra 1976; Robins-Mowry 1983; Yoshizumi 1995).

Finally, in the domain of popular culture and the mass media, gender bias has influenced the ways in which women were selected and portrayed. As already discussed, the Japanese preoccupation with the characterization of young girls as sexual objects is a trend found in magazines, comics, and movies that are increasingly aimed at young audiences (Funabashi 1995; Clammer 1995; Allison 1996). This public inclination toward young, dependent, and adorable female personalities is apparent in television as well. The age range of most personalities who appear on television is substantially lower and narrower than that of men—most falling between the late teens and the early thirties (quoted in Suzuki 1995: 78, 79).[6] Typically these television personalities are portrayed as middle-class, elegant, sensitive, average, or cute. These images stand in contrast to those of the disliked ugly-looking women (*busu*) and men (*gesu*), or older women (derogatorily referred to as *oban, babaa, obatarian,* or *kuso-babaa*—which literally means "a filthy old woman") and men (*ojin, jijii,* or *kuso-jijii*). These images are frequently the objects of public laughter and ridicule (1995: 79; my observation). The image of an ideal female personality on television is

---

6. This is based on a survey conducted in 1985 by the Forum for Citizens' Television in Tokyo.

paired with that of her ideal partner: the stylish, handsome, firm, and independent man who has the same class background.

Women who appear on news programs and variety shows are more often assistants rather than main hosts. Here, too, women are accessories that brighten up the studio atmosphere. In many Japanese television dramas that I observed, female actors who performed the role of the main character were, in the end, meek, feminine, and ideally obedient—however strong and independent they appear to be in the beginning.

These cases support the fact that sexual politics in Japanese institutions, social relations, and the mass media center on existing gender expectations that characterize women primarily as the dependent caretakers of the home. This characterization as represented in the idealized image of "good wife, wise mother" operates as a recurrent metaphor that presents Japanese femaleness as the object of societal domination. Since the dawn of Japan's modernization, this metaphor profoundly influenced the ways women were treated and portrayed in social, economic, and popular-cultural sectors.

FEMALE-LED YOUTH SUBCULTURE: ELEMENTS OF GENDER TRANSMUTATION

Disenchanted by the prospect of inequality as adult women, many young women try to avoid the stigma of traditional womanhood (*onnarashisa*) in Japan today by seeking alternative forms of femaleness. To be sure, these young women are not the first to oppose the ideology of male chauvinism in Japan. The history of Japan's sexual politics in the modern era encompasses a series of female-led movements that opposed the state's recurrent promotion of the "good wife, wise mother" ideology in its welfare, education, employment, sexuality, and reproduction policies (e.g., Tanaka 1975; Fujimura-Fanselow 1985; Joseigaku kenkyūkai 1987; Sasakura and Nakajima 1990; Kaya 1995; Satō 1995).[7]

---

7. In the 1880s and 1890s, activists and women's groups stressed a woman's right to participate in public affairs. Labor strikes by women began as early as 1886. In 1911, a female activist by the name of Raichō Hiratsuka founded Japan's first feminist organization, Seitōsha (Bluestocking society). Seitōsha published

In 1973, *Fear of Flying*, a million-selling novel by an American novelist, Erica Jong, was translated and published in Japan. It was a story of an adventurous heroine who overcomes her fear of flying on an airplane through her self-enforced trip to Vienna. She travels with her husband in order to attend a conference on psychoanalysis. Once there, she falls in love with a local psychoanalyst and takes off on a jaunt with this new lover across Europe, leaving her husband behind. The trip proves to be empowering: through this venture, the heroine attains her own brand of liberation—that is, she obtains the courage to step out of her home-bound lifestyle back in the United States. This fiction created a sensation in Japan, and the idea of women's personal liberation (*onna no jiko-kaihō*) became resonant enough among young adult women to motivate the media to brand a new concept, *tonderu onna* or "flying woman."

This idea caught the attention of Japanese women whose ages ranged between the early twenties and the early thirties (similar to the heroine's age). Self-affirmative womanhood became even more popular through an incident that occurred in March 1988. Agnes Chan, a former idol singer from Hong Kong who made her debut in Japan in 1972 at the age of seventeen and who subsequently married a Japanese producer, took her one-year-old son with her to a television quiz show on which she appeared as a guest. Such an act was unprecedented, and it ignited a discussion among actors and critics that became known as the "Agnes debate" (*Agnes ronsō*).

———————

periodicals in which female intellectuals discussed various social and legal issues concerning women. Shin fujin kyōkai (New women's association), founded in 1920, succeeded in achieving the repeal of the law that barred women from political meetings. In postwar Japan, the principle of democracy led numerous movements and organizations to emerge within the context of civil society. In the 1970s and 1980s, feminists such as Mitsu Tanaka, Ikuko Atsumi, Chizuko Ueno, and members of Gurūpu tatakau onna (Fighting women's group; founded 1970) criticized the idea of good wife, wise mother. They questioned the inevitability of women's domestic destiny as they examined the mechanism of societal domination as manifested in social institutions such as the state, family, and corporations (Uno 1993: 308). Other activists, pressure groups, and conferences were organized around specific agendas, such as the elimination of sexism in law, politics, employment, and education (e.g., Tanaka 1975; Joseigaku kenkyūkai 1987; Sasakura and Nakajima 1990).

The initiator was a senior singer, Noriko Awaya, who criticized Chan for having violated the etiquette of show business. For Awaya, bringing such a real-life scene as childrearing onto a television show was thoughtlessly inappropriate for a performer whose role was to provide her audience with dreams. Articles for and against Chan's conduct were subsequently published in popular journals; Chan herself wrote an article in the September 11 issue of *Chuō kōron* (better known in English as *The Central Review*) expressing her determination to fight against what she called "Agnes bashing." Her stance was supported by a feminist scholar, Chizuko Ueno, in the May 16 issue of *Asahi shinbun*, on the basis that Chan represented women's freedom of choice in public. This article shifted the gist of the "Agnes debate" from behavioral propriety in performance to the question of women's liberation outside the home.

The increased tendency for young Japanese girls to oppose the traditional image of femininity appears to be an extension of these earlier events. More direct reasons for young girls to adopt rebellious attitudes against adults have appeared recently. In July 1990, a high-school teacher (a middle-aged man) in Kobe City caused the death of a female student by jamming her in the school gate. The teacher closed the gate in order to prevent students who did not make it to school on time from entering the campus. The media contextualized this particular event within the larger, ongoing problem with the system of high-school education in Japan. This resulted in the so-called "school problem" (*gakkō mondai*) that generated negative images of high-school teachers as stubborn regulators who threaten students more than they educate them. Added to this was what might be loosely characterized as a "moral crisis" in high schools precipitated by a series of scandalous incidents in which teachers had engaged in sexual harassment, bullying, and overlooking of bullying among students. Alongside the emergent public distrust of high-school education and the corresponding call for a more "relaxed education" (*yutori kyōiku*), teenage women began to oppose what they saw as a filthy, male-dominated system in which those whose senses of morality were questionable authorize rules and impose regulations.

One of the most infamous forms of escapism for young Japanese girls in the 1980s was the cute style. By adopting this form, the most extreme case of which was to act like a child or in a *burikko* manner, young girls attempted to abandon any need to grow up and play the role of "good wife, wise mother." As popular culture has a tendency to do, the longing by these young women for eternal childhood was perpetuated by an influx of cute products, celebrated cute idols like Seiko Matsuda, and animated characters like San Rio's Hello Kitty.

But because the cute style had thoroughly penetrated Japanese society by the early 1990s, it has gradually lost its appeal as a form of rebellion. Moreover, there was an emergent perception that "cutesy" embraced fragile femininity, which continued to become objectified by adult men. To borrow from Tanaka, cute girls appeared to be "too weak and stupid," especially in the eyes of the newer generation of young Japanese women (Tanaka 1995: 85). Cutesy has become the subject of cynicism, and those who continue to embody the cute style today tend to be disliked as being too flirtatious or *kobi o utte iru* (selling one's favors to be attractive).

In the youth culture of the 1990s, a new image of adolescent femaleness, known as *gyaru*, or "gals," began to replace the older image of *kawaii shōjo*, or "cute girls." This image conjured up the figure of an assertive, self-centered young woman who is in no hurry to marry and who maintains a stable of boyfriends to serve her different needs (Robertson 1998: 65). *Gyaru* could be read as a Japanese form of the French *garçon* (*gyarusonnu*), one of the terms used in the 1920s to denote a group of self-assertive women who took militant approaches to the established world. These women rejected conventions to follow free and daring lifestyles at a time when people were weary from World War I. The booming leisure industries of the time offered new fashion, music, film, and other forms of innovative entertainment, and young women in particular embraced a sense of liberated femaleness by wearing sassy dresses, short skirts, cloche hats, and strapped shoes that offered them freedom of movement, versus the heavy and frilly Edwardian costume that the previous generation had to wear. *Garçon* were commonly spotted in nightclubs, drinking, smoking, flirting with young men who they picked up on the spot, and dancing frantic-ally to the syncopated rhythms of new music.[8] The media of the time called these "New Women." The attitudes of contemporary Japanese *gyaru* toward adults resemble this antisocial stance of French flappers in the 1920s and 1930s (Robertson 1998: 65). Silver-berg (1991) documents a trend that occurred in Japan during the 1920s and 1930s: young women modeled themselves after French *garçon*. Young, cosmopolitan women rejected the chaste and sub-missive domesticity of good wife, wise mother. They were called "modern girls," though this term is better known in abbreviated form, *moga*. The end of youth as anchored in the established proc-ess of female enculturation appears desolate in the eyes of contem-porary Japanese gals, providing them with a reason to abandon *onnarashisa*. Just as the French *garçon* did, Japanese gals of the 1990s have rejected the traditional traits of *onnarashisa* with the hope that society will treat them differently from the women of previous generations.

In the fall of 1998, a female student who was taking my class on Japanese culture and society in a Canadian university went to Ja-pan to conduct a research project on gal subcultures under my guidance. She was competent in Japanese and well informed on re-cent Japanese trends. Her experience of growing up in a commu-nity of Japanese immigrants at the same time as attending schools that catered to Anglo-Canadian norms and customs provided her with sufficient background to observe Japanese gals with a good eye for cross-cultural comparison. Her task was twofold: to ana-lyze contemporary Japanese gals with respect to linguistic, physical, and attitudinal aspects; and to compare these attributes of gals with the features of traditional Japanese womanhood.

Based on this research project, the student and I identified five subtypes of *gyaru*: *sukeban* (delinquent girls), *oyajigyaru* (gals who act like middle-aged men), *Amuraa* (followers of post-idol Namie Amuro), *kogyaru* (kid gals), and *gankuro* (tan-faced gals). These gal subtypes evolved in a sequence, and they could be differentiated

---

8. New styles of dancing called the "lindy hop" and "the Charleston" were popularized among these women at nightclubs, and these generally consisted of frenzied body shaking, toe turning, and arm swinging.

from one another in a strict sense, but they share one feature: all consist of young women in their teens and early twenties who adopt distinct language, physical appearances, and attitudes to express their resistance to *onnarashisa* (womanliness) as defined by the parent culture. In what follows, I will elaborate on the distinguishing features of the gal subtypes.

Sukeban

Members of this group emerged in the late 1980s. They typically wore colored socks and lengthened uniform skirts to protest the orthodox appearance of white-socked and properly uniformed high-school girls. These girls tended to use vulgar forms of speech that are associated with the male style. They are quiet but militant and ready to use aggressive language in order to strike at any potential opponents who could step in their way. One of the most notable linguistic features of this subcultural group is its members' use of the masculine first-person pronoun *boku* in reference to themselves instead of *watashi*, which is a form typically used by *onnarashii* women. The term *sukeban* was a combination of "militant female companions" (*suke*) and "gang leaders" (*banchō*). These girls were associated with male delinquent groups, otherwise known as *bōsōzoku*, or "speed tribes," for their typical appearance on motorcycles.[9]

Oyajigyaru

The name comes from the cartoonist Yukko Chūsonji's comic strip, which appeared in 1989 issues of a popular weekly magazine, *SPA!*. The comic depicted a group of young, carefree office ladies who adopted attitudes that resembled middle-aged men (*oyaji*). These women were bedecked in long hair and elegant clothing—appropriate for office ladies. Yet they were not reserved, obedient servants of men, as were the office ladies of previous generations. Taking advantage of their marginal positions in the workplace, earning disposable incomes at the peak of Japan's economic

---

9. For further details on Japanese motorcycle gangs and their antisocial attitudes, see Satō 1991.

growth, and enjoying their freedom as unmarried women, the *oya-jigyaru* characters in the story spent their leisure time drinking beer, dining out, traveling, playing golf, and gambling on horse races. They laughed at their male counterparts for having to work competitively for long hours. The similarity between *oyajigyaru* and middle-aged men is also reflected in the use of vulgar language in relatively informal social settings, spitting in the street, and urinating outdoors. The real-life *oyajigyaru* copied some of the personal qualities that the comic characters represented. By rejecting the traditional *onnarashisa* and enjoying some of the freedom of men, while avoiding the responsibilities of adult men, these women permitted themselves to live out a role that made them exempt from the social expectations of adulthood.

Amuraa

In 1995, a rising nineteen-year-old pop idol by the name of Namie Amuro sported sexy outfits that consisted of long blondish hair, sharply colored and thinly trimmed eyebrows, tight short pants, exposed navel, and long boots, creating a sensation in the fashion and cosmetic industries. Born in Okinawa, Amuro had dark skin and what her idol colleagues described as a "funny small face." Her performance incorporated dances derived from black hip-hop artists. Her style stood outside the typical image of Japanese beauty.[10] With the growth in Amuro's popularity, there developed a cultlike group of young women who adopted the Amuro style. The Amuro craze peaked between 1995 and 1996, with wannabes dying their hair, going to tanning salons, wearing provocative clothing, and dieting to attain Amuro's exotic look. The media developed a new term, *Amuraaa*, or "Amurors," to refer to these young women.

---

10. The media praised Amuro as one of the most outstanding pop divas of the 1990s. The March 10, 1995, issue of *SPA!*, for instance, introduced her as the "wonder woman of the century," commenting, "Looking around the Japanese entertainment world, one notices that it has been a while since idols who could sing and dance well enough have appeared. The rise of Amuro, a competent performer, will . . . certainly provide a new direction!"

Kogyaru

Translated as "kid gals," this group emerged out of *Amuraa* and acquired momentum among teenage girls on the streets and in the shopping malls of Tokyo. *Kogyaru* possess enormous buying power, provided by allowances, part-time jobs, and affairs with adult men in exchange for monetary support (acts known as *enjo-kōsai*). A typical *kogyaru* has blondish hair, dark skin obtained at a tanning salon, and a tough-girl attitude. She wears an altered school uniform that consists of excessively shortened skirt and markedly loose white socks. *Kogyaru* members tend to form groups, some of which are hierarchically organized with one gal standing out from the rest for being particularly tough. In addition to their habit of speaking loudly, happily, and informally regardless of where they are and who they speak with, *kogyaru* use codified language that incorporates abbreviated terms and exclamatory affixes. Two words that represent the *kogyaru* language are *choberiba* and *cho-berigu*, which stand for "enormously bad" and "enormously good," respectively. These words, which combine an exclamatory affix *chō* with abbreviates of English "very bad" (*beriba*) and "very good" (*berigu*), signal *kogyaru*'s transgression of female linguistic propriety. *Kogyaru* also utilize pocket bells and cellular phones as their major means of communication. Their perpetual inclination toward trends and their "girls just want to have fun" attitude have captured the imagination of the media and nation at large: they are considered a new breed of self-assertive adolescent women who are tired of the polite-girl stereotype.

Gankuro

The name is a combination of "face" (*gan*) and "dark" or "black" (*kuro*). It signifies the members' super-dark tans, which come with light-colored eye makeup, shiny lips, decorated fingernails, and bleached hair (most typically blonde with hints of light green, orange, yellow, or purple). Because of these distinct features, *gankuro* girls are often derogatorily referred to as "mountain women"

Fig. 3.1 Sample images of *kogal*: street *kogal* (left) and *kogal*
in school uniform (right) (courtesy of Miwako Afuso).

(*yamanba*), monstrous women that appear in Japanese folktales. Linguistically and attitudinally, *gankuro* girls are identical to *ko-gyaru*.

These subtypes illustrate the trajectories of female-led youth subcultures that transgress the image of traditional Japanese femininity (Fig. 3.1). Contemporary Japanese gals take their bad-girl look from the *sukeban*, their habits from the *oyajigyaru*, and their sexual appearance from the *Amuraa*, making up their own style that serves as an alternative to the socially accepted image of adolescent womanhood as the precursor to good wife, wise mother.

Although space is too limited here to go into much detail, the fieldwork that my student conducted among a group of *kogal* revealed that these gals gathered outside their high-school gate each morning in order to readjust their skirts to the regulation length, change their socks to school standards, and remove their makeup. They wished to convey the image of a pure youth that fits the ideal standard for Japanese students as defined by their school and reinforced by their teachers. If they did not, it would bring unwanted attention from the guidance counselor (*hodō-kyōkan*), which could lead to being branded a delinquent girl (*hikōshōjo*). The morning transformation was reversed after school as these gals hiked up their skirts, changed back into loose socks, applied makeup, painted their nails, and redid their hair (Hayashi 1998: 14). This observation captures the dilemma of contemporary Japanese gals enacting their adolescent female roles in a highly regulated social environment.

My student also reported a case in which one gal used excessively bold language in speaking to authority figures, especially adult men. Using a vulgar form of the second-person pronoun, *omae*, instead of its normal form, *anata*, this gal demonstrated her aggressive, confrontational, even insulting approach to someone whom she regarded as a male chauvinist. At home, she occasionally spoke aggressively to her mother, who became apprehensive and gave in to the gal's demands more readily. A member of the generation that continued to enact *onnarashisa*, this gal's mother was incapable of responding in any effective way. Subsequent interviews with the gal demonstrated her intention to provoke fear in authority figures, who do not expect such a speech style from young women in a public place. *Onna-kotoba* or the traditional way of speaking for women in Japan lacks expressive language, which handicaps women from conveying their ideas and feelings in a direct way. The gal relieved herself from this sort of constriction by utilizing bold language (1998: 14).

The delinquent style that the *kogyaru* represents and the magnitude of the gal phenomenon within a manner-sensitive population has bewildered adult critics. One of the most recent critiques is directed toward a type of activity conducted by some *kogyaru* members called *enjo-kōsai* or "financially aided affairs," which consists of seeking long-term affairs (multiple affairs in some cases) with adult businessmen who provide them with monetary support.[11] Miyadai (1994), who conducted extensive ethnographic research on this subject, gathered comments by parents and teachers, not to mention professional critics, who monotonously denounce *enjo-kōsai* as an immoral act that should not be tolerated. Belittling these criticisms by adult moralists, Miyadai points out that those who engage in what many may consider prostitution with adult men are far from imprudently objectifying themselves to their male patrons. Instead, these gals have a clear sense of self-control, which many Japanese adults lack, and they are far more capable than their parents would assume in dealing with men's sexual desires. They are also capable of developing their own marketing techniques to earn a living in a world dominated by adult politics.

It is in this power dynamic that the image-making legacy of the idol industry can be situated. The *kogyaru* phenomenon became so prominent in Japan by the late 1990s that the idol industry had to consider incorporating some elements of *kogyaru* into its construction of idol imagery. What resulted was an arena in which old and new images competed to establish a norm of adolescent femaleness. In what follows, I will compare two of these contested prototypes of adolescent selfhood, the cutesy versus the sexy, and examine how these two images are differently envisioned and strategically manufactured by their producers.

THE PRODUCTION
OF CUTE-IDOLS

The group of female idol candidates I studied intensively for a period of four weeks in September 1995 included four individuals who had just been recruited to an agency that went by the name of Cutie Smile Productions, Ltd. I will use as pseudonyms Erika (thirteen years old), Miho (fifteen), Yoshiko (fifteen), and Mayumi (seventeen). Erika and Miho were recruited on the street by the method known as "street-corner scouts" (*machikado sukauto*).

11, For an article written on this subject in English, see, for instance, the December 24, 1996, issue of *Newsweek* (pp. 50–54).

Yoshiko and Mayumi, on the other hand, entered the agency by winning audition contests.

All four of these individuals had dreamed about becoming celebrities since they were little, and like all other performers I interviewed, they perceived idol performances to be the first stage in their career-building process. Yoshiko's ambition was to become a "well-known idol-pop singer like Seiko Matsuda," while all the others vaguely wanted to become professional actors. Erika and Miho were less dedicated to their work because it was something they were asked to do, rather than something they had always wanted to do. In contrast, Yoshiko and Mayumi were fully committed. This contrast had a crucial impact upon their attitudes toward idol performances. Playing the role of pop idols provided Erika and Miho with negative pressure that they were hesitant to accept, while it provided Yoshiko and Mayumi with positive challenges that they were willing to face.

Cutie Smile Productions was a venture that had specialized in idol manufacturing since the early 1990s. Their trademark was to promote typically cute idols. The institute had as its motto "pure, honest, and pretty" (*kiyoku, tadashiku, utsukusu*), and its trainees were expected to appear before the public with such qualities on show. Eager to obtain greater public recognition, this relatively small agency became an active collaborator in my research project. Akihiko Nakahiro was a male producer and the main decision-maker in this agency. In his mid-forties, Nakahiro has been in show business for nearly half his life. He previously worked as an idol manager and fan-club organizer. One of his assistants, Tsuneaki Kusunoki, was a man who specialized in voice training, while a female assistant, Yumie Wakase, directed choreography. Both assistants were in their late twenties. The agency held concerts from time to time, where approximately five hundred fans, mostly men aged 20 to 35, gathered.

I followed the four candidates to two- to three-hour training sessions that took place three times per week in the evenings. All four individuals underwent intensive voice training, followed by dance lessons. At times, all four were trained together; at other times, one of them underwent an individual session while the others practiced on their own. These sessions took place in a studio that was located next to the agency's office space. While Kusunoki and Wakase instructed the trainees most of the time, Nakahiro interrupted whenever he felt it was necessary. Nakahiro called this interruption "quality control," which made sure that trainees could perform properly in the end; that is, the way he wanted them to perform.[12]

EMBODYING
ADOLESCENT FEMININITY

In projecting his ideal image of adolescent femaleness onto idol performances, Nakahiro was specific about how performers should speak and act on stage. He described his ideal image of young female personalities as "pure-hearted and lovable young girls who could attract young men." When I asked if he had any interest in targeting female audiences, he did not deny it, but said that such a concern was secondary. He said:

I specialize in producing female idols that play a classically feminine character. However, I am a man and not a woman. I will not be able to understand how women themselves really think or feel about their ideal role models. Even if I could imagine that for a moment, my imagination would eventually deviate from what women actually think, like, want, and need. On the other hand, it is easy for me to imagine the kind of girls that young men prefer to go after, simply because I myself grew up as a man. Thus, my primary work is to concentrate on the production of female idols that can be adored by male idol fans. Of course, I do not intend to reject female idol fans who are willing to come see our performances.

He focused on the production of an adolescent femininity that he could market primarily to a male audience, using his own gender identity as a way of honing his operation.

---

12. Ian Buruma (1984: 68) notes in his observation of idol choreography that idols are choreographed, directed, and drilled to such a degree that any spontaneity that might have been there to begin with stood little chance of surviving. This was exactly what happened with the four individuals I followed. This is also true of other Japanese, especially traditional, forms of performance, such as *noh* and *kabuki*.

In a voice-training session, Nakahiro demanded that the performers articulate their words with childlike innocence and enthusiasm. This appeared to be difficult for all four trainees, because they were not used to singing and speaking in such a manner. With a guitar in his arms, Kusunoki played a tune and made each trainee sing a lyrical line over and over again until he thought it was good enough, then asked the next trainee to do the same. Nakahiro occasionally stepped in to push the trainees harder toward refining certain parts. The following excerpt is a typical example of how this interaction took place—in this case between Yoshiko (Y), Kusunoki (K), and Nakahiro (N). My observation of each action in its immediate context is indicated in brackets.

The setting is as follows: Y practices singing with a microphone in her hands, K coaches the practice, and N observes the two from his seat at the back of the studio.

Y: [sings a line] "It's so wonderful to fall in love, but it's difficult to be loved . . ."

K: Stretch out this "loved" part. . . . Yes, that's good! All right . . . On to the next part. . . .

Y: "When one wants to capture the happiness, it's so difficult not to rush . . ."

K: Good! Okay, that's it. Good enough.

N: [looks frustrated] What do you mean good enough, Kusunoki! Can't you tell that the "happiness" part is not articulated right!? Do it once more!

Y: *Hai*! [a humble confirmation in Japanese] "Happiness" . . .

N: [looking frustrated] The whole line, idiot!

Y: *Hai*! "When one wants to capture the happiness, it's so difficult not to rush . . ."

N: Put more heart into "happiness," would you!? Like "happiness" . . . [demonstrates a childlike articulation]

Y: *Hai*! "Happiness" . . . [tries her best to sound childlike]

N: It's "happiness" . . . [demonstrates again]

Y: "happiness" . . . [repeats with a childlike smile on her face]

N: Try the whole line again.

Y: *Hai*! "When one wants to capture the happiness, it's so difficult not to rush . . ."

N: "Difficult not to rush" . . . [demonstrates]

Y: *Hai*! "It's so difficult not to rush . . ."

N: Too strong! Why can't you get the cutesy!? It's "difficult not to rush" . . . [demonstrates] Even try to overdo it!

Y: *Hai*! [looking a bit tense, she pauses for two seconds to take a breath] "When one wants to capture the happiness, it's so difficult not to rush . . ." [tries her best to sound childlike]

N: Next.

Y: *Hai*! "Let's have the courage to say I love you . . ."

N: "I love you" . . . [he demonstrates]

Y: "I love you" . . .

N: [three-second pause] Okay, go on to the next part. . . . [looks unsatisfied but leaves it as it is for now; signals Kusunoki to take over]

Nakahiro spoke in an authoritative voice that incorporated vulgar speech. He clearly contextualized social hierarchy, submitting Kusunoki and Yoshiko to his nearly coercive control. Tension filled the air during this extensive drill, and although the trainees tried to keep up, they could not in the end prevent themselves from having weary expressions on their faces.

Dance lessons focused on making predominantly feminine gestures. Rocking the body back and forth, turning the body left and right, moving the body in a bouncy way, and waving the hands were some of the most noticeable features. Pensive poses and melancholic expressions were made when ballads were sung. In these cases, the trainees held microphones in their hands and waved their bodies softly from left to right. In Nakahiro's words, the bouncy look signified youthfulness that bursts open (*hajikeru wakasa*) while the pensiveness stood for emotional instability (*jōcho fuantei*). These, according to Nakahiro, were the two main features of youthful femininity invoking empathy in the minds of the viewers (Fig. 3.2).

Over the course of the four-week training, Erika and Miho became increasingly frustrated. One day, Miho came out of the studio with tears in her eyes as Nakahiro scolded her for not getting the style right in spite of the long hours of practice. She subsequently recalled this event as one of the most unpleasant experiences she had ever had in her life. Miho said that the gestures required by Nakahiro made her look excessively shy, coy, and submissive, creating a fake personality that was no longer herself,

Fig. 3.2   Idol candidates undergoing a choreography lesson: the
producer of Cutie Smile Productions instructs a young novice
(top); the choreographer demonstrates a new choreographic
form before debutantes (bottom; photos by the author,
May 1995.)

and she felt extremely uncomfortable about it. Erika, on the other
hand, got some sense of how to enact the cute character designed
by Nakahiro, but she also felt uneasy. She said, "When I first came
[to this agency], I thought that I could perform like those recent
popular dancers who are more active and cool. I certainly don't
want to do what I am doing now for the rest of my life!" The way
in which Erika was trained to become an idol personality did not
meet her original expectations, and this reduced her sense of dedication to the idolization of self. Both Miho and Erika felt that their

sexualized bodies and images were out of their control, but they could not do much about it because it was their job (*shigoto dakara shikata ga nai*).

Wakase, who had worked for Cutie Smile, Ltd. as a choreographer for nearly three years, was sympathetic to the sense of discomfort felt by many of her trainees. She argued:

Sometimes I feel bad because the trainees have to play the feminine character that they don't really want to play. All of them face a struggle at the outset of their training period as they try to become someone who they have never experienced before. For those who are willing to overcome that struggle, however, there is a point in which they embrace the cute character as part of themselves. That's when they really grow. They become apparently more enthusiastic and confident, and their skills improve dramatically.

Candidates' willingness to compromise with the image of adolescent femaleness provided by the manufacturing industry influences the rate in which they acquire and develop skills. The statement also makes a significant reference to how a willful trainee may successfully mold herself into the institutionally designed image of adolescent femaleness from a certain point on as the result of compulsory practices. Unfortunately, during the period of my observation, I failed to see Erika and Miho grow in the way Wakase described. These two students continued to look uncomfortable most of the time, even pained. Their will to embody constructed gender roles and sexual stereotypes was apparently much lower than that of Yoshiko and Mayumi, for whom performance on stage was conceived of as a great pleasure in and of itself.

For Yoshiko, adopting an excessively cute and childlike character was simply one of many tasks she was expected to fulfill in show business—something she attended to seriously and energetically as a part of her expertise. When I asked her whether she ever felt uncomfortable about her performances, she replied: "Not really. It's my job and I enjoy doing it very much. I eventually want to become someone who is adored by anyone and everyone." This showed the association Yoshiko made between embodying the cute style and attaining prestige, which together constituted her identity as a performer.

The situation was quite similar with Mayumi, who was somewhat frustrated about her current status at Cutie Smile, Ltd.—not because she had to enact an undesirable character, but because she felt that she was not enacting the character well enough to deserve public attention. She said, "No matter how hard I try, I just can't get the details of the cute gestures right, but I have to master them in order to become an adorable public figure and be successful in this world." Mayumi perceived the embodiment of adolescent femininity to be necessary to the development of her career even though it was not natural to her. I then asked Mayumi was how she perceived the part of herself that resisted the enforced enactment of adolescent femininity. She said that although she considered the constructed image of adolescent femaleness as somewhat exaggerated, it was not far from her own personal qualities. She argued, "I think there are many qualities in myself, and being cute or childlike is one of them. It's just a matter of how well I could pull it out of myself. I would certainly act in a very cute way if I really wanted to win the heart of a man that I love. That's how I try to feel when I play the cute character." Mayumi considered the cute style to be part of the multiple personal qualities that made up her selfhood. Idol-training practices provided her with a means to pull out and refine this particular quality that existed inside her. Moreover, her statement shows that she perceived "cutesy" as a strategy that could be used to win the hearts of others, especially young men in the audience.

In sum, I found that performers had mixed feelings about embracing the crafted image of adolescent femininity. To the extent that these performers could accept the cute style as part of multiple identities that characterized their selfhood, and to the extent that they were willing to adopt it as part of their work, there was no reason to contest the image constructed by a male producer to serve the interests of male audiences. To the extent that the performers could not identify themselves with the sexist stereotypes of adolescent selfhood, the embodiment of the cute style was met with some degree of resistance. In the end, however, it was the sense of prestige and the accompanying sense of duty that characterized these performers as professional entertainers that held them in their places. They were aware that acting in whatever ways their producer told them to would lead to success. For some of these performers who saw themselves as having a meaningful life (*ikigai*) in the entertainment industry, compulsory practices were the foremost significant step in the process of developing the self.

I had to wonder whether the motto of Cutie Smile Productions— "pure, honest, and pretty"—actually meant that a woman had to mold herself into a personality that did not represent who she is. Did the motto indicate the construction of an artifice that covered up a capitalist intention to compete and succeed in the market? This did not sound very pure and honest from my point of view! When I asked Nakahiro to comment on this issue, he smiled ironically and said: "You know, there is no such thing as purity, honesty, and prettiness as such. Alternatively, you should ask yourself to whom you would appear to be pure, honest, and pretty. These are like colors. . . . You color the performers that way to make them look provocative in the eyes of their viewers. Nothing could really be purely white, clean, or crystal clear." For Nakahiro, purity, cutesy, and the like were instruments for achieving the single most important goal of a promotion agency: marketable personalities. In his commercially oriented worldview, beauty and ugliness (or purity and impurity) were two parts of a whole that did not conflict with each other. Reflecting the *shintō* view of ambivalence as discussed by Nelson (1996), Nakahiro justified his commercial stance. He argued that he was, in effect, purifying idols by bedecking them in cute and innocent appearances. He expressed no sense of guilt about fabricating cute images.

BECOMING VIBRANTLY SEXUAL

Body-Wave Agency (B.W.A.), founded in the early 1980s by Yoshinori Mukai, became the powerhouse of a new and emergent idol category, "idol dancers" (*dansu-kei aidoru*). Performers who belonged to this category were also referred to as "post-idols" (*posuto aidoru*) who marked the era in which idols could no longer attract the public by simply being cute. Well-known post-idols today include Namie Amuro (debut 1995), mentioned earlier; Rina Chinen (debut 1996); as well as groups such as MAX (debut 1995) and

SPEED (active 1996–99). The popularity of these personalities helped B.W.A. attract hundreds of applicants.

In June 1996, I visited B.W.A. and observed how the students performed. Nearly 200 students attended the agency to receive dancing and singing lessons at the time of my visit, paying the annual fee of 200,000 yen. Most students were young girls between the ages of 8 and 22. These students were recruited through a series of auditions, to which they applied voluntarily, wishing to pursue their performing careers. A former cute idol, Yasue, coached the students with three other female instructors. She came to the school after retiring from show business in the early 1990s, and eventually made herself into a dancing coach. For her students, however, Yasue was a big sister with whom they could feel familiar, rather than an official instructor and a former pop star.

Dancing and singing practices took place in a relatively informal and friendly atmosphere, but all students were very serious about their practice. Once lessons began, their eyes turned sharp, their bodies were filled with energy, and they were transformed from shy teenage girls giggling during off-time conversations to confident dancers who concentrated on brushing up their skills (Fig. 3.3). All students performed in a local public hall once every three months to demonstrate the fruits of their practices. I did not stay in Japan long enough to observe these events, but a B.W.A. secretary kindly gave me a videotape of one of these events, which I observed afterward. Actors in the recorded stage performance were as sharp-looking as they had appeared during training sessions. Their performances were met with loud cheers from hundreds of people in the audience, who were mostly young men and women. According to Yasue, B.W.A. students voluntarily organized these regular public performances.

Mukai stayed in his office next to the studio most of the time, where he met with guests from big industries and local bureaus to discuss business. He came into the studio occasionally to observe how things were proceeding, but he did not interrupt at all. Small children also took dancing lessons, and their parents accompanied them. These parents sat at the back of the studio to observe how their little ones performed.

Fig. 3.3 A scene from dance practice at the Body-Wave
Agency (photo by the author, June 1996).

EMPOWERING ONE'S BODY
AND SOUL THROUGH DANCE

The essential concept used by Mukai to characterize his students was purity instead of cutesy. Standing in sharp contrast to the same word used by Nakahiro, the Mukai version of purity did not represent a form of adolescent femininity that was designed to primarily serve the interests of male audiences. For Mukai, or Mukai-*sensei* (Master Mukai) as students called him, purity was the single, most important driving force in performance.[13] He argued: "To be pure is to enable one's energy to flow from within, without any external constraint. It enables the actor to act from the bottom of her heart and her soul. By being pure, she can open herself up to anything and everything, and give the performance all that she can. It's the primary step in becoming a professional actor." Mukai's idea of purity is an active concept used to signify the subjectivity of the actor, or the sentiment of acting with all one's being, rather than to represent an objectified self. When I asked Mukai as to how this idea of purity compared to the image of the cute idols, he said:

---

13. The word *sensei* is used in Japan to address teachers, professors, or others performing in a teacher-like role.

In my opinion, the purity associated with the so-called "cute idols" is a made-up image. It's made for the actors to put on a childish act in order to attract boys' attention and be marketable to them. In my view, this is far from being "pure." To be "pure" is to listen to your own heartbeat, which is to listen to your own rhythm of life. It has nothing to do with becoming someone else that you didn't originally intend to become. Dancing and singing do not consist of techniques that you are, or ought to be, forced to memorize by someone else. Surely, you can acquire some of these acting skills through compulsory training, but the beat inside you is not something you can acquire from someone else. You have to be yourself, and you have to rely on your own senses and be able to develop the beat. That's why you need to be "pure," that is, to be honest to your senses.

Mukai's intention is to distinguish the pure self, which enables the actors to empty their minds in order to absorb the essentials of the performance, from the pretense of innocence used more generally in the idol industry. Mukai encouraged his trainees to stylize themselves in accordance with the rhythm that they felt inside themselves, rather than providing these trainees with designed *kata* or forms into which they were forced to mold themselves.

I then wondered about the role of dancing lessons at B.W.A.: whether these lessons were compulsory practices that molded students' personalities into the Mukai version of adolescent innocence, which, after all, was another constructed image. When I asked Mukai about this point, he smiled grimly and replied: "Dancing lessons are simply designed to facilitate the students' energies that flow from within. Acting school provides a space where these students can get together, encourage each other, and direct their own senses toward developing specific styles of performance within the context of mutual support and encouragement." Apparently, Mukai did not see dancing lessons as compulsory practice, but more as an instrument for his students to develop themselves in their own creative way. Mukai wanted to provide a common ground for these students to stand together and dedicate their bodies and their souls to personal transformation—to becoming talented performers.

Lessons were organized into five levels, with the first level for beginners. Members in each level met twice a week: Saturday for voice training, and Sunday to practice singing and dancing. In voice training, students lined up in the mirrored studio, breathed into their abdomens, and practiced the musical scales as loudly as they could for about one hour. In dancing and singing practice, students spent the first thirty minutes repeating basic voice training, followed by one hour of moving their bodies rhythmically. Dancing was practiced in a free style, so every student invented her own body movements.

Yasue and other instructors taught basic dancing skills, such as how to make steps or turn the body around, but there was no choreography in any strict sense as in the case of Nakahiro's promotion agency. All the students overwhelmed me with their enthusiasm, and the heat from their bodies heightened the temperature of the studio, which was already hot and steamy. Because there was no air conditioner, students were dripping, but everyone felt that they were "having a good sweat" (*ii ase o kaite iru*).

Every student had a good reason to be there. One student, for instance, told me that she was a high-school dropout who had no idea what she wanted to do with her life until she came to B.W.A. and gained self-esteem via dancing. She continued:

I could be wandering out on the street without anything to do if I wasn't here. I could have even died on the street. What I learned here gave me a lot of confidence. I learned how to believe in my abilities. I can work hard now, and really enjoy what I am doing. I feel like I am ready to challenge any trial that I may face!

For this informant, B.W.A. and its style provided a good reason to exist in this world and challenge things in life. It gave her a pathway toward maturity. One could also say that the form of purity invented by Mukai gave her a sense of subjectivity: that she could be in control of herself and her own life, which had been uncontrollable.

Another student felt that the spirit of dancing helped empower her academic life and improve her grades in high school: she could concentrate on homework and prepare for examinations with a greater sense of confidence. The mother of a twelve-year-old student, wanting her daughter to acquire something meaningful in life, decided to take the daughter to B.W.A. when she heard of its good reputation. She said that both she and her husband were very happy that their daughter could acquire confidence in an encouraging environment. This and other positive statements provided by the buyers of the B.W.A. style sounded like religious testimonials: they all testified to the effectiveness of B.W.A. as an apparatus of self-transformation. Indeed, B.W.A. functioned like a religious institution by purifying the trainees and preparing them to face their lives with a positive spirit.

As part of the lesson, each student selected her favorite song from the list of choices and sang it in front of the group. Others chorused the selected song at the back. Every song in the list was upbeat. All students chorused each song as they raised their voices vigorously. Many of Namie Amuro's hit songs were on the list, and students repeatedly sang a line from her 1995 smash hit, *Chase the Chance*, which went "Hey Yo! Just chase the chance, the pathway that you believe in. . . . Dream is not something you simply envision. . . . It's something to accomplish!" The students stated that they liked Amuro's songs because of their upbeat rhythms and stimulating messages. Through such music, the trainees created their own training atmosphere that motivated their wills to perform.

Each student sang for nearly two minutes and gave way to the next student in line. Yasue stood at the back of the studio and played the role of disc jockey, changing the music every two minutes. She also danced when the music was playing. At the day's end, students formed a circle to reflect upon their performances. They discussed some of the problems they found during their practices, as a form of mutual encouragement. I was informed that Mukai would occasionally step in at this stage to provide a comment that would heighten the spirit of the class, although this did not happen when I was there. This form of group reflection is similar to the one observed in Japanese companies. As Rohlen (1974, 1986) reports, group reflection provides Japanese companies with an efficient means of personnel management by enhancing interpersonal bonds and mutual competition among the employees.

The kind of crafted femininity that I observed in Nakahiro's promotion agency was absent from B.W.A. What I encountered instead was an expression of vibrant sexuality that incorporated quick, sharp, and even aggressive body movements that mimicked the style represented by various black American hip-hop artists or American pop singers such as Janet Jackson and Madonna. All body parts waved dynamically with fast foot shuffles. Frequent fist-making made little dancers appear more powerful. Students occasionally made crotch-grabbing gestures and touched under their breasts when they danced, preening for the audience in an overtly sexual way.

Seeing young girls strike some of these poses was quite astonishing, and I even wondered if some of them really understood what they were doing. All these gestures were nearly identical to those made by Amuro during her stage performances, which, combined with her fashion, constituted a style that many people in the media referred to as an expression of a young girl's power. All B.W.A. students that I interviewed considered that this style was cool and sexy, and it symbolized *tsuyoi josei no jidai*, or the "age of powerful femaleness."

In one of the discussion sessions, I asked B.W.A. students to describe how they felt about enacting a vibrantly sexual performance. Some replied that they felt a bit ashamed but they generally considered it fun, liberating, and empowering. I asked Yasue to tell me how she compared this overtly sexual style with the style she represented back in 1988 when she was listed as one of 58 cute idols making their debut in the same year.[14] Yasue's reply indicated a significant emotional and attitudinal contrast. She said,

> The cute character I played back in 1988 was a made-up image that oppressed my individuality, and I did not enjoy trying to live up to that image at all. The only thing that kept me going was my hunger for fame. . . . I mean, my dream to be popular among many people. The kind of sexiness that I am expressing now through my dance comes from within myself. It's what I really am or what I could really be, and I don't have to fake myself or lose my control over it. It's really a great feeling. . . . I don't have to feel bad any more about going out of my way and trying to satisfy people with an invented personality.

These comments showed the willingness of Yasue and her colleagues to break away from the old image of adolescent femaleness

---

14. This count is based on Matsuzaka jazz hihyōsha's data book, *The Idolist Manual: Idol Pops 80–90: 80's Idol Singles Perfect Collection*, published in 1991.

through a new, self-affirming style of sexualized performance. Yasue and her colleague confirmed Mukai's indication that the pure self was not a compulsory image that was given to the trainees from above, but a form they were entitled to construct on the extension of an opportunity provided by their promotion agency. What is interesting about Mukai and other B.W.A. members' narratives on vibrant sexuality is that although it may be true that the trainees were being themselves and experiencing themselves, their statements of these selves are codified in terms of one *kata*: that of Namie Amuro. Perhaps, when such a *kata* is in its heyday, individuals who adopt it may not feel that it is simply another commercial form into which they are being shaped; when the form is passé, they may sense the fabricating aspect of such a form.

When I asked Mukai how he felt about underage girls acting in such a vibrantly sexual manner, he said, looking a bit annoyed:

Why can't girls be sexy if sexuality is something essential to them? Why can't they be pure about it, rather than trying to conceal it? Why can't they express it to the best of their ability? I think nobody has the right to tell them what they should do about their sexual energies, and much less how they should constrict them. They have to take sexuality in their own hands and express it in their own healthy, creative ways! It's all part of being oneself, and what's wrong with that?

These comments clearly describe the vibrantly sexual style as a means for young female performers to dignify themselves as persons with individual abilities. However erotic they may appear to be, performers who enacted this new style of adolescent femaleness felt empowered—unlike the falsely constructed and standardized image of sexual passivity that tended to constrict its actors' identities in the name of cutesy.

IDOL PRODUCTION AS THE
MANAGEMENT OF CONTESTED GENDER

The two observed images of femaleness in idol performances, the cutesy versus the sexy, are two optional images of sexuality. Audiences of different genders and related interests can choose and adore one of them as their ideal female style. These images also reflect dif-

ferent visions of the appropriate image of Japanese adolescent femaleness, which are then manufactured by male idol producers.

Cute idols advance a traditional adolescent femininity that idealizes the image of the future good wife, wise mother for young girls.
A derivation of the term *kawaisō*—meanings include pathetic, poor,
and pitiable, *kawaii* or "cute"—articulates a vulnerable, subordinate,
even disabled personality that deserves personal attention, care, or
support (Kinsella 1995: 221, 222). While the cute style may provide
young girls with a way of opposing their parents' culture with a
facade of eternal youth, it is also regarded as a signifier of frail
femininity. When female idols act cute and coy, they resign themselves to sexual subordination, just as those who conform to the
good wife, wise mother ideology agree to social subordination
along with domestic protection.

A shift away from the cute style toward a more vibrantly sexual
style in idol performances shows that young Japanese women are
breaking away from the traditional gender ideology in order to become more self-assertive. But the extent to which the vibrant sexual style contributes to the reification of female subjectivity in
Japanese society is open to question—at least from the perspective
of male viewers, who still consider post-idols to be sexually objectified. Moreover, the current popularity of vibrantly sexual idols
simply proves the point that young girls continue to gain their
agency in reference to the motifs that are given to them by the image-making industry. By generating a contested terrain in which
adolescent women can variably position and construct themselves,
the burgeoning industry continues to capitalize on the manipulation of female sexuality.

The contest between the two alternative images of femaleness as
manifested in idol performances, however, becomes more apparent
when one looks closely at the idol-manufacturing process. Performers' wills and attitudes count as important determinants of an
agency's success, and their will to perform is closely tied with their
choice of female identities. The compulsory practices of gender reproduction are self-enforced by those who can identify themselves
with what their agencies perceive as appropriate role models for
young girls (as in the case of B.W.A. students' reproduction of the

Namie Amuro style). However, those who see a gap between the assigned gender role and their image of self resist them (as in the case of performers who belonged to Nakahiro's promotion agency who had trouble accepting the cute style).[15]

Several idol producers I interviewed indicated that there had been self-expressive and punk-like, if not necessarily vibrantly sexual, idols who tried to represent self-assertive womanhood back in the 1970s and the early 1980s when the cute style was in its heyday. They said that these idol styles were marginalized at that time. They were never recognized nationally. One had to wait until the late 1980s for the appearance of militant idols that represented the "bad-girl" (*sukeban*) stereotype. The success of gender construction in idol performances depends on cultural timing as much as on the performers' willingness to perform.

Idol-manufacturing agencies coordinate performers and their fans in space and time in order to provide them with role models against which to evaluate, contest, and select appropriate images of adolescent femaleness. In this sense, the field of idol production itself functions as a mediator that bridges the gap created between the existing ideological expectations of gender roles and the actual lives of the consumers.

THE SHOWCASE OF
GENDERED PERSONALITIES

Two distinct images of adolescent femaleness are identified in the above discussion: on one hand, there is the passive, submissive, and childlike femininity expressed by cute idols; and on the other, there is the active, stylish, and vibrantly sexual femaleness represented by idol dancers. While both of these images are designed to be marketable, the cute style is currently disparaged on the ground

---

15. It was revealed to me by several sources after I left Japan that most performers who belonged to Nakahiro's promotion agencies left the agency for better image-making agencies. Apparently, Nakahiro's focus on adolescent femaleness was too narrow and outdated, and thus these performers could not sustain their careers on this basis. On the contrary, the B.W.A. business continued to boom, as many post-idols succeeded in the entertainment industry.

that it deprives female actors of control over their own bodies and personalities. Only when this sense of confinement is overcome because of the hunger for success, the pursuit of greater public recognition, or the will to transform oneself into a symbol of femininity, does the actor's attitude change, accepting the cute style as a necessity and even a joy.

On the contrary, the embodiment of the vibrantly sexual personality is desired by young female performers and audiences who consider it to be a way for girls to reassert their positive identities in an era when women are encouraged to be increasingly stronger and self-assertive. But it is questionable how socially or culturally empowering this image really is. In either case, the field of idol production has become a site where appropriate forms of adolescent gender and sexuality are contested.

The ethnographic observations presented in this chapter will contribute to the ongoing debate in gender studies about how gender roles and sexual stereotypes ought to be evaluated (e.g., Strathern 1981; Ueno 1987; MacKinnon 1989; Haraway 1991). In cultural studies, for example, McRobbie (1984) and Frith (1981) present different views on how fashion and dance gender young North Americans who practice them as part of their leisure activities. On one hand, McRobbie contends that dance provides American girls with a positive sexual expressiveness that contributes to the creation of a distinct cultural form in its own right (McRobbie 1984: 145). On the other hand, Frith argues that the cultural activities led by female teenagers, such as dancing and dressing up, can become instruments for female gender oppression. These activities reproduce the socially objectified position of young women that serves the purpose of pleasing men—however fun, stylish, and artistic they may appear to be on the part of young girls who practice them as a collective occupation (Frith 1981: 229).[16]

In light of the two ethnographic cases presented above, one can argue that both McRobbie and Frith's ways of seeing are valid, or that neither of them can stand alone. They are two different aspects of the same phenomenon. The sexualization seen in fashion,

---

16. This comparison is quoted in Lewis 1990: 38.

dance, or an idol performance can create a social space wherein the agents can be objectified even though they may perceive these activities as self-empowering practices. However, the fact remains that selfhood is shaped in terms of these symbolic forms that articulate the organizational needs of the group into which the subject is initiated. As Cohen (1990 [1979]: 46) rightly argues, normative symbols have ambiguous meanings, and it is this ambiguity that forges symbols into such powerful instruments in the hands of leaders who wish to mystify people for their own purposes.

Moreover, the very debate over which interpretation is appropriate can be manipulated by the industry in order to provoke public interest and empower itself symbolically as well as economically. In this way, the industry functions as a hegemonic apparatus. In its presence, people are systematically but deliberately, instead of coercively, rendered into gender roles. Fashion and dance feminize American girls with a sense of pleasure rather than that of oppression. Likewise, post-idol performances direct Japanese girls to find female subjectivity and creativity within their social roles, rather than outside them.[17] The style represented by Japanese post-idols becomes a symbolic force that molds Japanese girls' selfhood.

The relationship between theatrical imagery and gender ideology is found elsewhere as well. For instance, Hatley (1990) shows that competing genres, such as the all-male *ludrug* versus the female-oriented *kethoprak*, exist in Javanese performances, providing sites for performers to enact, and for audiences to contest, female gender roles and sexual stereotypes. Female personalities are constructed in these performances on the basis of different attitudes that performers and audiences develop toward gender roles and

---

17. This is similar to Allison's (1996) discussion of the lunchbox (*obentō*) as an ideological apparatus that enforces the gender roles of Japanese mothers. The creation of a school lunchbox involves elaborate and cute aesthetics, which encourage children to eat everything. Japanese mothers exercise creativity and playfulness through the everyday practice of making beautiful lunchboxes. At the same time, these expectations reinforce ideologies of household obligation and motherly commitment (1996: 96). Thus, Allison shows that cultural processes actively channel gender and sexuality in ways that maximize productive labor demands, rather than repress sexual impulses.

sexual relationships—in a society where women have ideologically ascribed characteristics judged as essentially inferior to those of men. The contemporary mass media promote a new model of middle-class women that, for all its surface attributes of modernity (Western-style fashion, jet-setting lifestyle, and educational achievement) is basically ideologically conservative in that it implies the traditional wifely ideal.

All-male casts in *ludrug* reproduce this image in terms of an imaginary contrast between the domineering, nagging wife and the soft and sexy young wife—both roles played by transvestite actors. This implies male antagonism toward dominant women and corresponding fantasies of subservient femininity (1990: 183–86; see also Peacock 1968: 74–78). Conversely, the *branyak/kenes* style in *kethopiak* (a genre of popular theatrical performance that has specific appeal for lower-class women) portrays progressive female personalities. The genre articulates women's frustration (or the sense of dissatisfaction that they could not otherwise express) with their lack of freedom in everyday speech and activity (1990: 197–201).

On the subject of contemporary Japanese popular culture, Rosenberger (1995, 1996), Clammer (1995), and Kinsella (1995) provide cases where specific styles of performance (e.g., the cute style) or products (e.g., fashion magazines) are shown to provide points of contradiction in a contested sociocultural terrain. Using these contradictions, women could gain their agencies (both as women and as female consumers), sometimes through taking multiple positions (McNay 1992: 42, quoted in Rosenberger 1995: 144). Female idol performances become a site for epitomizing the ongoing symbolic contest of adolescent femaleness, which nevertheless perpetuates the male domination of gender and sexuality.

4

Explorations in the Field
of Competing Styles

From the standpoint of business institutions, the value of idols is measured in terms of their commercial usefulness. The more an idol personality can attract consumers, inducing them to buy what they advertise and allowing the advertisers to make a profit, the more recognition she or he earns. To this end, all idol candidates try to develop their own styles that can attract people and distinguish them from coexisting rivals. With this in mind, the discussion in this chapter explores competition in the arena of idol production. I will describe strategies employed by promotion agencies to set themselves apart. The first section will introduce some of the existing idols as they are perceived by producers and fans.

Popular idol styles are often imitated by other candidates in their pursuit of fame. Many copycats subsequently try to derive their own forms to distinguish themselves from the originator as well as other imitators. The stylistic performance of an idol may last as long as the style is trendy, but trends quickly succeed one another. Performers and producers are thus constantly on the lookout for a new style that can inspire the public.

The question of style cannot be limited to the realm of subjectivity but must take into account its inextricably interwoven relationship with the dynamic power structure that characterizes the Japanese entertainment industry and consumer society today.[1] This means that the process whereby the field of symbolic production becomes an apparatus that defines the temporal status of taste is taken into account (Bourdieu 1993: 108). This process sets the chronological contrast between the newcomers and the established, the challengers and the veterans, or the avant-garde and the classical, in concurrence with the economic opposition between the poor and the rich, the small and the big, the cheap and the dear.

In such a context, the development of symbolic forms and their producers is subjected to the continuous creation of the battle between those who have made their names and those who have not yet established themselves. Those established are struggling to stay in view; while those who are new are fighting to relegate to the past the established figures, freeze the movement of time, and fix the present state of the field (Bourdieu 1993: 104–6). With this in mind, the second section of this chapter will try to illustrate promotional techniques developed by idols and their agencies. I will here include my own experience of being promoted, so as to provide a better picture of how stylistic promotion is planned and exercised. The story of my promotion will also clarify the relationship I developed as a researcher with my informants in the field.

The symbolic competition between different idols is not a practice of promotion agencies alone. Fans and audiences also participate in the politics of differentiation as they identify themselves with their favorite idols and group themselves against one another. The third section of this chapter, then, will discuss how members of the audience locate, distinguish, and root their individuality in the field of idol consumption in reference to a public event involving two idol groups, one idol duo, and a solo.

---

1. This point is inspired by Ewen (1988: 23), who considers style as the source of cultural power. Seigle's (1993) study on Yoshiwara brothels, which developed in Tokyo during the Edo period (1600–1868) as the only government-approved pleasure quarter in the region, shows how stylization served as a means for the class of courtesans to upgrade their social status—to empower itself as a group. One way in which the Yoshiwara lifestyle mobilized itself upward was through its convergence with the class of literati and artists. Yoshiwara became the popular subject of how-to books called *sharebon*, the contemporary equivalent of which are lifestyle magazines. It also became the popular theme of *ukiyoe* woodcut prints, making it the subject of "dandy" culture at the time.

UNCOVERING THE FORMULA
OF STYLIZATION

In Japanese mythology, the four main islands as well as some thousand smaller islands are considered to be the creations of the gods. Gods are also believed to inhabit these places, which are sometimes characterized as gods themselves. In mythical times, these *yao-yorozu no kami* or "eight million gods" interacted in many ways: some coexisted in solidarity, while others fought against one another; others made love and gave birth to the next generation of gods. Today, one can find places everywhere that are noted in connection with these gods and find shrines that people of regional and local communities visit to worship their gods. According to the *Kojiki* (The record of ancient matters), which describes the divine origin of the imperial line, earthly gods created Japan's archipelago by initiating practices that are known as *kuniumi* (giving birth to a country) and *kunizukuri* (constructing the country), in accordance with the directions given by the heavenly gods (e.g., Konoshi 1994: 118).

Idol performances resemble this creation myth in many ways: idols, equipped with their symbolic qualities, aim to establish their territories or "islands" (so to speak) within the market, and in the process interact with one another in various ways. Like gods, they create legends to be transmitted and shared by their worshippers. Behind all this are producers who, like ideologues who used *Shintō* to organize the rites of the state and attain their political goals, control the idol symbolism according to their visions of creation. One producer made this explicit in an interview when he said that nourishing the idols with one's social influence is the producer's *raison d'être*.

In his study of Bikkuriman Chocolate, a hit product that was targeted to children for consumption, Eiji Ōtsuka discovered that child consumers were attracted to a series of stickers that came with the chocolates as a gift rather than the chocolates themselves. These stickers featured animated figures—heroic and villainous—whose names and roles were briefly inscribed on the back in a caption entitled "The Gossip of the Devil's World." What motivated the consumers, according to Ōtsuka, was the fact that they could collect these stickers and in the process use their imaginations to create their own stories about how these figures interacted. In this, Ōtsuka sees a structural similarity with Japanese mythology. He argues:

In fact, there is no particular hero in the Bikkuriman series. There are heroic god-like figures called "heads" representing different eras, but none of these figures is a hero throughout the entire series. This structure is identical to that of the *Kojiki* in which the myth is centered on heroic gods who represent different eras, such as Susano'o, Ōkuninushi, and Yamatotakeru. There are altogether 772 gods in the Bikkuriman series, which is no match with the eight million gods, but Bikkuriman is systematized in such a way as to be compatible with Japanese mythology. (Ōtsuka 1990: 312)

Ōtsuka contends that children are constructing their own historical narratives in the process of consuming commercialized images—the kind of historical narratives that one does not learn to read and create in Japanese schools due to their mechanical focus on the mere memorization of dates and names (1990: 311).

Likewise, the series of stylized idols are consumed popularly as they appeal to people's sense of time, or senses of popular history, which is not limited to the recording of events that occurred at the level of, say, national politics and state economy. Idol fans and audiences enjoy creating their own epoch-marking stories as they relate themselves to their idols. The mass media function here as bystanders that direct these people's interests toward preferred readings of the time. The media offer descriptions of the idols and their performances that are similar to those captions that appear on the back of the Bikkuriman stickers.

I found many materials and activities that signify this mythological interplay among idols, promotion agencies, the mass media, and consumers. Writers on popular culture kept publishing genealogies that classified idols on the basis of styles. Fashion magazines featured articles that commented on the model role of each idol in fashion and lifestyle or provided rankings of popular personalities based on consumer surveys. Fans debated the validity of these classifications and rankings based on their own criteria.

When I participated in a get-together held by a group of idol fans at a restaurant, one fan pulled out two issues of *Bejeans*, a popular magazine for men. In it appeared articles headed "The 25-year history of idols as seen in record jackets." One of them, the June 1, 1995, issue, focused on the history of female idol soloists while the other, the July 15 issue, emphasized female idol groups. At the beginning of these articles were commentaries titled "All about heroine's memorial" (written in English) that laid the foundation of these particular narratives, such as this one:

In 1970, Yuki Okazaki played a heroine role in a TBS drama and had a sudden rise to popularity. In 1971 . . . , the *Three Girls' Company*, including Mari Amachi and Rumiko Koyanagi, dominated the Braun tube [i.e., television]. In the following year, idol [performance] . . . was established [as a genre] with the appearances of Megumi Asaoka, who sang along with choreography, and Miyoko Asada, who emphasized her friendliness in a drama.   (June 1, 1995, p. 24)

This genealogical diagram described the connections linking some important idol groups that appeared between the 1970s and the 1990s. Lists of idol names and captions that briefly described the idols' backgrounds followed these commentaries.

Members of the research group started to discuss these articles, making various comments about the list of idol biographies. One of the members, for example, questioned the association between two idol groups in the diagram saying, "I have no idea what this arrow means. How does the [idol group A] connect with the [idol group B]?" Another member offered his interpretation to this question: "They're probably referring to the big money spent on their planning." "Oh yes," replied the skeptic, "I remember that [idol group A] was advertised as what, a ten-million-yen project? Or was it a hundred?" The members compared different idols or idol groups on the basis of their social, economic, and historical statuses, to the best of their knowledge.

Sitting next to them, I was discussing with another idol fan his preferences for different types of idols. This fan distinguished first between soloists and groups, devaluing the latter as worthless. He said there was no point in adoring idol groups because they are *kikaku-mono* (planned things), by which he meant groups whose members were put together in the context of a certain marketing concept. I asked what was wrong with that, and he replied, "In these cases, the producers' concepts inevitably precede personal qualities. This goes against my belief in the principle of idol production, which is to put heart [*kokoro*] into nurturing each of the young candidates as an individual personality."

Putting heart into doing something has an important implication in Japanese culture. Japanese often make moral judgments in accordance with the presence or absence of sincere motives toward others. The morality of *kokoro* or *magokoro* (true heart) is a culturally emphasized notion that supports the Japanese sense of social obligation. Heartedness signifies the pure self, which is identified, morally, as sincere, selfless, and altruistic—in contrast to the impure self, which is identified with pursuit of selfish interests (Lebra 1976: 162; 1986: 364). From this standpoint, I thought that the idol fan to whom I was talking tried to devalue idol groups morally because they exposed commercial interests, rather than the producers' willingness to provide careful attention to a performer's personal development.

Before long, other idol fans joined our conversation, and a heated discussion developed on the topic, "Is there a royal road to idol marketing?" The fan to whom I was originally talking insisted upon his view that idol production had to focus on human development rather than the pursuit of commercial interests. However, another fan said that there was no royal road to idol marketing. Other fans replied to this, expressing their mixed feelings about the issue. Subsequently, the topic of our conversation shifted from preferences based on idol types to that based on the details of existing idol personalities. In the end, everyone enjoyed the debate on idol appropriation, just as they would enjoy appropriating history by identifying what is good and what is bad in the tales of struggle related to some territorial power. Such a debate was a common occurrence in meetings held by other idol research groups. In these meetings, some fans frequently brought new and inspiring references for idol taxonomies, providing other members with points of entry into the field of idol contestation.

LEGENDS OF IDOL CREATION

Ambitious idols and promotion agencies constantly competed for prestige, which always revolved around the politics of stylistic differentiation in which actors tried to develop their own trademark. Some of these trademarks such as "sexy idol" were visually oriented; others like "purity idol" were based on personal qualities; and still others such as idol actors emphasized their acting skills. There were also child actors whose ages ranged between eight and thirteen.

Oscar Promotion, Inc., with its emphasis on the idea of beauty (*bi*), established its territory and is known today as the "kingdom of 1,300 beauty queens." The agency has been promoting a series of idolized fashion models since 1970. Sei'ichi Koga, the president of this agency, describes his reason for creating it in an article that looks back at its 25-year history. His mission was to develop a new standard of beauty by inhabiting the gap between what he considered to be the developed beauty standard of the West on one hand and the backward beauty standard of Japan on the other. As Koga elaborates:

[During the fifty postwar years,] Japanese beauty has been rarely recognized in international beauty contests as well as the worlds of cinema and fashion. This indicates the fact that Japanese beauty has not reached the global level. If the entertainment industry is . . . the "industry of dreams," I thought that people [who work in it] must have a sense of beauty that can be compared to that of Europe and North America, nations that champion our dreams. . . . That is why I started Oscar Promotion. . . . In Europe and North America, it was becoming a common practice for fashion models to . . . perform in movies, stage, and television programs. In Japan, however, there hasn't been a place for fashion models to expand their activities as actors or singers. Thus, I started Oscar Promotion . . . as a producing system to create stars out of fashion models. The business strategy [we used] to establish this system was . . . to send high-quality campaign girls to various image-up campaigns that became a popular practice among corporations in the 1970s. . . . Subsequently, these girls developed a wide range of talent activities and became the first star talents who grew out of fashion models in Japan as they won recognition not only as visual models but also as talented performers. (Koga 1996: 116)

This suggests that there should be recognition of the Japanese sense of beauty in its own right, rather than the expectation that the industrial-Western standard of beauty should be the one that prevails. Koga's agency has been trying to initiate such a recognition through the popularization of a new idol relic. The Oscar's recent master model, Kumiko Gotō (debuted in 1987), was advertised as *kokumin-teki bishōjo*, or the "nation's beautiful girl," creating a public sensation and adding the new concept of "beautiful girl" (*bishōjo*) to the genre of adolescent celebrities. Koga's agency reacted by holding annual audition contests that attracted thousands of applicants each year.

Another agency, Johnny's, became successful after its emergence in 1967 by focusing exclusively on the production of young male idols. Their first product was a group by the name of Four Leaves (1967–78), whose popularity lasted through the next decade. This agency has dominated the male side of the Japanese idol market ever since, producing a stream of big names over the years. These include individuals such as Hiromi Gō (debut 1972) and Toshihiko Tahara (debut 1979), as well as groups such as Hikaru Genji (active 1987–93), named after a playboy member of the royal family in the classic of Japanese literature, the early eleventh-century *Genji monogatari*, or *The Tale of Genji*, and SMAP (debut 1993). These idols and idol groups appealed to thousands of young female fans. The ultimate message to be delivered by both the performers and their promoters was that each of the performers was unique and had great potential vis-à-vis the others.

Yoshiharu Noda was a president of an emergent promotion agency, Yellow Cab, Ltd. (founded in 1980), and his trademark was "large-breast idols" (*kyonyū aidoru*). Over a span of fifteen years, his career involved producing such popular figures as Shinobu Horie (1984–87), Reiko Katō (debut 1990), Fumie Hosokawa (debut 1992), and Akiko Hinagata (debut 1995). These personalities repeatedly appeared in magazines and television commercials in bikinis.[2]

---

2. The company's name, Yellow Cab, reflects the sexual stereotype about Japanese girls that emerged in the 1980s as Japanese women overseas became known for their openness in having affairs with men. "Yellow," in this case, refers to the skin color of Japanese girls, while "cab" refers to taxi, signifying how easily

In an interview, Noda explained to me his reasons for developing this particular style:

In the past, there were two types of performances in Japanese show business involving young female performers: the white type and the pink type. The white, called idols, sold images of purity. They were publicly adorable for their "cute and healthy" images, as you know. On the contrary, the pink, called porn actresses, sold their nudity . . . to satisfy men's sexual desires. Considered obscene, their performances were limited to mature audiences. For most idols, appearing in bikinis was as far as they would go in terms of exposing their bodies in public space—albeit shamefully. My idea, then, was to develop a new style that would fit between these two categories. I wanted to nurture [young female] performers who could attract greater numbers of people. I wanted to transform these performers gradually, from a physically exposed personality that appears in bikinis and appeals to boys to an experienced actor who can impress people of both sexes and all ages. Since there has been a strong emphasis on motherhood in Japan, I recruited young women who I thought could symbolize Japan's future motherhood. This is how those idols with large breasts emerged. They are the glamorous symbol of motherhood. As the Japanese saying goes, to be big is to be good. So, I wanted to capture people's attention with a big symbol of motherhood in producing female actors.

Noda thus rationalizes bringing this new style into the idol market in an attempt to promote his agency's name. In the struggle for social recognition, certain concepts, or pseudo-concepts, are produced as classifying tools that create meaningful similarities and differences through the process of naming (Bourdieu 1993: 106). In Noda's case, "large breast" is one such concept that helped him create a new position beyond those in the market at the time, namely, cute idols and porn stars.

I pointed out, somewhat suspiciously, that the large-breast style he was advocating might become a subject of criticism due to the existing public norms about sexuality. Noda confidently replied that although the style he developed surprised people in the beginning, they eventually got used to it in the end. No matter what people thought, they made the performers famous by talking

---

these girls can be picked up on the streets. Noda adopted this name to parody the popularity of Japanese girls in the world and signify the sexual attractiveness of his company's idols.

about them. Apparently, the "large breast" motif became a style that appealed to the public. Noda added, "Things become problematic when one does it secretly or thoughtlessly. When you are reasonable and are capable of demonstrating your reason to the audience, you will eventually be able to convince the public. In my experience, that's the way [Japanese] people are in general." Indeed, Horie (who died of cancer in 1987), Katō, Hosokawa, and Hinagata all turned out to have successful careers.

A busy promoter, Noda was on the move constantly. My first meeting with him took place in a hotel cafe during the time of his coffee break. This interview was interrupted by a call and was resumed only upon my second request to get together two weeks later. When I arrived the second time, Noda was giving instructions to his assistant on his cell phone. Working papers were spread across the large table he occupied at the cafe. They contained profiles of candidates in bikinis. As I peeped into these profiles, curiously, Noda told me that they were performers of the new generation, and that he was running back and forth to the offices of event organizers and record companies to promote them.

In his study of product development, the advertising consultant Nobuyoshi Umezawa contends that there are conceptual and artistic sides to all items designed for consumption. The former refers to how much an item can stimulate the wants of the consumers, and the latter to how well it can satisfy the consumers and make them feel that they want more (Umezawa 1984). The field of idol production is full of concepts developed by promotion agencies in order to differentiate themselves from others. Producers are constantly seeking individuals who fulfill these concepts. Eminent styles evolve when performers, backed up by inspiring concepts, manage to perform well and develop themselves into marketable personalities.

CRITERIA FOR IDOL MARKETING

In the competitive world of consumer capitalism, the survival of idols depends on how much idols can continue to attract people and sell their images. Most of the agencies and media institutions with which I came into contact conducted consumer surveys, known commonly as *tarento kōkando tesuto*, or "talent adorability tests," to determine which idols were favored by the audience and why.

In the process of investigating how idol popularity is measured by respective agencies, I met Masanobu Naitō, a producer who worked at Dentsū Corporation. Dentsū is a leading advertising agency in Japan and serves as a matchmaker between promotion agencies (which offer talents) and marketing corporations (which hire talents selectively for advertisements to heighten the image of advertised products). In our meeting, Naitō showed me a pile of materials that related to the research he conducted in 1993 and 1994, which he thought might be of some use for my research. The project aimed to index the popularity of existing female idols, identify the components of their popularity, and create a formula that could predict the marketability of newcomers for advertising purposes.

What distinguished Naitō's research from others was his focus on producers' needs rather than consumers' demands. He explains in the opening of his research report:

Projects that seek to determine how well talents demonstrate their appeals to the average majority of consumers . . . are certainly important and necessary for those who take part in advertisement. However, relying solely on such a greatest common measure can be problematic because it drives all corporations to choose any talent as long as she or he is popular and this may lead to tedious recruitment programming, and because the balance of power between advertisers and talents may become skewed to the talents' side, creating situations in which advertisements set off talents without contributing to the successful advertising of products, and the appearance of celebrated talents in a variety of advertisements may reduce the efficiency of individual advertisement. In either of these cases, corporations will have to suffer from sacrificing a high contract fee without getting much in return.

Naitō's intention here was to shift his advertisement-research perspective from that oriented to consumer taste to that which takes in more of the producers' insights. In his view, the overemphasis on adopting existing celebrities in advertisement discourages the creativity of advertisers. Driven by this cause, Naitō conducted interviews with twenty individuals he called "professionals" who handled talented performers on a daily basis and examined their perceptions of talent marketability in advertisement. Participants included presidents of promotion agencies, directors of television stations, producers of record companies, publishing agents, free-lance writers, and advertising agents. Through an elaborate statistical analysis, Naitō tried to postulate what he called an "objective measure to judge the latent ability of performers" (1994: 4).

Despite the use of technical terms, detailed charts, and diagrams, Naitō's study did not strike me as anything more than a survey in which he and his team of professionals ranked 250 female idols of their choice and then classified them into three categories using Umezawa's criteria. These categories included "stars," who can be hired any time because of their excellence in both concept and performance, "firecrackers," who should be hired with reserve because of their excellence in concept but obscurity in performance, and "slow starters," who will slowly and gradually develop their popularity due to their excellence in performance. Above all, I had a problem accepting his account of talent marketability that, after all, did not consider the very claim it made against other studies: the relationship between talents and *advertised commodities* in a specific context. Nevertheless, his research pointed out three conventional elements that are considered important by the professionals for promoting idols. These, in Naitō's words, are: providing something "unexpected" (*hen*), which gives the viewers an impression that the actor is unusual; something "tempting" (*waku*), which refers to sexual appeal; and something "able to induce" (*do*), which appeals to certain values that the public finds inspiring.

These three aspects identified by Naitō were apparent in many television commercials, a notable example of which is a lipstick commercial that featured Takuya Kimura, a celebrated male idol and a member of the popular idol group SMAP. In this television commercial, produced by a leading cosmetic company, Kanebō, as part of its spring 1996 campaign, Kimura appears naked in bed, covered in a white sheet, awakened by the touch of the hand that has just colored his lips red with lipstick. Red lines on his cheek signify traces of his struggle against this forceful hand during sleep.

Accompanying street posters featured Kimura, bedecked in long hair and red lips, facing the viewer. The poster highlights Kimura's face as well as the advertised product.

This advertisement was unexpected because it reversed Kimura's gender identity while maintaining his charm. As one female informant put it, the handsome Kimura had become a beautiful Kimura without provoking any sense of incongruity. This switch from the female subject of the male gaze to the male subject of the female gaze is unexpected not so much because Kimura turned female, but rather because the expected gender message was inverted. Kimura was slotted into what had conventionally been a female position, reversing the existing gender patterning. The extent to which this advertisement tempted the audience is evident from a well-known fashion magazine survey, conducted in 1995, that ranked Kimura number one among all male idols in terms of "who young women want to sleep with the most." The message advocating the power of the lipstick—that could transform the beauty of one of the most adored and handsome male idols in the country—induced a large number of female consumers. It captured the attention of a news reporter from *Yomiuri shinbun* who in the March 21, 1996, issue wrote:

Kanebō adopted Takuya Kimura from the popular group SMAP in its spring campaign, creating a sensation. Thanks to the "Takuya Kimura effect," 2.5 million units of the lipstick named "Testimo II" were sold in two weeks following the campaign's opening on February 16. This is so far the top sales record in [the history of] the company's campaign. The campaign, which overturned the common assumption that women are the main actors [for lipstick commercials], developed when an executive director of the company . . . happened to ride on the same bullet train with Kimura. Being surprised by the craze created by female fans in the train as well as the station yard, the director arranged to hire Kimura in a hurry.

This quote itself is a good indicator of Kimura's strength in all three aspects of talent popularity: the reporter confirms that Kimura, an attractive male idol, impressed the audience with the image of the advertised lipstick by overturning gender expectations. Thus, the director's attempt to surprise, sexually attract, and lead the public in the creation of a beautiful life was recognized as successful.

THE NORI-P PHENOMENON

How, then, are idols promoted to meet the demands of both the industry and consumers? Masahisa Aizawa, the vice-president of Sun Music Productions, told me that idol production can be compared to creating a kingdom headed by an idol:

A good kingdom excels [others] in technology and leadership. The skillful use of technology can cultivate things that can enrich the livelihood of people, while good leadership is necessary to create solidarity among the people. A kingdom is not built in one day, so one must take time to activate a series of constructive events and earn people's recognition and trust. A kingdom is not possible, either, unless the king or queen and his or her supporting staff are talented. When they cannot hold people together, the kingdom will collapse sooner or later.

This quote relates to the general emphasis on long-term planning and long-term relationships in Japanese corporate institutions. The continued existence of the firm is idealized in many Japanese companies, as well as the continued existence of workers in the firm. Corporate systems such as lifetime employment and hierarchical promotion motivate workers to work hard consistently—even though these systems may not apply equally to all workers (e.g., Murakami and Rohlen 1992; Ito 1992: 369). Long-term planning in the idol industry consists of a promotion system that in principle enables successful candidates to grow and benefit the industry over an extended period. With this preface, Aizawa elaborated on how he went about promoting Noriko Sakai, one of the top-selling idols in Japan as well as in other Asian countries.

Sakai was one of several hundred applicants who participated in the agency's annual audition contest. Aizawa explained, "She did not make it to the final cut, but I saw potential in her. She was very small, cute, and had an unusually lively, 'burst open' kind of image that caught my attention. I thought it would be worth promoting her to see how far she could go. Now that I look back, it was the right decision on my part." Aizawa revealed his decision to adopt Sakai in an agency meeting and arranged a trip to Fukuoka City on Kyūshū island to bring Sakai back to Tokyo. In order to draw out the liveliness in Sakai and mold it into a marketable personality, Aizawa and his newly organized staff issued a debut campaign.

In Aizawa's view, the popular-cultural scene at the time of Sakai's debut was dominated by women in their twenties, who included university students and office workers. Emergent feminist movements, which led, on the one hand, to the promulgation of the Equal Employment Opportunity Law (EEOL) in 1985, extended, on the other, to the realm of popular culture. This created a phenomenon in which young women above the legal drinking age gathered in large discotheque-bars to dance on high stages in showy costumes. Their buzzword was "Express yourself!" The media facilitated this trend by highlighting tight, fancy styles of dress, which they called "body-conscious fashion" (*bodikon fashion*), and which signified liberated office ladies.

Aizawa's goal was to promote "a new style of identity for younger boys and girls headed by a cute, sixteen-year-old Sakai" that could equal the strength of the established youth culture led by older women. He also told me that the "junior market," involving children whose ages ranged from six to fifteen, was considered a significant source of investment in Japan during the 1980s. There is a research estimate of as much as 10 trillion yen in gross product (a large portion of which came from allowances). In Aizawa's view, attracting at least a portion of this segment of the population with a new style was not a bad idea.[3]

Given this socioeconomic background, Aizawa exercised his strategy for promoting Sakai, the first of which was to highlight Sakai's child-friendly image by making her an advocate of childlike handwriting and slang. The former refers to an unusually round handwriting that altered the shape from a previously vertical, stroke-oriented Japanese script. The original forms of this handwriting developed among high school students in the 1970s. The latter has to do with a deliberately mispronounced speech style mimicking the speech of a toddler incapable of adult pronunciation. Aizawa's cultural strategy was to associate Sakai with these existing popular culture items representing infantile cutesy and innocence,

---

3. This research refers to Yoshida 1984.

make them Sakai's trademarks, thereby establishing Sakai as an adorable leader of her generation.

Apparently, one of the first things Sakai did after making her debut in 1987 was to invent her own infantile speech style, which became known as *noripiigo*. *Noripiigo* is literally "*noripii* language," in which *noripii* is a cute characterization of Sakai's first name, Noriko. The transformation from Noriko to Noripii (later inscribed as "Nori-P") would be the equivalent of transforming names from, say, Marcela to Marcelita in Spanish, or Rob to Robbie in English. In *noripiigo*, words such as *kanashii* (sad) and *ureshii* (happy) were altered into *kanappi* and *ureppi*, respectively. New words such as *mamosureppi* (very happy) were invented, in which the *mamos* part refers to the size of happiness signified by an animated image of a mammoth, which connotes the idea of largeness. Sakai appeared on television and used these forms as a part of her stylized promotion. *Noripiigo*, inscribed in rounded characters, appeared with her cute images in a vast quantity of magazines and comic books. Even a dictionary called *Noripiigo jiten* was published by a major publisher, Shōgakkan, in 1989.

Aizawa and his company had no demographic data demonstrating the success of this promotion campaign. Aizawa himself did not know how many children and young adults adopted *noripiigo* and Sakai-style handwriting in their everyday life. He did tell me, however, how excited he and his staff were when they saw *noripiigo* appear as an item in an annual dictionary, *Gendai-yōgo no kisochishiki* (Basic knowledge of contemporary terminology). This, according to Aizawa, convinced them of Sakai's success in terms of cultural influence. Sakai's rise to popularity during this period is indicated by her continuous appearance in some of the nation's pop-music countdown programs such as *The Best Ten* and *The Top Ten*.

According to Yamane (1990), childlike language such as *noripiigo* created a teen craze that developed into a vital form of popular culture throughout the 1980s. Following this view, Kinsella (1995) observes:

The spread of cute-style handwriting was one element of a broader shift in Japanese culture that took place between the mid-1960s and the mid-1970s in which vital popular culture, sponsored and processed by the new

fashion, retail, mass-media, and advertising industries, began to push traditional arts and crafts and strictly regulated literary and artistic culture to
the margins of society. At the same time as Japanese youth began to de-
base written Japanese, infantile slang words began to spread across the
nation—typically coming into high-school vogue for only a few months
before becoming obsolete again. . . . There are . . . a few examples of deliberately contrived childish speech such as *norippigo* [*sic*] officially invented by idol Sakai Noriko, alias Nori P . . . , [which] consisted of
changing the last syllable of common adjectives into a *pi* sound.   (Kinsella
1995: 224, 225)

Thus, Kinsella acknowledges the contribution that chubby handwriting and *noripiigo* made to the construction of popular culture
at large. Kinsella further suggests that chubby handwriting and
noripiigo, as well as other forms such as childlike fashion, represented a female-led youth subculture that refused to cooperate with
the established social norms. Young people who participated in
this subculture celebrated physical appearances and social attitudes
that contributed to the creation of an adolescent utopia in an affluent socioeconomic environment—where young people could be
liberated from the filthy world of adult politics (1995: 220). Aizawa's intention, as demonstrated above, specifies this point in
terms of the symbolically competitive positioning of junior adolescents against young adults.

    Strategies for promoting Sakai did not end in language, however.
The staff invented a cute animated figure, supposedly invented by
Sakai herself, called Nori-P chan, and collaborated with Glico,
Japan's leading confectionery company, to bring to market choco-
lates and ice creams featuring Nori-P chan (Fig. 4.1). The staff further created franchise stores called Nori-P Land in various amusement parks across the country. People could visit there to eat
Nori-P candies or buy T-shirts, stuffed toys, stationery, and other
goods related to Sakai and her alter ego, Nori-P chan, for souvenirs.
Seeing success in all these areas, the promotional staff organized a
fan club whose members were called "Nori-P zoku," or the "Nori-
P tribe." Monthly newsletters were published to celebrate Sakai as
well as advertise her activities; and aside from her regularly produced songs, the *Nori-P chorus* (*Nori-P ondo*) was released by a record company, Tōshiba, to which she belonged.

Fig. 4.1 On the cover of a Noriko Sakai fan club newsletter called *Nori-P Times* (no. 87), images of *Nori-P chan* appear above Sakai. This advertises a newly opened variety store called Nori-P House where various Sakai-related products are sold. The form of chubby, rounded cute handwriting mentioned in Chapter 2 is incorporated in order to enhance the cute and lovable image of Sakai.

In effect, Nori-P became one of the nation's most adorable personalities of the late 1980s. Male university students considered her their ideal little sister, while members of her own generation regarded her as their adorable colleague. Those younger than her treated her as their ideal elder sister. Apparently, these terms relate to the idea of fictive kinship. Kinship terms are extended in Japanese speech to all kinds of people in order to enhance empathetic identity (Suzuki 1976). The use of relational terms, such as "big sister" (*oneesan*), "big brother" (*oniisan*), "mother" (*okaasan*), and "father" (*otōsan*) outside family contexts is found in groups of traditional female entertainers (*geisha*), organized crime groups (*yakuza*), and artisan communities (Dalby 1983; Seymour 1996). Such a use served the purpose of establishing sociological kinship as a means to strengthen or maintain social bonds among members who are not originally related by blood.

This strategic mechanism shows how producers, as part of their stylistic promotion, link the personal qualities of the young performer with a wider social issue or cultural climate, enabling the image of the performer to be marketed as a role model throughout the stages of personal development. What I failed to examine in reviewing this dynamic with Aizawa, however, was how Sakai herself perceived this development of the self. This examination, I thought, would offer answers to some of the important anthropological research issues on identity formation that takes place in capitalist institutional settings: the advantages and disadvantages of transforming oneself into a popular personality; whether the performers have a sense of self-control; the extent to which they can exercise power; whether they become disillusioned by the image fabricated by the institution to which they belong; and the way in which they negotiate public image with image makers. My failure to answer these questions by approaching Sakai was partly due to her tremendously busy schedule—the official reason provided by the agency, which protects the images of its talent from outsiders.

BECOMING AN
IDOL-LIKE PERSONALITY

One way for me to handle these research issues regarding the strategic process of myth-making was to experience the process myself—to be produced as a differentiated figure in the field of symbolic production. The opportunity was given to me by Akio Nakamori, who took pleasure in promoting unique individuals within the range of his power and network of people. Nakamori described some of these individuals in columns that he wrote for popular magazines. I met Nakamori in the summer of 1995 at an audition contest where both he and I participated as judges who evaluated idol candidates. Nakamori knew my name from an article published in the July 9, 1995, issue of *Sunday mainichi* that out-lined the content of my idol research project, which I had pre-sented in a press conference.

Being Recruited

In our first short conversation, which took place during a lunch break, we introduced ourselves and shared some of our thoughts about idols and the Japanese entertainment industry. When I ex-pressed the need to gather ethnographic data that would allow me to examine idol performances as contemporary symbolic rituals, Nakamori said he would provide me with any support that he could. Later, I invited Nakamori to my research base, an old wooden house belonging to a relative of mine, which I called the "Laboratory for Research in Cultural Idology." After a long chat during which I told him more about my research, Nakamori re-quested that I take part in his idol-promotion program. "I want to make you an idol!" he said, to my surprise.

Being Transformed from Researcher
to Idol-Like Personality

As a columnist who wrote about popular culture in one of the na-tion's most widely distributed weekly magazines, *SPA!*, Nakamori held a meeting with his regular publishing staff and discussed pro-ducing my public image. The image he envisioned of me was that of an "idol professor" (*aidoru hakase*) who came to Japan from a Canadian academic wonderland to analyze idols. Then, one of his staff members called me to confirm my participation. There was cultural play here in that I was Japanese, presented as a curious im-port from Canada, which raises a more general issue of cultural presentation in Japanese mass media. For instance, Creighton (1995) indicates that foreigners are frequently adopted in Japanese adver-tisements to reinforce the idea of Japaneseness. Foreigners, particu-larly Caucasians, are considered the bearers of highly valued inno-vation as well as violators of traditional Japanese norms. Their depictions in advertisements fit into Japanese advertising images of fantasy, where one can become personally carefree and innovative, sacrificing the traditional emphasis on maintaining the status quo. In providing representations of foreigners as fantastic outsiders who contrast with Japanese images of themselves, Japanese advertisers highlight the distinguishing features believed to define the Japanese. In doing so, they reinforce collective self-identity (Creighton 1995: 136; see also Ohnuki-Tierney 1987; Brannen 1992). In my case, however, someone Japanese was transformed into the exotic who is more expert on Japanese than the Japanese, and who could contribute innovative insights into Japanese idols and their sociocultural importance.

This positioning of me in relation to the cultural self and other is similar to the advertising technique used in the 1984 *Exotic Japan* campaign of the Japan National Railways. *Exotic Japan* was a mass-media campaign designed to enhance the popularity of domestic tourism. In her analysis of posters used in this campaign, Ivy (1988) indicates that the phrase "Exotic Japan" (pronounced in Japanese fashion as *ekizochikku Japan*) is written in *katakana*, the script used to transcribe foreign words. The goal was to represent Japan as if it had been interjected as the foreign, the nonnative, something that entered from the outside. Since place-names that are written in *katakana* are by definition not Japanese, *ekizochikku Japan* establishes Japan as non-Japanese seen through Japanese eyes on the level of script (1988: 25, 26). At the same time, *Exotic Japan* invokes the stereotypical image of Japan as seen through the eyes of outsiders (especially English-speaking Westerners): visions of the triumvirate of Japanese exotica, namely images of geisha, cherry trees, and Fujiyama (the Western mispronunciation of *Fuji-san*, Mt. Fuji). In doing so, the message appropriates Japan from the perspective of a foreigner looking at Japan, while the inscription indicates the subject position of a Japanese person looking at things foreign. What is considered to be identical is set apart and imagined as incompatible and therefore different (1988: 26). In the story-making campaign launched by Nakamori, this same movement was applied, transforming my image into something exotic, different, unusual, and therefore interesting.

According to the way things happen in the hierarchy of Japanese mass media, when a writer proposes to write about a celebrity, a staff member from the publisher takes the issue to the editor in chief, who in turn discusses the issue with higher authorities. Once permission is granted, the staff member reports to the agency to which the celebrity in question belongs. Once the consent is obtained from the agency, an interview schedule is arranged. The writer interviews the celebrity and produces a rough draft of the article on the basis of obtained information, while staff members, in consultation with the writer and copywriter, design the layout of the article and calculate the number of words to be written.

The ability to convince people plays a significant part here. The writer, his publisher, and his publishing staff frequently make encouraging comments to the talent and her or his agency in question. In my case, the staff member who called me said, "Nakamori-*san* thinks that you are really extraordinary. He says you are a star who turned up like a shining comet, and he is willing to promote you all the way this year! We really look forward to seeing you take part in our project! Could you give us your most serious consideration?" I told him that it would be my pleasure to participate.

An interview was scheduled at my residence, and Nakamori showed up with his assistant, Kazuhiro Yoshimura. I, on the other hand, asked Toshio Fujiwara, my first key informant, to be my agent, and guide me on how to go about being produced. Given his expertise in the entertainment world, I thought Fujiwara would be an appropriate manager for me. He kindly agreed and came to the meeting that day. After we briefly introduced ourselves, Nakamori started to explain the main point of his project.

I am going to produce Aoyagi-*san* because I thought his unique personal quality and his research topic would have a great appeal to many readers [of our magazine *SPA!*]. I am going to make him the first star-scientist to ever touch on the subject of idols! This will be a sensational topic for feature articles. At the same time, this will help Aoyagi-*san* develop his research contacts with a large number of people in the industry, who will surely recognize his name and make contacts easier. I am going to take a four-step approach. First, I am going to make Aoyagi-*san* appear in my *SPA!* column, surprising the readers and making them wonder who this person is. Then, Aoyagi-*san* will outline his research project using the space of my column, attracting the reader to a unique research project that never existed before in history. Then, he will write another article providing a case study of idol performances. By the time his research is finished, he will write another article that looks back to his fieldwork experiences. How does this sound?

As everyone agreed, Nakamori described how interesting my house as a place was, and that he wanted it to appear in his feature article. He then told Yoshimura to look around:

Look at this place—a finely preserved old wooden house. Such a house is becoming increasingly rare in a city like Tokyo! Besides, look at all the idol goods, and posters, autographs, and photos on the walls. The scene demonstrates how successfully Aoyagi-san's unique research on idols is developing. In addition, look at the [Buddhist] alcove and the [Shintō] altar he has next to his idol photos. . . . This is just a perfect site for the feature article, don't you think?

Immediately after Nakamori made this comment, Yoshimura (Y) opened his mouth and started to provide his vision of the first article's layout. Nakamori (N) responded to this, and conversation quickly developed between the two:

Y: This wall with autographs and photos can be made into a background, and we can take a picture of idols standing in front of it.
N: Yes, but we need another one outside where they stand by the garden gate . . .
Y: That's two photos there, and . . .
N: We have to make this house the subject, not idols.
Y: Yes, that's right. I wonder who would be appropriate to bring here.

Following this exchange, Nakamori decided to arrange for some idols to participate in a photo shoot. When Yoshimura started to propose many possible scenes that could be considered, Nakamori interrupted and said, "Well, we've only got fifteen minutes or so for photographing. Besides, Shinoyama-*sensei* has the final say on what scenes to shoot. Just give him the rough idea of this house's layout."

I listened quietly as Nakamori and Yoshimura negotiated their plan to put me in what I thought was *Nakamori bunka shinbun* (Nakamori culture newspaper), a three-page, black-and-white column that appeared in *SPA!* in which Nakamori discussed popular culture issues every other week. Realizing, however, that they were planning something much more serious when I heard them utter the name of Kishin Shinoyama, Japan's leading photographer, whose many works featured female pop stars, I panicked and interrupted their fast-flowing conversation. I asked, "Please wait a minute! Are you talking here about putting me on the cover where Kishin Shinoyama displays his artistic photos of some of the most celebrated people in Japan?" Looking astounded, all three people around me started to laugh at my ignorance. Nakamori said, "What did you think it was that we are discussing here? You are going to appear on the front page!"

Overwhelmed by the magnitude of the exposure, I expressed my hesitation to participate. I strongly felt that I was not qualified to appear in a prestigious magazine space that was usually occupied by celebrities. I thought that once I had exposed myself in such a way, I had to prove to the readers that I was in fact an outstanding scholar. I did not think this was possible when I had not even finished my Ph.D. dissertation. It was too late to pull back, however. Nakamori replied that he had already arranged an appointment with Shinoyama. To cancel it was a great offense, he said. Following Nakamori, Yoshimura said, "What are you intimidated about? You are unique. There is no question about that—unless you are faking your identity. You are really an idol researcher from Canada, aren't you?" Fujiwara followed up on this and said, "I wondered that, too. Maybe he is just an idol fan who wanted to approach idols by pretending to be a researcher from Canada. I've seen cases where some fans fake their identities to get better access to their favorite idols. Maybe you are one of them . . . !" Fujiwara joked, and everyone started to laugh. I was embarrassed, and my attempt to veto my appearance on the cover page of *SPA!* was overruled.

Being Produced

A week later, on October 25, 1995, nearly thirty people, including performers, managers, Nakamori and his staff, Fujiwara, and myself gathered at my residence. The first to arrive on the scene were Shinoyama's assistants, who came with equipment to set the place up for photography, followed by performers and managers. There were three rooms in the house plus a kitchen and a washroom, and

I opened one of the rooms to be used as a dressing room for the participating idols. As for performers, one idol group (nine members) and five individuals were present altogether. When I asked Nakamori "Are we not inviting any big names?" after his arrival, he replied, "No, they can't be here because they would be the center of attention if they were. Our central theme is this laboratory and you, Aoyagi-*san*, not necessarily idols." This statement opened my eyes to the status of performers within the hierarchy of fame that is considered in producing feature articles. Indeed, talent, fame, and power cannot be separated in the world of entertainment: the person who is considered talented or has demonstrated the potential to be popular gets to play a better role.

The sense of competition between different idols as well as their agencies was expressed in the way participants interacted (or "disinteracted" to be more precise) with one another on the scene. When the performers sat shoulder to shoulder in the dressing room to do their makeup, they hardly spoke; neither did their managers who stood waiting for them silently in the living room. The fact that these people kept their psychological distance from one another and reserved openness only for those who they considered to be the event organizers or mediators (in this case Nakamori, his staff, and myself) told me how crafty they were in their attitudes toward interaction. My laboratory space was soon divided into territorial segments, and tension filled the air. The site became a field of symbolic competition.

Nakamori brought a lab coat with him and asked me to put it on. His aim was to dress me up as a scientist and make me strike a pose with my idol specimens in one cut. He also wanted to use "Laboratory for Research in Cultural Idology" as an official name to appear in the title page of the *SPA!* article. The image of a scientist was going to be my trademark, indeed my style. "You shall be called 'idol professor' from now on!," he exclaimed. Since all participating models were young women, I felt uncomfortable about the way my public image was being constructed. I told Nakamori that I was not really planning to look like a Lolita maniac who took pleasure in objectifying, experimenting, and dissecting young female idols as if they were guinea pigs. Nakamori was insistent, however. "Don't you worry," he said, "readers will know that this is part of an image-play, and they will come to understand who you are when they read your upcoming articles. Besides, you are a social scientist who came here to analyze idols, aren't you?" Overcome by my will to put myself into a scientific experiment (one that examined how the audience would react to my style), I went ahead and wore my lab coat.

After ninety minutes of preparation and waiting, Shinoyama arrived with his crew. A noisy house with people chatting suddenly became quiet, and everyone started to look tense in the presence of this 58-year-old legendary photographer. Shinoyama had received awards in art, including one from the Ministry of Education in 1973, and published best-selling photo albums such as *Silkroad, Tokyo Nude*, and *Santa Fe. Santa Fe*, published in 1991, became a best-selling collection of photos in which an idol, Rie Miyazawa, struck poses, naked, in the desert landscapes of New Mexico. It created a public sensation because it was considered to be the first photo album in which a well-known idol appeared naked at the height of her popularity—where the convention has been that idols appear naked only when they do not sell well. Naked images of Japanese, particularly Japanese women, appear in late-night television shows, ads, and products directly or indirectly defined as part of the sex trade (*fūzoku*). Nude representations of Japanese for everyday, mainstream products and businesses are not common because they are considered culturally inappropriate (Creighton 1995: 137). Thus *Santa Fe* was sensationally challenging to the social norm at the time.

Appearing to be in a rush, Shinoyama first told me when I introduced myself that he wanted to look around the house quickly. It took him a matter of five minutes to do so. Yoshimura followed him around, adding a few extra words to clarify the plan of the scene that had already been arranged (Fig. 4.2). Taking the images proposed by Nakamori into account, Shinoyama decided to do three cuts: the first cut had an idol stand by the door; the second had me sit in front of a line of idol-group members; and the third had four other idols stand in the backyard of the house. He

Fig. 4.2 A scene from *SPA!* photographing: Kishin Shinoyama
inspects the layout of the site while idols and promoters get
ready for the big day (photo by the author, October 1995).

gave a few directions to his assistants, who then moved briskly to set
up the equipment so that their master could get to work. For each
of the three cuts, two to three test photos were shot. Upon shooting
these test photos, Shinoyama called Nakamori and me to see
whether they were okay. "What do you think, Professor!? Is this all
right!?" he would ask me, making an overly respectful gesture, corresponding to my image-motif of being a researcher of pop idols.

In one of the test photos, the model had a relatively serious expression on her face, which I thought was inappropriate because
idols generally smiled all the time. When I informed Shinoyama of
this, he said, looking offended, "This professor throws cold water
on my photography!" Those observing around us were all intimidated by the exchange. Expressing one's personal opinion before the
group or to the authority is considered risky behavior in Japan, and
people seldom do this without a good reason with which everyone else can eventually agree. It was apparent that I had violated
this rule. Shinoyama, however, ordered the model to smile and
quickly took another test shot. Then, he showed it to me and asked,
"What about this time, Professor!? Is this what you wanted?" Con-
sidering Shinoyama to be an international-class photographer who
handled English without any problem, I purposely replied to him

Fig. 4.3   The first cover-page of the
November 15, 1995, issue of *SPA!*

in English, "I don't think I like it . . ." Then, just as his face was
about to show anger, I added, "I love it! There's no problem!" My
goal was to reflect the idea that foreigners, or *gaijin*, can get away
with violating cultural norms because foreigners are not expected
to be competent in the cultural norms (Creighton 1995: 137). Here,
code switching between two languages served as a useful strategy in
expressing a mixed identity (Gumperz 1976; Auer 1998). By switching from Japanese to English, I also shifted my cultural identity,
positioning myself as if I were a foreigner who lacked the ability to
communicate in a Japanese way. My effort to compensate humor-
ously for the tension I had created worked. Shinoyama replied,
"No problem!" with a smile on his face, and everyone looked relieved. Fujiwara, who was quietly observing the situation, later said
that at first he couldn't believe that I challenged Shinoyama, but

was glad to know that it was a gag after all. I wondered whether Shinoyama was truly offended, to which Nakamori replied that it was no problem because I was an expatriate from Canada who could get away with violating norms anyway. Thus, I was allowed to violate the Japanese rule, but only because I was denied my Japanese identity.

The fruits of this event appeared in the November 15, 1995, issue of *SPA!* as part 268 of the front-page series called "Woman Catch the News." The title I gave for my research base appeared as the heading on the first page, at the bottom of which were the profiles of me and the idols who appeared in the article. The idol who marketed her futuristic image was featured on this page (Fig. 4.3). I appeared as an idol scientist in the following centerfold page, which, in fact, was a composite of two photographs taken in different rooms (Fig. 4.4). This was followed by the page on which the photo taken in the backyard appeared next to a column written by Nakamori (Fig. 4.5). The column introduced me and my research in the form of a tale. The excerpt below shows its mystical orientation:

I visited him one deepening-autumn day, getting off at the Myōgadani subway station and walking along the quiet neighborhood of Bunkyō district [in Tokyo]. . . . Next to a grassy backyard was a time-honored, isolated wooden house that had probably been there for a half-century or so. When I rang the doorbell and stood there waiting, the squeaky door opened and a roaring voice that said "Welcome . . ." was heard as if it arose from the bottom of the ground. A man with shining glasses and lab coat appeared before my eyes. As I entered the mansion guided by this man with a lab coat, I shouted "Wow!" in surprise. Young girls were smiling everywhere. . . . There was a large number of idol goods including photos, autographs, CDs, and albums! The man was the famous idol professor, Dr. Hiroshi Aoyagi, and this was his secret idol research center!! After a long talk, I excused myself and started to walk away from the research center, it was late at night. . . . As I heard strange voices at the back, I returned [to the center] with stealthy steps, and peeped between the sliding screens. . . . Alas! One after another cute idol girls appeared like spirits and danced joyfully, and the mad idol scientist in his lab coat was smiling, looking satisfied! Is this a dream, reality, or illusion? Or is this the professor's idol black magic!? When I regained my consciousness, there

Fig. 4.4   The second cover-page of the November 15, 1995, issue of *SPA!*
featuring the researcher as a "scientist."

was only a dark back street of Myōgadani. . . . The professor's idol re-search center was entirely out of sight, and there were only grass and trees before my eyes.

Nakamori had developed a story much like native folklore, in which I was projected as a charismatic personality who came to Japan from an exotic land to play with magic using idols.

Outcomes

It did not take long for me to see the result of this stylistic promotion. Within a few weeks after the article was published, I began to receive telephone calls from publishers requesting me to provide commentaries to their feature articles on idols or to write an essay about them. One television station contacted me to appear on a variety show, which I politely declined; I asked the staff to contact me again when my dissertation was complete. When I interviewed fans, many of them asked me for my autograph. For some of them who asked me for a short quote, I wrote, "They are just idols, but

Fig. 4.5 The third cover-page of the November 15, 1995, issue of *SPA!*, which shows a column by Akio Nakamori next to the photo of four cute-style idols in the grassy yard.

they are cultural symbols . . ." in order to signify the anthropological research value of idols regardless of their popularity. Some idol candidates, claiming to be my fans, also approached me.

Although I enjoyed being in such an adored position, I could not simply indulge in having a good time because some skeptics questioned my position. One day, I was approached by another individual who had been promoted by Nakamori long before me. He wanted to have a chat with me, so we went out to do what many Japanese white-collar businessmen (*sarariiman*) do in Japan, namely, after-work drinking. There was nothing particularly important about the content of our conversation, but the man kept expressing his interest in hearing stories about my background, my research project, and how I met Nakamori and reached the point of being promoted.

As conversation opened up after several bottles of sake, the man, who had been reserved until then, started to reveal his true feelings. "Hearing all your stories," he said, "I think you are just a graduate student who is interested in studying idols." When I replied that this was the case and asked him what he was trying to get at, he said, "Well, I suppose many people who read that article in *SPA!* would think that you are a braggart!" When I pursued his reason for making this statement, he explained that there was no reason for a student to call himself a "professor," and much less was he qualified to become a center of national attention by appearing in one of the nation's best-selling magazines, simply because the topic of his study was interesting. Realizing that I had become a nail that stuck out, only to be hammered down by this white-collar worker who also appeared in *SPA!*, I asked what qualification he thought he had to appear in the magazine as a "wonder man." He said he neither used his real name nor exposed his face in the article that talked about him. When I discussed this issue with Nakamori later, he told me not to worry about it. He said that what I experienced was simply a form of jealousy, and that it was easy for many Japanese to get jealous with one another over the slightest difference— although they themselves have "no guts to act with personal dignity." Nakamori thought that this was a negative quality of the Japanese due to the strong cultural emphasis on group conformity: "Whenever they want to express themselves, they tend to do it secretly, indirectly, or innocently. This is why Japan can never have strong leadership in international politics, you know. Japanese are not used to expressing themselves."

Thus, as much as my appearance in *SPA!* provided me with an excellent opportunity to participate in the cultural practices of celebrities, it was a bizarre experience for me: I became an academic turned entertainer, or observer turned observed. Certainly, the constructed public image of me had its roots in my personal qualities and my long-held identity as an ethnographer. Yet my "excess value" (so to speak), which led me to earn popularity and become a marketable personality in the world of mass media, was due to the style bestowed upon me by the image-making machine. In this sense, the characterization of me as an idol professor was an enforced identity rather than a quality that I could accept as part of myself.

Fabrication of image is a frequent practice in idol production, and indeed it is necessary for idols to embody styles, differentiate themselves from coexisting rivals, impress consumers, facilitate their marketability, and develop their careers (Inamasu 1989). My own experience of becoming a unique personality that was not exactly myself indicated that I could use it to hold a privileged position in the industry, which allowed me to have my voice heard in public, get jobs, and obtain a greater symbolic capital. Elsewhere, an emergent idol who has been fabricated by her agency as "an internet specialist who grew up playing with computers since she was a little child" told me that she had to study hard to acquire computer skills so that she could live up to the artificially constructed public image (which nevertheless allowed her to play a model role in the computer market). Her skills in using computers and in particular her abilities to create a home page and communicate with fans through e-mail, at the time, were emphasized by the members of her promoting staff. Seen in this light, mythical stories function as a cloak to symbolize performers and display them in society as meaningful commodities, whose values are auctioned by their users.

THE ARENA OF

SYMBOLIC COMPETITION

Backstage at events involving multiple idols and agencies was no place for me to conduct interviews with my informants. As much as they were closed-mouthed, they had eyes and ears that opened everywhere trying to read others' thoughts. Should any misbehavior occur, it became the subject of subsequent gossip, which, in some cases, led to scandals. Each agency protected the image of its idols carefully, and interaction between different agencies rarely took place outside mediation by a field overseer and staff, who in turn concentrated on directing the stage performance. Partly because of their need to appear adorable, idols looked relatively relaxed and friendly, and some of them talked with one another at times. Still, they were very much aware of their limits. Most of the time, they appeared innocent, indifferent, and interested only in playing their roles on stage.[4]

---

4. I found it most difficult on my part when I followed my informants from one agency backstage and met the people I knew from another agency. Caught between the two (or more), I had to worry about not being considered a spy. I

This tension, created by the symbolic competition between different agents of idol performances, is not limited to the domain of production. In many events in which two or more idols or idol groups appear, the competition is provoked by different groups of fans and audiences as well. Yano's study of fan organization in Japan shows that the very popularity of the public figure becomes defined by the devotion of the followers, and these followers make a person into a public, symbolic figure—the star (Yano 1997: 336). The fan can become a private surrogate for the star who shares vicariously in her or his fame and triumphs. As Yano indicates: "One becomes a surrogate through internalizing the other, through empathy. The empathetic internalization is complete. In Japan a fan is she who publicly takes on the responsibilities and obligations of the star, upholding the star's image, anticipating the star's needs. Through the created bonds of surrogacy, a fan takes on the burdens (and glory) of stardom" (Yano 1997: 337). Thus fans, working as surrogates, turn the contest of style among different idols in the field of production into a contest of identities among themselves. As much as stylistic competition shapes and is shaped by the way performers interact, it also determines and is determined by the way fans act toward one another, as well as toward their idol vis-à-vis other idols.

On a late, cold afternoon in November 1995, approximately 2,500 people lined up before a large hall that stood in a recreation area known as Ōmiya Sonic City in Saitama prefecture, just outside Tokyo. The public event people came to see was a concert organized by the state's Ministry of Public Welfare, which collaborated with promotion agencies and the mass media, as part of the United Nations' ten-year anti-drug campaign, which began in 1991. The ministry was particularly concerned about the recent increase in the number of drug-related problems in Japan, and it sought to advertise its campaign on the local level and educate people about the dangers of drug abuse.

I was invited to attend this event to observe the performance of the Seifuku kōjō iinkai, or the School Uniform Improvement

---

purposely avoided going backstage when two or more agencies invited me to the same event.

Committee, also known as S.K.I., an idol group that emerged in 1993 as a "facilitator" (so to speak) of the high-school uniform re-newal project organized by the Tokyo-based school uniform com-pany Satō Sangyō (founded in 1900). In the late 1980s, the company launched a campaign that aimed to renew high-school uniforms for young women under the slogan "collective beauty" (*shūdan-bi*). Uniforms have been a tool by which Japanese schools and compa-nies reinforce the value of uniformity, and the idea of collective beauty adds an element of beauty to this collective ethos of group conformity (e.g., Ōtsuka 1989; cf. Tanioka and Glaser 1991).

What started as an experiment in a few high schools became a national sensation as the project appealed to the fashion sense of female high-school students across Japan. In Tokyo and its vicinity, many students are now known to choose their high schools for their uniforms, although this may not be the *only* reason for their selection. In 1993, the industry organized S.K.I. as the signifier of this trend, hiring seven young women to perform as fashion mod-els. Eventually, the group extended its activities to the realm of idol performances, appearing on television shows, producing music CDs, and holding a series of concerts. I followed S.K.I. members' activities over a period of one year.

The anti-drug campaign concert functioned as an instrument for the government to attract and educate people in the name of enter-tainment and by virtue of the symbolic quality of idols. Such inter-play between education and entertainment is a common socializing strategy used by Japanese institutions outside the school context.[5] The pure, healthy, righteous, and friendly images of cute idols

---

5. In her study of department stores, for example, Creighton (1994) shows that large marketing institutions develop theme parks and play floors for children, along with shopping clubs for their mothers. In these amusement spaces, activities are developed in such ways that participants can interact and learn behaviors that are considered appropriate for one's status (or class), age category, and gender through goods and services that stores offer. While stores present their offerings and activities in terms of educational development themes, they also struggle to make them appear pleasant, playful, and fun: that is, something to which participants can look forward. Retailing amusements in Japan are cloaked in appeals to education, which is given a high cultural value in Japan (Creighton 1994: 40).

helped endear the campaign to the public. The main attractions of this event included Tomomi Nishimura (debut 1986), the mascot personality of the campaign, the idol duo Wink (1988–96), the idol trio Melody (debut 1993), and S.K.I. As for S.K.I., the group's claim to be the representatives of righteous schoolgirls and its past involvement in welfare activities (e.g., donating part of the money made from its concerts to the World Wide Fund for Nature), provided it with a chance to perform in this campaign concert.

The event was organized into two parts: the first, greetings, consisted of a series of speeches made by officials; and the second, Yes to Life Young Festival, consisted of stage performances featuring idol participants. After glancing at the line of audience members, I entered the hall and observed officials in charge passing out campaign posters and packages containing a program, brochures, and a souvenir telephone card. Then, I situated myself in one of the seats at the center of the hall. People flowed into the hall before long, and the three-hour event started on schedule at 6:00 P.M.

The majority of those who entered the hall first were idol fans, who had spent hours waiting outside long before other people started to form a line. As they rushed into the hall, they quickly grabbed posters and packages and occupied front seats as they divided themselves into four factions. It was like being in a multiparty parliament where members of different political parties occupied different sections: conservatives to the right, liberals to the left, and so on. Some fans appeared in distinct costumes to express their identities creatively. Others brought flashlights and had to surrender them to officials on the grounds that they disturbed other people in the audience.

In the first part, the minister and the governor appeared, giving speeches that said, "Drug abuse has been a problem in our country since World War [II]. It is becoming a serious problem in recent years especially, and it is our wish to prevent it. Drugs are dangerous not only because they can cause damage to your health, but also because they can destroy your family." The fact that the end of World War II was chosen in this speech as a temporal marker is interesting, because it marked Japan's surrender to the allied forces of the West and the beginning of the U.S. occupation. There is an implicit linking of the drug problem to the time when Japan re-engaged with the Western world. This further suggests a subtle underlining of the idea that drugs were not originally a Japanese problem but a foreign one—a kind of reasoning that derives from a tendency to see foreigners as standing in contrast to Japanese self-images. In a social environment where foreigners are often represented as overtly breaking the conventional rules of Japanese society, Westerners are seen as egoistic and contravening as compared to the essential Japanese values of collectivity and social harmony (Creighton 1995: 136, 137, 144). Drugs, which symbolize Western egoism, pose a moral threat to the Japanese. Idols, representing the images of Japanese adolescent purity, are used as a symbolic force that aims to counteract against this foreign threat.

After the last speech, everyone was asked to stand up and sing a campaign song called *Yes to Life*. Nishimura appeared on the stage to sing the lyrical lines of this song with the audience. Throughout this ritual, two female high-school students who sat next to me made cynical remarks about the campaign. They did not think it was possible for the state officials to prevent drugs from coming into Japan and spreading among young people, as was the case in the Tokyo area at the time. They wanted the officials to finish their boring speeches and start the concert, which was their reason for being there. Parents who brought their children were at my back, and they were attending the ceremony more seriously. As they observed the data presented by the officials, they made comments like "Drugs are becoming a pretty serious problem, aren't they?"

Once the event reached its second part, the atmosphere changed drastically. Fans who sat quietly during the first half transformed themselves into energetic and noisy cheering squads. Naturally, different sections reacted to different idols that appeared on the stage. They shouted, clapped their hands, raised their arms, and jumped up rhythmically as their idol(s) sang. Some fans hooted "Rubbish!" (*dasai!*) as fans from other factions cheered their idol(s). Those who sat behind these enthusiastic fans stood in their seats and observed the stage performances by the first two groups, Melody and S.K.I., in progress. Many of those who sat around me laughed at the scene. Some referred to the fans in the cheering squads as a "bunch of weirdoes," while others made fun of what they thought were artless performances by groups that they had never seen before.

Events involving multiple entertainers are arranged according to seniority in Japan, and newcomers commonly appeared before those who have been performing longer. The seniority rule does not apply when exceptionally popular and important performers are invited. In this particular campaign-concert, the stage performance proceeded according to the hierarchy based on seniority, and it matched nicely with different levels of public recognition attained by each participant. This was reflected in the number of fans that were present as well as in audience reaction.

When Wink appeared on stage, many people stood up and cheered, causing the rest to stand up and clap their hands as the duo sang songs including smash hits. Winner of the 1989 Japan Record Award, the duo popularized their images of innocent babes between the late 1980s and early 1990s. Unlike those of the first two groups, Wink's set featured live bands and stage effects. Along with the fancy, frilly costumes that they wore, the set created an illusion that they were singing in a European forest, which evoked a sense of romanticism in the minds of the viewers.

As far as I could tell, nobody laughed or made fun of Wink's performance, which led me to realize that the more recognition the performers attain, the more seriously they are viewed by the audience. Giving famous performers their serious attention represented a kind of respect to them—like that given by Japanese students to a respected teacher. Yet one of the two female high-school students who stood next to me told me that their doll-like images looked somewhat outdated, when I asked them about the style represented by the duo. The style they preferred was much more vibrant, as represented by Namie Amuro—with whom the generation of teens today could better associate themselves.

What interested me all the more was the fact that some of the idol fans who cheered other groups stood in their seats while the rest of the people stood up to dance along with Wink's melody. Other fans walked out of the hall while Wink's stage performance was in progress. Apparently, these acts were significant. When I subsequently interviewed one of the fans who walked out, he said that he was there only to show his support for the idol he adored:

I don't care how popular other idols are. I don't care if anyone wanted to make fun of my idol. I take pride in supporting my idol—especially when she is not considered so good by others. If we [the fans] don't support her, who will? People are generally mindless. They're probably there simply because the event was fun, or because it included someone famous. . . . They wouldn't think or care about putting their heart in supporting someone they can adore, but we do. I was there to support someone I find worth supporting and not to go with the flow of an event with a bunch of mindless people!

This fan expressed his indifference and even hostility and therefore differentiated himself and his group of idol fans from other members of the audience.

THE FIELD OF
COMPETING IDOL STYLES

This chapter has delved into the mechanism of idol promotion. It showed how styles are used as instruments for idols and their fans to interact meaningfully and to differentiate themselves from their rivals. The system of idol production demonstrates a striking structural similarity with the religious arena in which sacred figures are signified and contested. In either of these cases, competition tends to promote convergence on a unity of identity rather than resulting in social chaos. To this end, idol consumers identify themselves with a particular idol as an object of their worship, taking pride in their activities of support, while promotion agencies work hard to package performers as appealing figures and to contextualize promotional campaigns.

Public events in which the competition between different groups of idol promoters and consumers take place are similar to *matsuri* or *shintō* festivals. In a typical *matsuri* event, representatives from different local districts prepare portable shrines. Each of these miniaturized shrines in which the spirit of a local guardian (*kami*) is believed to reside is sturdily built and elaborately decorated. Local representatives carry these portable shrines on their shoulders and take them from their districts to a ceremonial ground at the time of festival. At the ceremonial ground, these groups compete with each other over the demonstration of their shrines' distinctive appearances as well as their spiritual liveliness. There are occasions in which one group of carriers collides with another group with an intention to push opponents out of the ceremonial ground at the height of their excitement. In much the same way as this *mikoshi katsugi*, or "shrine-carrying," public events in which different groups of idol fans compete over the adoration of their idols constitute a ceremonial arena of symbolic competition.

From the standpoint of an outsider, the symbolic competition between idols and their styles appeared to have occurred within a homogeneous social category. Watching my informants form a group around their favorite idol and oppose other groups was, to me, like watching *donguri no seikurabe*, or "a bunch of acorns fighting over their height" as Japanese would put it. In other words, many of the things idol fans considered important, worth disputing, seemed rather meaningless. Moreover, for someone who could not appreciate the symbolic value of idol performances to the extent that idol fans did, the community of fans that revolved around an idol appeared cultlike: a community of obsessed individuals who had nothing much to do other than libidinously consume young female characters that are provided by the market.

5

Following the Trajectory of
an Idol Superstar

Seeing an average child grow into a big star is what makes idol performances all the more exciting.

If successful, an idol will become an undisputed leader who can stand on
the mountaintop of popularity. Climbing up this mountain is not easy,
however. On the way, idols must face various obstacles. Only those who
overcome these obstacles with their patience and charm can win the
hearts of many people.

To be a star is to establish a personal style that can guide the public: that's
what all idols strive for.

These comments taken from interviews with idol producers indicate that establishing the self (*jiko kakuristu*) is considered a significant goal for idols. Whether they are the cute-idols that dominated
the Japanese pop-music scene between the 1960s and 1980s or the
post-idols that had become more pervasive in the 1990s, young personalities who become stars present highly stylized images.

Producing an idol is expensive, and it involves cautious calcula-
tions by producers. An interview with a record company director
revealed that the average cost for producing an idol is 30 to 40 million yen, and very few idols actually contribute greatly to the
companies' profit-making. This director saw idol production as an
act of charity for girls and boys who wanted to chase their dreams
and become famous. However, spirited idol candidates attempt to
take charge of their assigned roles and use them as instruments to
develop their own style—to prove to the public that they indeed

managed to establish themselves. The industry takes advantage of such a spirit, exploiting the labor of willing candidates, in hopes of profiting from these individuals as they are marketed in commodity forms. Expanding on this point, the current chapter will follow the trajectory of a successful idol, Seiko Matsuda. It will demonstrate how the mass media transformed her speeches and activities into publicly shared narratives that constitute a form of contemporary folklore. It will also demonstrate how Matsuda used these media-constructed narratives as sources of self-empowerment. Her controlled reactions to these narratives allowed her to transform herself from a cute girl to a mature woman without losing stardom in the context of present-day Japanese mass society.

Recent studies on folklore provide a productive framework that emphasizes the dialogue between tradition and innovation in the actual conduct of social life. As Bauman contends, a performance-centered conception of folklore or oral literature can reveal how the individual can creatively interact with tradition in a dialectic that is played out within the context of situated action, viewed as a kind of social practice (1992: 33; see also Bettelheim 1976; Bruner 1984). Elsewhere, Bauman elaborates: "Oral performance, like all other human activity, is situated, its form, meaning, and functions rooted in culturally defined scenes or events—bounded segments of the flow of behavior and experience that constitute meaningful contexts for action, interpretation, and evaluation" (Bauman 1986: 3). This performance-centered concept of folklore allows for the understanding that oral literature is grounded in the complex interplay of communicative resources, social goals, individual competence, community ground rules for performance, and culturally defined event structures.[1]

---

1. Bauman defines performance as a mode of communication, a way of speaking, the essence of which resides in the assumption of responsibility to an audience for a display of communicative skill, highlighting the way in which communication is carried out, above and beyond its referential content. From the audience's point of view, the act of expression on the part of the performer is thus laid open to evaluation for the way it is exercised, for the relative skill and the effectiveness of the performer's display. Performance is also offered for the enhancement of experience, through the present appreciation of the intrinsic qualities of the act of expression itself. Performance thus calls forth special

Building on Bauman's viewpoint, my ethnographic purpose in this chapter will be to put in perspective the politics of representation as played out among the performer, the mass media, and the audience. The performer tries to represent herself in a positive way by initiating activities that can inspire the public; as the provider of information as well as the coordinator of public opinion, members of the mass media try to produce sensational reports about a performer and her activities; and members of the public shape and re-shape the performer's image based on what they see, hear, and read. The idol's songs and speeches, as well as rumors and commentaries about her, are all components of the contemporary urban folklore that build her public image as a cultural symbol.

The life of Seiko Matsuda, one of Japan's most celebrated female pop singers today, illuminates this process of idol packaging. A girl named Noriko Kamachi came to Tokyo to become a successful idol, and she was transformed into a pop diva called Seiko Matsuda. This transformation was partly due to the effort made by Kamachi herself, and it was partly made possible by her promotion agency and its network, which backed her up. The transformation was also the result of Japanese public, who recognized Kamachi's diligent stance in idol performance. I have chosen Matsuda as the subject of this particular investigation because she has been one of the most frequently discussed public figures in the mass media.[2] Since her debut in 1980, the industry has been successfully marketing Matsuda's maturation process. Matsuda is considered to be a model (*otehon*) for the transformation of the self for many female idols and young women. Matsuda's life history shows how she was represented as someone who managed to earn her celebrity status with a tremendous amount of enthusiasm, patience, and cleverness, developing her own distinctive style. I will also examine what influence this representation has had on those watching her or following her.

---

attention to, and heightened awareness of, both the act of expression and the performer.

  2. Some of my informants considered Matsuda one of three chief examples of Japanese idols. Two others were Hiromi Gō and Momoe Yamaguchi (retired in 1980), both of whom dominated the entertainment scene in the 1970s.

I will not recount in detail the events of Matsuda's life or investigate who Matsuda really is. Rather, my intention here is to understand, through the analysis of a set of publicly presented narratives, the cultural forms and processes by which this girl, who is now a superstar, has been portrayed visually, orally, and in print over time.[3] I became interested in Matsuda's success story because the various accounts associated with this superstar express collective dreams, desires, and myths about selfhood and identity in Japanese society. Matsuda broke new ground in the symbolic construction of self. At the same time, this selfhood of hers is situated in the flux of changing values and lifestyles that signify the era of internationalization in Japan.

DRAMATIZING ONESELF

In Japan, celebrated heroic personalities embody processes that are culturally virtuous, such as disciplining the self (*jishukisei*), developing the self (*jiko-hatten*), discovering the self (*jiko-hakken*), renewing the self (*jiko-kaizō*), evaluating the self (*jiko-handan*), and recovering the self (*jiko-kaifuku*). Their lives are dramatized by the leadership campaigns of the Japanese mass media in a form that might be termed *jinsei-gekijō* (life theater). Such a dramatization process involves standing up against various trials (*shiren*) imposed upon the self by other individuals, groups, or institutions; overcoming feelings of inferiority (*rettōkan*); and establishing one's self as *ichinin-mae*, or a creative, responsible person. Though codependent on others, the *ichininmae* acts in harmony with one's individuality. It is premised that these are things that not many people have the courage to do, and viewers can therefore acquire from courageous individuals a fuller sense of self-confidence (*jishin*) as well as insight into the meaning of life (*ikigai*) (Mouer and Sugimoto 1986: 195–200).

Seiko Matsuda represents this process of self-accomplishment in Japanese culture and society. In the December 23, 1988, issue of *Asahi Journal*, feminist critic Chikako Ogura evaluated Matsuda's defiant characteristics:

---

3. I am here inspired by Portelli's study of subjectivity in oral history. For further details, see Portelli 1991: ix.

In the sentimentalism that lies at the core of the Japanese-style relationship between a mother and a daughter, the daughter cannot betray her mother. In the wet and sticky [i.e., benevolent] family organization of Japan, it is proven that the sexuality of a girl cannot be expressed freely. . . . Seiko, on the other hand, does not [conform to this rule]. Even though she is told that it is a customary practice for a Japanese woman to give up what one has now [i.e., career] to acquire a new happiness [married life], or that she has to grin and bear many things [in life], Matsuda asks back "Why?" and desires to have both [marriage and career]. She never lets go of something once attained: until now, such an attitude has been criticized as selfish, and it has not been admissible for a woman in Japan. Yet Matsuda does it without hesitation. (Ogura 1988: 1287; my translation)

The tension Ogura sees in Matsuda between female sexuality and the structure organizing the moral courses of action in families is perhaps more cross-cultural than specifically Japanese (cf. Collier, Rosaldo, and Yanagisako 1997).[4] Nevertheless, Ogura provides an account wherein the very sexuality that creates the human need for families becomes the point that the family institution tries to control.

In agreement with other critics, Ogura describes such an attitude as heroic because it challenges the existing system and facilitates social change. She contends:

[Matsuda] teaches a happy girl the concrete strategy of maintaining her happiness [without giving up anything]. Don't hand over to him the woman's ability to control her own sexuality. Dislike an old-fashioned man; there is no need [for a woman] to suffer [from limiting her activities to the home] by becoming a wife and a mother. Why not go into the system and break down those rules and codes about being a wife and a mother? . . . One will have to make a great effort to get what she wants. She is demonstrating these things. She is telling young women to grow up just as happy as she was during her girlhood. (1988: 1287; my translation)

---

4. In her song, *Girls Just Wanna Have Fun* (released in 1984), Cyndi Lauper sings, "I come home in the middle of the night, and my mother says 'When are you going to live your life right?' Oh mama, ain't we not the fortunate ones? Girls just to want to have fun." This is a good example of the family/sexuality tension in American popular culture. A similar form of tension is apparent in Madonna's *Papa Don't Preach*. In both present-day Japan and North America, young women perceive family as an ideological apparatus that keeps sexuality in line with social conformity.

In detailing the process whereby Matsuda deploys cultural norms, social standards, and moral principles to establish her style, I looked at articles and oral narratives about Matsuda. Her stage performances were also crucial. I used autobiographical essays written by Matsuda as well as other publications that discussed her in order to bring purported accounts of her dreams and desires into relation with her public image, her social relationships, and the institutions that support her career. Her experiences undergoing the process of establishing the public self-image are important to this understanding. There is a rhetorical problem with media sources, however: their contents are selectively organized, and the information they provide is presented to meet the interests of the writers and publishers. To compensate for this problem, I employed oral narratives that include commentaries on Matsuda's performances provided by idol producers, media agents, and fans. These comments offer insights into the ways Matsuda's style is adopted by her audiences as part of their own personality creation beyond the boundaries of the mass media.

Examining Matsuda's stage performance in concert reveals how she enacts her style before the audience, and how the audience reacts to this in an immediate context. Idol concerts typically function as showcases for performers to demonstrate their achievements. The interactions that take place in Matsuda's concerts are how her style is publicly shared in the form of a life history.

FROM MAIDEN TO SAINT:
THE BIOGRAPHY OF SEIKO MATSUDA

If genus *Idola japonica* can be classified into two species, cute-idols and stylish post-idols, whose qualitative differences signify a "genetic mutation" that occurred in the span of a decade or so, Seiko Matsuda is a personal manifestation of this transformation. Matsuda embodied the change in style from an innocent cute-idol who begged for public support to a confident pop star whose activities are almost always the source of public inspiration.

Most important, Matsuda is considered in Japan today to be a symbol of accomplishment. Her life is a testimony to the fact that a woman can challenge the world in spite of many obstacles and establish herself as a successful entertainer, homemaker, mother, shop owner, seductress, and independent worker simultaneously. As Kawanobe et al. (1994) put it, paraphrasing a comment by Matsuda, what distinguishes her from many other idols who simply market dreams is the demonstration that these dreams are there to be achieved via one's will to act: "The very source of Seiko Matsuda's popularity is her way of life that puts dreams into practice. She gets everything she desires. Seiko's dream is not simply a dream. There are steps to [reach] it. And it is her tenacity and enthusiasm to which many women [in particular] are attracted" (1994: 32; my translation). This statement specifies the way in which a dream can shackle human desire. Allison (1996: xv) notes that desire in present-day Japan is produced in forms that coordinate with the habits demanded of productive subjects.

The dullness and arduousness of the tasks Japanese must execute over a lifetime, starting in childhood (e.g., discipline and effort), are made acceptable by a process of internalization that makes the habitual desirable, rather than by an external structure (e.g., fear of failure in school). Escape from the habits of labor seems possible through everyday practices of pleasure in consuming (1996: xv). Matsuda's statement (as restated by Kawanobe et al.) implies that many Japanese women can attain a sense of subjectivity from Matsuda, who shows them the importance of having dreams in life, holding onto them, and working hard to achieve them. The internalization of Matsuda's lifestyle for these women, in turn, is made possible through the everyday consumption of her performances.

Matsuda was born Noriko Kamachi in 1962, in Kurume City of Fukuoka prefecture, which is located on the southern island of Kyūshū. One of her first public appearances was as an actor who played a young female character in a drama that was targeted to adolescent audiences, which demonstrated her cutesy image. Matsuda subsequently performed roles in radio programs and made her debut as a singer in April 1980 when she released a song called *Hadashi no kisetsu*, or *Barefoot Season*. Matsuda began her career as a cute-idol belonging to one of the big idol-promotion agencies,

Fig. 5.1 Seiko Matsuda in her typical cute, naïve look. This
example appeared on the cover of Matsuda's essay book,
Mō ichido anata (You once again) (1981, Wani Books).

Sun Music, but she became independent in 1989 and established her
own agency. Winning various musical awards from prestigious associations of Japanese pop music, such as Japan Music Grand Prize
(Nihon kayō taishō), Matsuda cultivated her expertise in the Japanese pop-music scene. In 1989, Matsuda released a duet with Placido
Domingo, followed by the release of a song entitled *Right Combination* in 1990, which was a duet with Donnie Wahlberg, a former
member of the American teen-idol group New Kids on the Block.

What distinguishes Matsuda from many other idols is not only
the fact that people of all ages became familiar with her performances but also that she has maintained her stance as a long-lasting

Fig. 5.2   Seiko Matsuda as a well-established pop diva. This image
appeared on the cover of the July 1995 issue of *Monthly
Kadokawa* (Kadokawa shoten).

idol who remains adorable even after she married and became a
mother. Where most of the so-called idol talents would retire from
the entertainment world after getting married or would move on
and become mature actors, Matsuda hung on to her role as an idol
role model—she was even called a *mamadoru* or "mom idol." Her
success as an idol-pop singer can be measured in part by the fact
that between 1980 (the year she made her debut) and 1993, she released 25 number-one singles and sixteen number-one albums, making more than U.S.$500 million in sales.[5] These figures are consid-
ered extraordinary, given the average life expectancy for idol-pop
singers of two to three years (contracts with agencies and record
companies are normally two to three years). Most of these young
singers are not expected to cover the high cost spent on their production. These events contributed to the Japanese public image of

5. For further details, see Kōdansha 1993: 1286.

Matsuda as a self-established and self-controlled idol-pop diva (cf. Figs. 5.1 and 5.2).

THE PROJECTION OF MATSUDA IN PRINTED MATERIALS

Newspapers, magazines, and essays about and by Matsuda played important parts in constructing Matsuda's public image. These materials can be classified according to the kinds of knowledge they generate. Newspaper articles on Matsuda are full of spontaneous remarks about the latest events and activities related to Matsuda. Tabloid magazines aim to criticize and ridicule Matsuda on the basis of what she did and said. Idol magazines and newsletters for fans try to promote Matsuda's image in a way that satisfy her supporters. Autobiographical essays, written to modify her public image, reveal Matsuda's reactions to these characterizations. There are also academic references that analyze Matsuda's personality and activities from psychological and sociological standpoints. In what follows I will elaborate on the constructions that occur in each of these categories. Translations of all quotations and excerpts from Japanese sources are my own.

Tabloids

Tabloids articulate whatever events might be of interest to the public and present them in their most immediately available details. Unusual events, calamities, and personal incidents are common, and many of these stories are exaggerated or intentionally fabricated by promotion agencies or news outlets. Stories on celebrities are often aimed at fomenting scandal.

Tabloid articles commonly appear in the *jōhōshi* or "information magazines," such as *Shūkan Post*, *Shūkan gendai*, *Shūkan hōseki*, *Shūkan Asahi*, *Shūkan Yomiuri*, *Sunday Mainichi*, *Shūkan taishū*, *Asahi geinō*, *FOCUS*, *FLASH*, and *FRIDAY*. Some of these magazines focus on political and economic information, while others emphasize manners, customs, leisure, and entertainment. Some magazines that include tabloid articles, such as *Josei jishin*, *Shūkan josei*, *Josei Seven*, *Bishō*, and *Shūkan myōjō* (ceased 1991), target women. These are heavily loaded with information on entertainment, romance, food, and fashion. Other magazines, such as *Weekly Playboy* and *Monthly Takarajima*, are rich in information about female entertainers, sports, as well as love and sex—issues that are presumed to be particularly attractive to a male readership. There are also a variety of tabloid newspapers, including *Hōchi shinbun, Sankei shinbun, Nikkan Sports,* and *Tokyo Chūnichi Sports.*

One can also tune into the "wide shows" on private-television channels that are tabloid in nature. Many of these programs are shown in the morning for businessmen or during the midday for housewives. As much as people criticize the intrusive quality of tabloids, or the tendency of these tabloids to "mess around with people's private lives in the name of freedom of speech" as one informant puts it, they enjoy consuming them. Many people I talked to characterized Japan as a "gossip society" (*uwasa-shakai*) and considered tabloids to be an apparatus designed to accommodate such a social environment.

Matsuda is undoubtedly one of the most frequently discussed subjects in tabloid news. My survey at Ōoya sōichi bunko in Tokyo, an archive that specializes in popular journals, revealed many more articles featuring her than any other celebrated idol. I will limit myself to the minimum number of tabloid articles on Matsuda, however, and my accounts of these articles will be superficial. This is due to the negotiations between myself and Matsuda's promotion agency about the controlled content of this chapter. When I presented the original draft of this chapter to Matsuda's promotion agency in order to make sure that no part of it would substantially offend Matsuda, the agency spent nearly two months reviewing it. After obtaining opinions from Matsuda, her families, and those who worked with her, the agency requested that I omit all data that would potentially jeopardize Matsuda in the future or provoke bad memories. As much as this decision was frustrating to me, I appreciated the time the agency took to attend to my requests. Finally, I tried to maintain my point on Matsuda's symbolic significance—her power to overcome social challenges in the process of establishing her own style in a form of public signifier—without extensively discussing negative representations of her. Examples that I selected here are intended to demonstrate the general style in which events were reported. I will provide some accounts of the influence of these articles upon their readers.

Most frequently, tabloid articles try to expose what they regard as the realities of Matsuda's private life—especially her romances, marriage, motherhood, and sexual relations—that contradict her purified public image. These aspects were all carefully followed up over time and covered under cynical headlines. For example, articles about her romance were variously introduced as:

The catastrophic affair of Seiko . . . and [its] shocking reasons: Seiko's tearful press conference, four-year romance in treasured photos, the truth behind the sudden breakup   (*Shūkan josei*, Feb. 12, 1985)

Seiko breaks up: the complete story of her four-year romance   (*Josei jishin*, Feb. 12, 1985)

As for Matsuda's marriage, the tabloids wrote:

Seiko Matsuda—complete notes on their [luxurious] 200 million-yen wedding! Long carpet, curtain, hairstyle, makeup, surprises, the map of the area in which their new home is located, the interior of their love nest, etc.—complete coverage   (*Josei Seven*, July 4, 1985)

Seiko Matsuda—detailed coverage of her honeymoon in Hawaii with 28 pages of graphic color photos and articles   (*Shūkan myōjō*, July 11, 1985)

Apparent in all of these cases are the intentions of tabloids to turn Matsuda's private life into a public spectacle as part of their mission to symbolize her as a monstrous personality with unlimited desire.

Matsuda's willingness to follow her career path even after marriage and motherhood was reported as follows:

Seiko may get divorced in February, May, or August because of her return to show business!   (*Scholar*, Oct. 10, 1987)

A good business period for the shrewd Seiko Mama? This time she is running a boutique   (*FLASH*, Feb. 18, 1988)

Independence came prior to marriage: the loud laugh of Seiko Matsuda, who ran away from home duties   (*FOCUS*, July 14, 1989)

Dream and hope for Seiko Matsuda, an isolated former idol and a selfish mom-idol in Japanese show business   (*Shūkan taishū*, Sept. 4, 1989)

These articles try to provoke collective resentment by attacking Matsuda's qualifications as a mother. She is depicted as a villainous, self-centered woman who seeks a career by sacrificing her life and duty at home. Together these narratives emphasize Matsuda's attitude as one that is unconventional, controversial, and thus intolerable from the perspective of "decent" Japanese.

One may argue that these examples of contemporary folklore in which an idol is signified as a villain can be added to the existing body of popular Japanese literature on suffering, especially maternal suffering, which is attributed to ostensible celebrations of personal sacrifice in Japanese culture. In many novels, movies, and television dramas, heroes and heroines surrender themselves for the good of the others, delighting audiences with a sense of *anshin*, or "peace in heart." It is wonderfully reassuring for these audiences to see that other people's problems, even in fantasy, are worse than their own. Maternal characters play a crucial role here as they enhance guilty sentiment and hidden aggression (Buruma 1984: 24, 25). In popular-cultural texts, mothers always appear as a kind of scapegoat who make every possible sacrifice for their sons and daughters with minimal or no return.[6] Nobody's fate can possibly be worse than theirs. Seen in this light, the media's exposition of Matsuda's career as well as her life course to marriage and motherhood as difficult is an appeal to the Japanese public ideal of motherhood.

Rumors, more recently known among young people as *kuchi-komi* (an abbreviated form of *kuchi communication*, or "word of mouth"), play an important role in implementing group control over individual courses of action. Gossiping is a commonly practiced form of social control that reinforces such culturally emphasized ideas as *sekentei* (public appearances), *menboku* (face, honor, or reputation), and *tatemae* (a form of self-expression that conforms to public norms, standards and principles), not to mention *haji* (shame)—a concept that has been discussed in detail by Benedict (1946) as a prominent Japanese value. Gossip evokes in the

---

6. In dramas, mothers are often betrayed by their children, who eventually abandon them as they grow up to be adults. Yet they are presented as ever-forgiving mothers who pour out their affections constantly as they endure their suffering or who simply smile beatifically (Buruma 1984: 25).

minds of the Japanese a concern that their activities are being watched by others.[7] Tabloids operate as incessant watchdogs; they put celebrities on trial and thereby challenge their exercise of symbolic power.

While the manner of reporting in tabloids is itself ethically questionable at times (by intruding upon the performer's privacy), tabloids call upon their readers to evaluate who did what with respect to customary rules, ethical codes, and moral values. Tabloids reproduce what is considered appropriate in society. Thus, for example, Matsuda who became a mother is accused of neglecting her husband and her child when she tries to continue her pursuit of an entertainment career. The implication is that she is going against the traditional role of good wife, wise mother. Likewise, she becomes prey to scandals when she appears to be overly childlike and therefore provokes in the minds of the viewers the sense that she is acting inappropriately for her age. One can find many headline reports of Matsuda's extramarital affairs that aim to construct a public image of Matsuda as a morally intolerable person. In these ways, tabloids try to function as watchdogs that hammer down the subject whom they see as standing out.

For Matsuda, as much as for any other well-known Japanese idol, tabloids are elements of social pressure that interfere with her intention to keep her public image clean. Being clean is crucial for maintaining one's popularity as a star in the Japanese entertainment industry, where pop stars that soil their image are likely to lose their jobs. In early 1988, Matsuda in a press conference scolded reporters who attempted to scrutinize her family relations. This act simply aggravated the situation. The February 4, 1988, issue of *Shūkan myōjō* and several other publications pointed out the absurdity of a public role model revealing her anger, appealing to the norm that one should not publicly expose anger in Japan.[8]

---

7. For a concise and elaborate discussion of the Japanese emphasis on group-controlled behaviors, see, for example, Mouer and Sugimoto 1986.

8. One is reminded of an old hero-tale, *Chūshingura*, here. Based on a true story, it talks about a lord named Naganori Asano who loses his temper at a meeting held in the shogun's castle. Asano draws his sword in an attempt to attack Kōzukenosuke Kira, another regional lord who kept picking on him. Charged with disrupting the social order and public harmony for personal reasons, Asano

Matsuda, however, was aware of the outcome of her reaction against the tabloids, and it has been her policy to neglect them in most cases, as she reveals in one of her essays:

My life as Seiko Matsuda . . . can be said to have been full of struggle with part of the mass media [called tabloids]. I changed my way of thinking at a certain point, however. Although I was protesting in the beginning because I could not hold my anger, I started to ignore them from then on. This is partly because I could not afford to protest each time [a story about me was published], but more importantly because I thought protesting would only make me fall into the snare that they spread. I managed to become more cautious. . . . I told myself that I would not act under the influence of their imagination. I started to play innocent so that I could keep myself aloof from the imagination and artifice of those who make a lot of noise about scandals. (1986: 141, 142)

This indicates the determination of a super-idol to use the signifying qualities of idols such as innocence as a strategic means to surpass and thereby overcome challenges imposed by the organizers of public opinion. Over the years, Matsuda managed to transform herself from the prey of tabloid criticism to the predator of Japanese mass media by developing a technique to take advantage of her celebrity status.

Promoting Articles

Idol magazines such as *Bomb!*, *Heibon* (ceased 1987), *Momoco* (ceased 1994), *Myōjo*, *Potato*, and *Up to Boy* provide elaborate data on idols' personal backgrounds, ideas, and activities. In the feature article, "Seiko Matsuda: A Twenty-Year," in the March 1983 issue of *Bomb!*, for example, eight pages of color photographs of Matsu-

---

is ordered to commit *seppuku* (an authenticated form of suicide in which the subject cuts open his abdomen to atone for the shame he had caused). Subsequent episodes speak of 46 of Asano's servants, led by Kuranosuke Ōishi, who avenge their lord and assassinate Kira. The shogun later orders the 46 men to commit *seppuku* as well. The story celebrates the loyalty and bravery of these 46 men, but it also moralizes the tragic outcome of losing one's temper in public. I remember as a child my father used this story as an example to teach me about the importance of patience in one's dealing with public affairs. "Never expose your emotion," he told me, because "if you do both you and your associates will lose face and end up suffering."

da (some of which have promotional quotes on the side) are followed by a 31-page article that includes her personal history: when
and where she was born, which schools she attended as a child,
what she wanted to be as a young girl, behind-the-scenes stories of
her debut, first concert, performances on television, and so on.
Subsequent pages include supportive comments (from her colleagues, producers, and managers), stories of her dedication as a
performer, personal messages, list of released singles and albums,
astrology, and palm-reading. This article ends with a handwritten
letter from Matsuda to her fans, calling for their continuous support and encouragement.

Fashion magazines, such as *Non-No, Men's Non-No, Popeye, An-
An, JUNON, McSister, Hanako, Seventeen, Olive, Duet,* and *Potato,*
also included many cover pages and special interviews that promoted Matsuda and other pop stars by representing them as models in fashion, lifestyle, and romance. Other popular journals dealing with more general topics in popular culture, such as *SPA!,
Views,* and *Monthly Kadokawa,* also offered feature articles on
Matsuda in a style of presentation similar to that of the *Bomb!* article mentioned above, but with a somewhat more analytical overview of her life, ideas, and activities.

An eight-page article in the April 6, 1994, issue of *SPA!* called
"The Way of Life Called Seiko Matsuda" ("Matsuda Seiko to iu
ikikata") exemplifies this more analytical style. Commemorating
the fifteenth year of Matsuda's career, this article gives Matsuda the
title, "super-lady who made all the dreams of Japanese women
come true." Its centerfold features a computer-graphic image of Japan in the ocean on which Matsuda stands gigantically as a Statue
of Liberty—with a torch in her hand, smile on her face, and feet
placed on Tokyo.

The first column of this article, written by Akio Nakamori,
characterizes Matsuda as an innovative idol who represents Japan.
This opening is followed by another centerfold in which the editors make connections between Matsuda's activities and a series of
fads involving young Japanese women over the span of a decade.
For example, Matsuda's childlike performances not long after her
debut influenced many other young female performers to act in a

childlike manner. The rumor that Matsuda had an eyelid operation had an influence on the increasing number of young women getting cosmetic eye surgery. Matsuda's wedding influenced women to put more emphasis on having a luxurious wedding. When Matsuda became pregnant and had a child, many young women followed her. Matsuda's success in the boutique business facilitated career-consciousness among women. This listing, which the editors claim to have produced on the basis of thorough research, tries to explicate Matsuda's cultural influence by showing how Matsuda influenced changes in the collective behavior of Japanese women. Certainly, practices such as cosmetic surgery and career consciousness predate Matsuda, and these practices were not rare. The editors try to show that resurgent cycles of already existing trends among Japanese women are additionally affected by Matsuda.

Underneath this list is another column that portrays Matsuda as a pioneer of Japanese womanhood. Part of this reads:

How can the life of one woman over the past ten years or so stir up the curiosity of so many women? She [i.e., Matsuda] is scandalous enough to double the sales of women's magazines. . . . A rapidly increasing number of women are sympathizing with the way of life called Seiko Matsuda and are feeling much easier [than ever before] about devoting themselves to living according to their desires. Time is about to catch up with Seiko. What sort of guide can Seiko, who has been an evangelistic figure for Japanese women in terms of lifestyle for ten years or so since her debut, provide from now on for all those women who are becoming the agitators of their own desire? The value of Seiko Matsuda will depend upon the next ten years [of her activities].   (pp. 38, 39)

This portrays Matsuda as a leading figure of the time—what many Japanese call "a person of the time" (*toki no hito*) or "a person who constructs the times" (*jidai o kizuku hito*). This article is followed by a two-page list of interview comments from different audience groups that signifies Matsuda's leading sociocultural role:

Transvestites: "Seiko-*chan* is an eternal symbol of cuteness."

Young mothers: "I am working hard by making Seiko-*chan* my spiritual support."

Students of Tokyo University: "We want to follow Seiko's enthusiasm."

High-school gals: "Seiko-*san* provides us with the model for our lifestyle."

Finally, supportive comments by Matsuda's fans are followed by a concluding remark by the editor summarizing how Matsuda represented the youth of the 1980s. According to this remark, Matsuda's wavy hairstyle and her frilly fashions were imitated by many other idols and young women of the same age group, while her fresh, active personality inspired them.

Although there is a certain degree of variation in their content, all supportive materials on Matsuda applaud her unique personal qualities and her achievements with an elaborate discussion of how she was able to accomplish so much. In this way, they counteract tabloids that try to estrange her from any meaningful existence in the realm of public entertainment in contemporary Japan.

Analytical Essays

Aside from popular magazine articles, there are essays that glorify Matsuda through elaborate analyses of her lifestyle and philosophy. Perhaps the two classic examples from this category are *Blue Tapestry* (*Aoiro no Tapestry*) by female cultural critic Mariko Hayashi (published in 1982), and *A Treatise on Seiko Matsuda* (*Matsuda Seiko ron*) by a feminist sociologist Chikako Ogura (published in 1989). Other publications include "Is Seiko Matsuda an Evil Woman or Is She a New Woman Who Lives the Times?" ("Matsuda Seiko wa akujo nano ka jidai o ikiru atarashii onna nano ka"), *Seiko Matsuda: Women's Revolution* (*Matsuda Seiko onna kakumei*), and *All Women Like Seiko Matsuda* (*Onna wa minna Matsuda Seiko ga suki*). In a large bookstore that I often visited in the Shinjuku district of Tokyo, I found a section dedicated to essays about Seiko Matsuda written by cultural critics, freelance writers, editors, sociologists, and psychologists, most of which appeared between 1994 and 1996. Every time I visited, I saw young female workers and female high-school students examining them. I occasionally observed couples and groups talking to each other about Matsuda's extraordinary characteristics as they examined some of these items.

The book by Hayashi is unique in the sense that it was written as a dialogue based on interviews that the writer conducted with Matsuda. Several people recommended this book as a necessary part of my idol research. It elaborates Matsuda's background and experiences, as well as her ideals at the time she had turned twenty years old. Becoming twenty has a special meaning in Japan: it is the year in which one is recognized socially as *seijin*, or "adult." In this book Hayashi identifies two opposing characteristics in Matsuda: an average young girl who dreams about being together with a reliable male partner, marrying him, and having a happy family life to which she can retire from her current work in show business; and an ambitious individualist who wishes to be independent, active, and self-reliant. If Matsuda is a role model for Japanese women, this characterization represents the ambivalence of Japanese female existence.

In her book, which was introduced to me by some of my female informants as "one of the most sensational books on Matsuda," Ogura takes this point further and suggests that both of these characteristics are equally realistic for Matsuda:

Many women criticized Matsuda's childlike quality . . . , the *Seiko white* [or her cute and pure appearance] . . . , and rejected it as nothing more than flattery toward the young men's dream [of an ideal woman]. These women were implying that the real Seiko is the *Seiko black* [which is her ambitious and egocentric side]. . . . However, both white and black are the real Seiko. As Matsuda says [in her interview with Hayashi], being a professional is not putting on a mask [of a fake child], but becoming one itself [when necessary].   (Ogura 1989: 21; italics mine)

Ogura stresses that ambivalent selfhood is a constructive part of Matsuda's expertise. In a thorough examination of Matsuda's activities, comments, and songs, Ogura concludes that Matsuda's way of life can enlighten many women of her generation by encouraging them to take their decisions about romance, womanhood, and femininity into their own hands. Staying outside the established system, or the ideological role of good wife, wise mother, enables women to be free to choose between conformity and resistance (1989: 228, 230).

However differently they are packaged, other essays demonstrate common themes that ultimately converge on the point made by Ogura: Matsuda's personal strength, which enabled her to overcome various struggles imposed upon her by the society. These characteristics earned Matsuda an unshakable position in Japanese society as a female role model. Somewhat like fables, these essays bring to the readers' attention certain events that marked the stages of Matsuda's personal development and indicate how she managed to resolve each of these problems. In doing so, they provide the readers with a series of guidelines to cope with life problems. Kawanobe and others (1994), for example, demonstrate how Matsuda's tenacity allowed her to become a successful entertainer. A strong sense of accomplishment led Matsuda to come all the way up to Tokyo from one of Japan's southernmost towns, Fukuoka, to perform in spite of repeated failures in audition contests. This spirit of accomplishment eventually led Matsuda to sacrifice her marriage and family for the sake of her career (1994: 22).

In a prologue to his essay on Matsuda, Inoue (1996) states that his intention was to examine Matsuda's lifestyle as a way of over-coming one's handicaps, complexes, and a sense of failure. Matsuda, he says, was neither a beauty nor a genius by nature: her legs were bow-shaped, and she suffered from the belief that she was over-weight. She had a local accent, which is considered backward in Japan. She also had nervous breakdowns due to the scandals in her life. However, it was her positive thinking and incessant effort that stylized a way of life that many people, particularly young women, found inspiring (1996: 11–13). These are but a few examples showing how writers identify aspects of Matsuda's *raison d'être*, or define her social values, in such a way that they can stimulate the readers' sense of self-improvement. Most of these pieces are targeted to young women who are likely to find much to share with Matsuda in terms of their ideas and attitudes.

Autobiographical Essays

Aside from books and articles written by journalists and cultural critics, there are many essays that are purportedly written by idols themselves as first-person accounts. Speculating that many of these essays might have been ghostwritten, I asked several producers about their authenticity. Their answers revealed that some essays were ghosted, while others were written by idols themselves under the direction of their promotion agency. Although I could not determine the authenticity of Matsuda's essays, I will, in this section, read them as texts that reflect her points of view as a public persona.

The first series of essays written by Matsuda was *Ryōte de Seiko* (Seiko in both arms), published soon after her debut in 1980. One essay was published each year during the subsequent few years of Matsuda's career, commercializing each stage of her personal development. *Ryōte de Seiko* sketches Matsuda as a novice who had dreams about becoming a popular, adorable personality. The second essay, *Mō ichido anata* (You once again; published in 1981), commemorates the crucial first two years of Matsuda's career as a novice. *Seiko 20-sai: ai to uta no seishunfu* (Seiko 20-years-old: a youthful chronicle on love and music; published in 1982) signifies the importance of reaching adulthood. These essays were recommended to me by my informants, who had been influenced by Matsuda. Another book, *Seiko* (published in 1986), said to be written by Matsuda under her married name, Noriko Kanda, is a reflective autobiography commemorating Matsuda's marriage with Masaki Kanda. These essays are extremely valuable to readers who want to take their knowledge about Matsuda beyond rumors that are constructed by tabloids or third-person accounts in magazines. They detail in a single volume an extraordinary individual's own account of her ideas, activities, and experiences—especially her thoughts about herself, her reactions to the ways she was treated by people around her, her courage to take control of her own career, and messages she wishes to deliver to the readers.

Each of these essays discusses a wide range of issues—work, romance, marriage, womanhood and manhood, sex, stories about memorable events in the past, current activities, and future prospects. More important culturally are recurrent themes related to self-development. Training in social membership and the cultivation of the individual have been serious enterprises in Japan for centuries, and they are regarded as imperative to the creation of an orderly society, individual quality, and personal fulfillment (Rohlen 1986: 327). Many parts of Matsuda's essays contribute to these cultural enterprises by interweaving her own experiences into issues that are related to socialization in the pop-idol industry. For example, three of Matsuda's essays have this to say on interpersonal relationships:

Seiko is very happy now. It's because there is someone like you who are supporting me. I feel really glad that I became a singer. I am beginning to feel that even someone like me can look out for myself. (Matsuda 1980: 16)

The fact that I am here today owes much to your support. Thank you!!— I am sorry for such a blatant statement, but this is my true feeling. The staff members of Sun Music, those of CBS/Sony, those of various TV and radio stations, and every fan who has been supportive of me since my debut, thank you very much. There were many joyful events on my way here, but there were sad and bitter events as well. In all these moments I said to myself, "Seiko Matsuda is not alone. Seiko is here because she is together with her staff and her fans," and because with clenched teeth she worked hard. I am [insignificantly] small, but I do not want to forget to keep up [in life] with my earnest desires. (Matsuda 1981: 24)

[As I was touring around for my concert] I became increasingly exhausted. When I faced my fans who cheered me, such exhaustion easily vanished. "There are so many people who are supportive of me all across Japan!" This fact very much touched my heart. It encouraged me to work much harder from now on! (1981: 59)

It has been three years since I made my debut. All this time I have been running with all my might. I did my best to live up to your enthusiastic support. From now on, too, I wish to walk along with you all the way. (1982: 21)

One after another, [aspects of] the new world come surging at me. A new passage opens before my eyes. There is no turning back for me. I can only march forward, and forward. Because everyone takes me by the hand, I can march onward. (1982: 127)

These comments reflect the high value given to interpersonal relationships in Japanese society, which, rooted in the psychology of dependence (*amae*), encourages close emotional ties. Two prominent Japanese concepts that emphasize the importance of social ties are *giri* and *on*: *giri* signifies the sense of social obligation, and *on*, or "beneficence," signifies the tendency to feel appreciation for what others have done on one's behalf (Doi 1973; Suzuki 1976; Befu 1986). Interpersonal relationships are stressed in reference to these concepts, which indicate the importance of togetherness as well as mutual support. In her essays, Matsuda repeatedly expresses how much she feels obligated and thankful to those who support her, including fans and staff members. She is projected as a benevolent person in order to appeal to the readers' sense of empathy.

If dependence offers an emotional ground for establishing interpersonal ties, responsibility enables Japanese actors to coordinate their ideas and behaviors toward the maintenance of that solidarity. Matsuda's essays certainly reflect this, as the following excerpts show:

During the rehearsal [of my concert], dozens of cameramen were taking photos as I was singing. People in the band, lighting staff, equipment staff, and sound editors—when I thought that everyone was working hard on my behalf, I could feel that I was about to do something very important, and I felt extremely responsible. (Matsuda 1980: 27)

[When I acted in drama for the first time] I was caught up, and I made many mistakes. I had a particularly difficult time with my accent, which I could not get right. Tears streamed from my eyes, really, because I felt bad for my co-actors who had to wait for me for a long time. The fact that such a beginner like myself took away the precious work-time of famous actors made the sense of responsibility come home to my heart. I felt so bad that I couldn't stand it. (Matsuda 1981: 27)

In Japanese families, schools, and places of work, the moral value of becoming a responsible adult who can adequately perform one's social role is emphasized (Lanham 1979; Rohlen 1986). Matsuda's essays demonstrate this value by indicating her sense of responsibility: she wants to do her best as a performer for her assistants, supporters, and coworkers.

Elsewhere, essays touch on the importance of self-cultivation in stories of Matsuda's experience of struggles, challenges, and the overcoming of suffering at important moments of her life:

My father's dream was to have me attend a university . . . and then make me a cute bride. In that sense, I let my parents down, and I am an undutiful daughter. Nevertheless, I just didn't want to have any regrets [in my life], so . . . I pled [with my father to give me his support]. Then my father slapped me even before he ended saying, "If you want to be a singer so much, get out of this house at once!" I patiently kept my dream. . . . People from the record company and the production came to see my father and had a talk with him, many times. As a result, my father eventually changed his opinion toward giving me permission. Yet, he did not tell me, "You can be a singer" until the very end.   (Matsuda 1980: 138, 140)

Before making a record debut, it was decided [by my agency] that I should perform in a television commercial, so I took an audition for an ice cream commercial first. I failed this one completely, however. Without being disheartened by this, I took the audition for Shiseido's commercial called "cheek dimples" [advertising a cosmetic product] this time. There was this thing called test-filming, and I changed my hair style and washed my face [before the camera] many times. . . . I remained as a finalist, but there was a sudden reversal at the very end. . . . I don't have any dimples on my cheeks!! It was decided that there was no point in using a model without any dimples to advertise a product called "cheek dimples." I worked hard to perform in the audition, and I was rewarded for this in the end, and they allowed me to sing the image-song instead of acting as the model.   (Matsuda 1981: 30)

The concert held in Kyūshū in the late summer of 1983 was one huge ordeal for me. As such, summer concerts make you exhausted because you have to run around the whole country in the middle of the heat. Besides, there were two stage performances, daytime and evening, each time. Work for a TV station in Tokyo was added onto this, and I was quite anxious by the time I reached Kyūshū. . . . On the evening stage, I lost the sense of what I was doing. My legs were not firmly placed on the ground. My throat was dried up. My voice faded out. Before long, gastric juice came up to my throat. I tried to endure it as hard as I could. I encouraged myself to keep singing with a smile on my face. If people who took the trouble of coming to see found out that I wasn't feeling well, they probably wouldn't be able to enjoy. . . . And if I collapsed, the place would be in chaos, and people would be in shock. "I feel sick a little, but I think I can keep up till the end," I said to the staff when I came down from the stage for a change of costumes. The staff knew that I didn't eat at all before the concert, and they seemed much more anxious than me because they saw me dripping greasy sweat from my pale face. I changed my costumes, pushed back the gastric juice that came up, and made strenuous efforts to sing.   (Kanda 1986: 66, 67)

I was shocked when I first found [an article] in a [tabloid] magazine indicating that high school and university students of my generation say "Your legs are Seiko-ed" (*ashi ga Seiko-tteru*) after my bowlegs when they see a bowlegged person. Then, when I looked at my legs they were indeed bowlegged. . . . Although I have given up thinking I can change this [there is nothing I can really do about them], I have been . . . reminding myself "not to be Seiko-ed" wherever people are watching.   (1986: 104, 105)

These comments portray Matsuda as a willing and patient individual who manages to conquer difficulties, such as her father's negativity and her physical shortcomings (not having dimples, being exhausted, and being bowlegged), to accomplish her goals. This reminds the reader of a popular Japanese phrase, *shoshi-kantestu* or "carrying out one's original intention," which signifies the importance of fulfillment through intention and discipline. Readers are led to believe that once Matsuda intends to do something, she does not let go of it until she accomplishes it, even if it involves much suffering.

Lebra (1976: 75) contends that as part of the development of the self, individuals in Japan work hard to attain success in educational and career pursuits. Strenuous effort (*doryoku*) and suffering (*kurō*) are expected of a young person who has ambition. While the above comments represent Matsuda's experiences of suffering, other passages demonstrate her expectations about effort.

At the time of my debut, I couldn't express my opinion in interviews at all, thinking "I cannot say this" and "I cannot say that either." It's not that people in my agency told me not to say anything unusual. Although it was the case that I could go ahead and express my ideas, I was bad at doing so. That is why I was misunderstood by many people and hated by women [who called me a childlike person]!! Starting this year, however, I am expressing my feelings and thought in terms of my own opinions. (Matsuda 1981: 146)

Let me tell you about my image of what an adult is and what a child is. The image of an adult is to be able to take responsibility for everything that one does, without troubling anyone. The image of a child is to work furiously. As for me, both of these conditions apply. It's true that I am working hard, and it is also true that I wish to act with a sense of responsibility. . . . To be more precise, I am still a child, but I am making efforts to become an adult. (1981: 158)

Many times, I was asked, "If you had a choice between a love affair and a career, which would you choose?" I answered, "Both of them are equally important." I am sure that I can love someone no matter how busy I am with my work. . . . Even when I loved one of my coworkers, I hardly got confused [between work and private business]. . . . In my high-school years, whenever I fell in love with a boy, and if this boy and I had a similar grade . . . , I studied hard so as to demonstrate that I wouldn't fall behind him. . . . It was the same when I entered this world [of show business]. I worked hard when I had to. When someone I liked was working near me, I worked harder not to be defeated [by him]. I felt at the time that my lover ought to be my strongest rival at the same time. (Kanda 1986: 22, 23)

These comments paint an image of Matsuda as a child working hard to become a responsible and opinionated adult. The idea of effort is valued in education and career. Yet the statement about children working "furiously" suggests that even something like aging does not simply happen—one should make efforts to grow up. This echoes a prominent Japanese perception that childhood is regarded as the time to play, and that this play is part of the child's work which contributes to her or his self-development. As in the phrase "the child's work is play" (*asobi wa kodomo no shigoto*), the child is expected to play hard as much as the adult is expected to work hard. As an enthusiastic role model for adolescents, Matsuda enacts the image of a young girl who works hard and plays hard. As the last statement suggests, even youthful romance motivates Matsuda to work hard with a will that is as mighty as that of her male partner.

Not only do these essays demonstrate Matsuda's positive attitudes toward life, but they also encourage the readers, especially young women who wish to overcome male domination, to be positive about their lives as well. Although these examples are directed to readers at large, other parts of Matsuda's essays try to capture the hearts of specific groups of people. In Matsuda's 1980 essay, for example, she wrote:

For those of you who think you are no good: I often feel the same way [that I am no good], too. In such times, I decided to think this way: that this is not just my problem. It happens to everyone. Although it is seldom expressed, we all are trying hard to cut out a path through it, you know. If you think, "I am no good," people around you will strangely start to think that you are no good, and if you think, "I am not popular," you will indeed become less and less popular. I suppose things often do not turn out the way you want them to, but rather because of this, one cannot live without believing in the possibility of the self. It's not fun, is it, if you don't challenge every possibility there is, thinking, "I can do it if I try"? (Matsuda 1980: 197, 198)

For those of you who cannot make friends: youth without a friend may be lonesome. I thought about how to make a friend who can encourage me and be encouraged by me, who can help me and can be helped by me. This is what I think: for example, if there is someone that one can feel, "Ah—This person looks all right," then she or he should open her or his heart [and approach this person]. Otherwise, that person will not open her or his heart either. If one wants to have a friend, she or he should try to be a friend for someone, too. I think that not having a friend does not necessarily mean that there is no one there to talk to. It's simply that there is no close friend, or real friend, or someone with whom one can share understanding, or to whom she or he can honestly reveal her or himself. (1980: 199, 200)

For those who are brokenhearted: It's wonderful to be in love, but somehow it's accompanied by disappointments. I think it is hard not to feel sad every time you lose your love. . . . Yet, I think those without any experience of being brokenhearted are boring. I think that one can become stronger as a person and more understanding toward other people's feelings through disappointments in love. There are many beautiful things on earth, I think. . . . Beautiful flowers, beautiful sunsets, beautiful scenery. . . . If there is a heart to feel beautiful things as beautiful, your heart will be polished beautifully. If so, I think that you will meet a wonderful person once again. (1980: 202–4)

By providing thoughtful and encouraging comments on some potential problems that commonly beset growing adolescents, Matsuda—the cutesy idol—becomes a pop philosopher who provides her audience with symbolic power for self-development or transformation.

All the lines presented above, published between 1980 and 1986, explicate Matsuda's dedication to her performances and her audience, as well as to the development of her personality over time. Matsuda is represented as someone who has transformed herself from an inexperienced, support-seeking girl to a confident and established performer who has mastered the skills needed to lead a meaningful life as an adolescent. All this is based on the assumption that youth—a category to which Matsuda and the readers of her essays belong—is a progressive state in which one is expected to actively explore the world, cultivate her or his way of life, and seek after her or his dreams. Another part of Matsuda's essay explains:

I think that youth is about taking a risk. To bet [one's life] on something so that one can think "This is it"—be it in study, sports, or romance . . . is what makes that person youthful. . . . It's all right to make mistakes, really. In my case, I jumped into the entertainment world because I wanted to entrust myself to this kind of a risk. One of the reasons that my parents opposed it . . . was that the entertainment world is a world full of the unknown. "It is much safer to graduate from high school, attend a university, learn the tea ceremony and flower arranging [typical subjects of bridal training in Japan], and get married to someone nice," they said. Although I think it is very important to be safe or simplistic [about one's life], I feel like I would not have been able to prove to myself that I had had a life when I was young if I simply followed my parents' path.   (1980: 206)

Matsuda suggests the view that personality development is made possible through challenging explorations during youth. Elsewhere, readers are repeatedly reminded that they are growing up together with Matsuda. The prologue of *Seiko 20-sai* states, "I want to walk along the same youthful path with you—that is my [i.e., Matsuda's] wish" (Matsuda 1982: 21; brackets mine).

By combining Matsuda's life story with prescriptive messages for her young readers, these essays try to saturate the consciousness of young people with the ideology of Japanese capitalism concerning personal approach to life: that is, the notion that personal success can be achieved through hard work. Thus, the idol Seiko Matsuda advises fellow adolescents to take active part in the adult social order, or initiate themselves into it, without losing their sense of self-esteem. In doing so, Matsuda functions as a role model not only in fashion but also in how to live life. She is depicted as a bright, cheerful, hardworking, healthy, honest, patient, positive, and progressive personality who, with internal strength and will power, manages to learn from her mistakes and march forward in life.

STAGING THE LIFESTYLE

On a hot and rainy July 7, 1995, several acquaintances and I went to observe a concert by Matsuda. It was the first of three days during which she was performing in Budōkan, a hall that can hold an audience of around 10,000 people. Matsuda's concerts were by then famous for the speed with which their tickets sold out, and the tickets for this particular concert were sold out fifteen minutes after their sales had begun. Thanks to the help of Ikeda-*sensei* (a pseudonym), a university instructor who kindly managed to reserve a ticket for me through a contact he had with a salesperson, I was able to attend the concert without much difficulty. I became acquainted with Ikeda because of our mutual interest in Japanese popular culture. Known for his study of Japanese celebrities, he was one of the first helpful persons I contacted in the field. On this day, he attended the concert with two of his former students who worked in media institutions. These people also provided me with their assistance while I was in the field.

Since Budōkan is surrounded by a small park, it took some time to get to the hall's entrance from the main gate. On the way, I encountered many yakuza-looking ticket scalpers who approached me persistently saying, "Hey *niichan* [brother], do you want a ticket? I have a great seat for you." After fifteen or so minutes of walking, I found a table around which a crowd of people gathered and competed to buy souvenirs of this concert. These souvenirs included videotapes, photo albums, concert pamphlets, T-shirts, caps and pins, all of which featured Matsuda. "It's 3,000 yen. Thank you very much!"—the loud voices of clerks mingled with the noise created by customers who tried to push each other out of the way to get what they wanted. Then, one after another, these customers departed from the table with bags in their hands, looking satisfied.

The doors opened at 5:30 P.M., one hour before the concert began. I was waiting toward the front of the crowd that was repeatedly told by the security personnel to form four lines. There were people of both sexes and all ages in the crowd. Some came alone, while others came as couples, families, and groups. As we went up the stairs approaching the entrance, security personnel checked our bags to make sure that we did not have a camera or tape recorder to carry inside. Once I entered the large hall, I went to my reserved seat, located at the front row in the second-floor balcony of the three-story theatre. Looking around, I noticed a gap of about five meters between the stage and the front row of seats. Security personnel were everywhere, reminding me of the fact that I was attending a concert given by Japan's most famous female pop star. Recalling a scene from 1980 in which this same individual performed in front of a small crowd on a street corner of Tokyo as part of her debut campaign, I felt how times had changed. Matsuda who used to be just one of many friendly-looking idols had grown to be a big star.

The long-waited moment arrived at 6:30 P.M. A great uproar rose from the hall packed with people; the lights became increasingly dim and the whole area grew dark. Once the curtain was raised, a giant screen emerged, and the music began to play. There appeared the image of Matsuda on a black-and-white screen, dancing and singing around a shiny silver bar, dressed in an equally shiny silver costume. As the audience shouted with joy, Matsuda on the screen went on singing, "Your white finger strokes my body! You cast a spell on me . . ." This opening song, bedecked with terms such as "white finger," seemed to reflect Matsuda's attitude about her extramarital affairs with American men (the latest of which, being discussed by tabloids at the time of the concert, involved one of the dancers from New York whom she had hired).

As I watched Matsuda on the screen, I asked myself what kind of message she was communicating in this particular part of her performance. After some thoughts, I settled on a twofold interpretation. First, Matsuda was trying to justify her own extramarital affairs, which took place abroad. Second, by making this a style she was trying to show women in the audience that they had a right to take actions into their own hands, and that extramarital affairs are not necessarily bad, if handled discreetly. In agreement with this interpretation, one of Ikeda's former students later pointed out that Matsuda had inflamed the so-called extramarital affair boom (*furin boom*) in Japan today. Indeed, extramarital affairs became a common topic in television dramas at the time, and some of my acquaintances went on to have such affairs. To be sure, extramarital affairs have always existed in Japan, although according to cultural projections, it was usually assumed that men took the initiative in these affairs. What distinguished this new trend, represented by Matsuda, was the idea that women were taking the initiative.

This idea led some media critics to argue that Japanese society has recently become more immoral than before.

With a blast of fireworks, followed by another delighted shout from the audience, the screen went down and Matsuda appeared on stage with seven back-up dancers (four men and three women). She performed a series of rhythmical songs with dancing under colorful flashing lights. Seeing her dressed in a black costume and moving in a sexy way, a man near me turned to his female partner and said that she looked just like Madonna. This reminded me of some scenes from Madonna's music videos such as *Lucky Star* and *Like a Virgin*.

After the sexually expressive performances came a series of ballads. Matsuda reappeared alone on stage with a fancy, frilly costume, coming down the stairs to close the distance between herself and the audience. The special-effect fog contributed to the creation of the image that Matsuda was coming down to the audience from the sky. This was followed by her reappearance in a more childlike, doll-like costume. Her hair was curled and had ribbons on top. A highlighted set design that included gothic-style churches and rococo-style houses added to the effect. A closer observation of the stage setting showed the presence of a suspension bridge, which evoked the idea that this wonderland was New York—a point confirmed subsequently by Ikeda and his former students. New York has been a major source of Matsuda's inspiration in performance since her first visit in 1983. She frequently visited this city to acquire the techniques of American-style performance as represented by Broadway musicals, though the tabloids suggest that she goes there on vacation to "engage in extramarital love affairs."

In one of her essays, Matsuda recalls her visit to a concert by Billy Joel as one of the most enlightening experiences that she had had in New York. In 1983, Joel invited Matsuda to his concert in Madison Square Garden. Matsuda was overwhelmed not only by the size of this concert but also by the way Joel caught the hearts of his large audience and made them all stand in joy by the power of his songs (Kanda 1986: 258–60). Matsuda revealed in her essays that there was much to obtain from this concert experience (e.g., 1986: 260). For those in the audience who were familiar with this background, the symbolic meaning of Matsuda's emergence from the exotic landscape on stage was all too clear: Matsuda had accomplished her dream by mastering the skills of American performances and returned from New York to demonstrate these skills before the Japanese audience.

Internationalization has been on the national agenda since the dawn of Japan's modern era. In this historical setting, the West has been a point of reference as well as a national goal—in reference to which Japanese people have been trying to define and redefine their national identity (e.g., Ohnuki-Tierney 1990). In this setting, returnees from overseas are viewed as a catalyst for positive social change. Their acquired foreignness is considered to be a resource for Japan's internationalization (Yoshino 1998: 29). Kelsky's study of women's internationalism in Japan (1996) is particularly interesting in this regard because it shows how some young Japanese women can inhabit hybrid transnational spaces that radically destabilize Japanese national identity. These women construct a national binary between backward Japan and advancing Western countries and implicate transnational spaces in Western agendas of modernity (1996: 29). The West, particularly the United States, is imagined as a kind of utopia: the source of freedom, opportunity, and new lifestyles. Western men, especially American men, are represented as women's allies against Japanese men, who are imagined as conservative, feudalist, and sexist. Many young internationalist women in Japan believe that they can discover a "new self" (*atarashii jibun*) and remake themselves through their contacts with Western things and Western men (1996: 31–37).

The meaning of Matsuda's stage performance becomes clearer in light of these studies. The cultural implications of the "white finger" in the song that opened the concert, her extramarital affairs with American men, and her "style '95" become obvious. Images of exotic whiteness, American men, stage settings that resemble New York, and frilly costumes become instruments for Matsuda to create a transitional social space in which she positions herself as a symbolic role model for internationalist women. Matsuda presents herself as a new woman who can break out of the constraints of tradition and away from those who try to control her (her family, promotion agencies, or the force of domination typically represented by adult Japanese men). In doing so, Matsuda demonstrates that a new woman can take her life into her own hands. Matsuda's performances act upon Japanese audiences, especially young female ones, as a powerful source of progressive imagination.

One concert technique used by Billy Joel is to program a medley after his new songs have been introduced. He then points his microphone at the audience and leads them in singing some of his earlier songs. The technique creates nostalgia and unity in listeners. This same technique (which I observed as a participant at a concert by Joel in 1993) was used by Matsuda at the end of her concert: she called this the "let's sing together corner." When she announced that the first song in her medley was going to be *Tengoku no kissu* (Kiss in heaven), the members of the audience, who were already standing, reacted immediately with a shout. Then many of them jumped up and down with joy. Matsuda then pointed her microphone at her audience and the dialogue in music began. Matsuda had her audience sing the first part of the song, and she sang the second part. Finally, both Matsuda and her audience sang the rest of the song.

As everyone in the audience sang along with Matsuda through the medley, Matsuda went up on the bridge that was set on the side of the hall so that she could get a better view of the entire audience. This spatial movement had symbolic significance: the bridge was enhanced with cable designs, creating an illusion that she was standing on a New York suspension bridge. Matsuda moved back and forth between this bridge and the center of the stage, establishing a symbolic linkage between her Japanese audience and the imagined exotic landscape, filled with stylistic inspiration.

Those who looked the most excited during this medley performance were Matsuda's long-term fans, most of whom occupied the front rows. These fans distinguished themselves by wearing uniform T-shirts. Cheering squads held paper fans (*uchiwa*) in their hands and cheered Matsuda in rhythmic unison. When Matsuda started to sing her last song, a 1981 smash song called *Natsu no tobira* (The summer doorway), the cheer became one big rhythm of harmony executed by the entire audience in the hall:

Key: C = Clap; J = Jump; (( )) = Boundaries of nonlyrical utterance

Round 1a. Matsuda: To me who cut my hair,
ka-mi o ki-itta wata-shi-ni
| |
Audience: C C C C C C C C C C C ((*Seiko!*))

Round 1b. Matsuda: You said, "You look like another person."
chi-gau hito mi-tai to-
| |
Audience: C C C C C C C C C

Round 2a. Matsuda: You seem a little embarrassed,
a-nata wa su-koshi te-re-ta yo'o
| |
Audience: C-CC J C-CC J C-CC J C-CC J

Round 2b. Matsuda: you start walking ahead of me.
ma-e o a-ru-i-teku-
| |
Audience: C C C C C C C C

Round 3a. Matsuda: To be honest, "You look beautiful"
ki-rei-da yo to hon-to wa
| |
Audience: C C C C C C C C C C ((*Let's go, Seiko!*))

Round 3b. Matsuda: is what I wanted you to say.
i-itte ho-shi-ka-a'tta-
| |
Audience: C C C C C C C C C

Round 4a. Matsuda: You are always hesitating
a-nata wa i-tsumo ta-me-rai no
| |
Audience: C-CC J C-CC J C-CC J C-CC J

Round 4b. Matsuda: beyond the cloak.
ve-eru no mu-ko-o ne-
| |
Audience: C C C C C C C C C C

Round 5a. Matsuda: ((*Everybody together!*)) *Fresh! Fresh! Fresh!* . . .

| |

Audience: *Fresh! Fresh! Fresh*! . . .

(Used by permission of JASRAC, license No.0313709-301)

Matsuda had established an empathetic unity between herself and her audience by the time the concert reached its finale.

During the course of the concert, Matsuda shifted her style from the vibrantly sexual performance of recent times to the more familiar, cute performance of the past. Indeed, Matsuda took her audience backward in time, using her songs as the vehicle of exploration and unity construction. In Ikeda's analysis, this transition from the present "mature" style to the past "innocent" style represented the process by which Matsuda's Japanese identity is reconstructed. Matsuda demonstrated that she was an established Japanese idol who has mastered American performance.[9] "Certainly," said Ikeda, "Matsuda has reached the finest stage that a Japanese performer can ever reach! She is the idol of all idols." One of his students, a 27-year-old female publishing agent, added that Matsuda was "Japanese after all" (*yappari Nihonjin*). The concert she had just seen made her feel "overwhelmed in the beginning and relieved at the end" (*saisho wa attōsareta kedo, saigo wa hottoshita*). This combination of exotic inspiration and national identity (or pride), or the transition from one to the other, in her opinion, was source of the power of Matsuda's performance. She said:

I think it is relatively easy for a person with such fame, money, and interest in overseas life to run away from Japan and not come back. Yet, Matsuda would not do this. She frequently goes to New York or Los Angeles where she learns about leading Western performance and fashion, but she never emigrates there. . . . She brings back home what she has digested abroad as her own style, which everyone now looks up to. This, I think, is her strength. . . . She probably knows that her opportunities lie here in Japan where everyone knows her very well, supports her very

---

9. This point is very similar to that made by Kondo (1992) in her observation of Japanese fashion designers, who find their sense of identity and accomplishment in acquiring, mastering, and overcoming the superior modes of Europe and North America.

well, and continues to expect a lot from her. Her true identity is as a Japanese idol, and I think she is very much aware of it.

Matsuda's commercial value depends on her role as a cultural symbol. Matsuda performs as a Japanese role model whose passage toward establishing the self has been shared, followed, or debated. Her style has become the source of inspiration for many people in constructing their own gender and national identities in this age of internationalization.

DRAMATIZING IDOLHOOD

The present chapter examined Seiko Matsuda's life history as illustrated in a variety of media sources. In doing so, it revealed how the process by which a nation's role model developed her identity is dramatized as a form of contemporary folklore. According to this urban folklore, the Japanese virtue of accomplishment is realized through a rite of passage consisting of a series of struggles in which the young actor wishing to publicly express herself faces social pressures and overcomes obstacles. In the case of Seiko Matsuda, these pressures and obstacles included family resistance, physical deficiencies, negative tabloid coverage, and heavy workloads. Matsuda is represented as someone who overcame these obstacles and developed a style in which her confidence is portrayed. This process of self-establishment provided her audiences, especially young women who seek to transgress traditional forces, with sources of inspiration. Maturation toward individualization is carefully traced and described by the media, critics, and consumers, allowing Matsuda to win social recognition upon the public's acceptance of her as a diligent person who works hard to accomplish her dreams. In discussing Matsuda's performance, my informants, producers and consumers alike, said "Asoko made yaretara sugoi!" meaning, "Being able to do that much is admirable!" This signified Matsuda's status as an unshakable role model in Japan today.

In establishing a style, Matsuda transformed her image from a dependent novice to a confident superstar. In this process, she is projected as someone who has breached traditional Japanese norms, particularly those regarding gender, and deconstructed the conventional image of appropriate Japanese womanhood—the good wife, wise mother. By doing so, Matsuda has contributed to the liberation of Japanese women from the home. That is, her life and her performances have elevated the importance of a woman's personal choice over that of her family duty, or the importance of self-esteem over group conformity.

Matsuda's more recent role as an international pop star evokes in the author's academically oriented mind the images of scholars, such as Amane Nishi (1829–97), Yukichi Fukuzawa (1835–1901), and Umeko Tsuda (1864–1929), or politicians such as Toshimichi Ōkubo (1830–78), Takayoshi Kido (1833–77), and Hirobumi Itō (1841–1909), who pioneered Japan's national development in the late nineteenth century by becoming emissaries between Japan and the industrialized nations of Europe and North America to which they looked up as sources of inspiration. These pioneers of Japan's nation-state traveled to countries such as Great Britain, France, Germany, and the United States to study science and technology and bring back to Japan anything they considered useful for "public education" (*kokumin kyōiku*).[10] By importing the style of Western popular performances and making them accessible to Japanese audiences, Matsuda became a contemporary pioneer in the development of Japanese popular culture. Whether in science, technology, lifestyle, or entertainment, the Japanese have always looked to Europe and Anglo-America with *akogare* (longing). In such a setting, Matsuda adopts the role of a leader in appropriating these inspirational sources as she incorporates them into her own style.[11]

The study of how a legendary idol such as Matsuda is socially constructed contributes to the understanding of the process in

---

10. See, for example, Beasley 1972, Bolitho 1977, and Jansen 1980 for further details.

11. Matsuda's CD debut in New York in 1990 and her advancement into the U.S. market, which signify her international success, are likely to have meaning for Japanese audiences in terms of enhancing Matsuda's role as a pioneer of lifestyle in popular culture. However, she is hardly known in the United States. A few American informants of mine vaguely remembered seeing her in news programs on television when she was first introduced as a Japanese Madonna. They were generally cynical that this previously unknown personality would ever make it in American show business.

which the media, interacting with the audience, generates a belief system around an idolized personality. In this signification process, idols, considered the "maidens of contemporary Japanese pop culture," are shown to operate as charismatic centers, while producers come to function as priestly facilitators of innovative beliefs. Members of the audience, on the other hand, are made into the followers of lifestyle represented by the pop diva. Although Matsuda's career offers a good example of how the idol industry conducts the business of symbolic transformation by capitalizing the maturation process, her case is by no means unique. In the field of idol production, establishing the self through style is a common endeavor, as the producers' statements at the outset of this chapter demonstrate.

It is said that before Matsuda there was Momoe Yamaguchi, and after Matsuda came Yū Hayami, Noriko Sakai, Hikaru Nishida, Rie Miyazawa, Yuki Uchida, and Namie Amuro, to list a few examples of female idols. These idols are considered to have developed their styles as they competed over bigger shares of an economic and symbolic pie.

6

Idol Fans and the Adoration Cult

This chapter concerns activities of idol fans that contribute to the shaping of adolescent female role models in contemporary urban Japan. Idol fans are participants in symbolic interactions through acts of idol consumption; understanding the significance of these interactions can illuminate how young female actors are meaningfully constructed and how practices of idolatry implement existing discourses on gender. Stuart Hall (1980) contends that popular cultural forms at any given moment in history can inscribe ideological themes that nevertheless allow audiences to generate preferred, alternative, or opposed readings from them. Potentially meaningful articulations of a specific form must be understood in terms of the dialogic relationship between the ideological themes and their recipients (quoted in Mukerji and Schudson 1991: 41). Lisa Lewis takes this a step further and demonstrates the ethnographic importance of audiences that, acting as creators of collective tastes, influence the way ideologies are contextualized in their society (Lewis 1990). This study of idol consumption as a constitutive practice will build on these perspectives.

Audience preferences in the case of the idol-pop phenomenon inspire idol producers to develop new themes. Some producers with whom I spoke during my fieldwork paid very close attention to what was going on among buyers. They were ready to incorporate any aspect of consumer lifestyle that they thought would be worth

Fig. 6.1   In a university event organized by an idol study group, enthusiastic students interact with their idol of the year (photo by the author, May 1995).

signifying. I also witnessed cases in which young, creative idol fans turned into producers as they reached adulthood and entered the world of show business. Both of these situations represent the ways in which fan tastes and opinions were more or less directly applied to the production of female idols. This chapter looks at the ways idol fans become active participants in idol engineering and influence the social gendering of adolescent personalities.

Inevitably, part of my discussion will focus on a conspicuous group of idol worshippers called *aidoru otaku*. Roughly translated as "nerds," *otaku* refers to those who fanatically consume what they like. As for idol *otaku*, extensive consumption encompasses acts such as the elaborate collection of idol goods, frequent attendance at idol concerts as well as fan conventions, and taking part in voluntary support groups (Fig. 6.1). Devoted idol *otaku* publish their own newsletters and magazines as ways of exposing their knowledge about, and their dedication to, their idols. It is also a common practice for idol *otaku* to turn their rooms into shrines (so to speak) elaborately decorated with idol goods. Through ritualized acts of idol consumption, idol *otaku* operate as connoisseurs of pop idols. Their actions reflect a fetishism that may be characterized collectively as the "idol cult." In this sense, idol consumption can evolve into a phenomenon that resembles secular religion.

The role *otaku* play as active and creative consumers has attracted much scholastic attention in recent years. Just as I was finishing up my fieldwork in Tokyo in 1996, I heard from some of my informants that a new course in the sociological study of *otaku* was being offered at Tokyo University. At the time, people around me (academics and businessmen alike) considered the fact that *otaku* had become an academic subject to be studied in Japan's most prestigious university as outrageous. These people regarded the subject as too "trashy" (*bakakusai*) to be studied seriously in academic institutions. The instructor of the course on *otaku* at Tokyo University was Toshio Okada, who characterized himself as a connoisseur of Japanese animation. For the course, he used his recently published book, *Otakugaku nyūmon* (Introduction to otakuology). In this book, Okada claims to provide an insider's account of the *otaku* subculture. He defines an *otaku* positively as a possessor of extensive knowledge about particular areas of popular culture for which he or she has a passion. Such a person can use this knowledge to decode the meanings in popular cultural forms that other less interested recipients cannot (Okada 1996: 33; see also 1997).

Working on the extension of such a view, the journalist Shin'ichi Kiyotani published a book, *Le Otaku: France otaku-jijō*, in 1998. This book detailed how enthusiastic Japanese animation fans in France organized conventions wherein they demonstrated their knowledge of, and enthusiasm for, Japanese animation by impersonating their favorite Japanese animation characters (Kiyotani 1998). This complements another work called *Otaku: les enfants du virtuel* in which French journalist Etienne Barral analyzed *otaku* as a transnational trend (Barral 1999).

More recently, Sharon Kinsella (1998, 2000) traced the trajectory of amateur comic fans or *manga otaku* in Japan, arguing that they had developed a "twilight sphere of cultural production" that operated alongside the growth of the commercial *manga* (comics) industry since the 1970s (Kinsella 1998: 294, 295). Kinsella applies the notion of "shadow cultural economy," an analytical concept developed by John Fiske in order to explain how enthusiastic consumers of popular arts organize a socioeconomic order that lies outside the economic order of the industry but shares features with the industrial order. Active consumers can influence the industry from time to time (Fiske 1992: 30). Kinsella demonstrates the *manga otaku* phenomenon as a case in point: *manga otaku* use the services of small offset printing companies in order to publish their own works in cheap form, and distribute editions of these individual representations within their circles. This subsequently developed into seasonal conventions known as "comic markets" or *komiketto*, enabling the rise of small venture companies that publish amateur *manga*, followed by the appearance of large shops that cater to the specialist demands of amateur *manga* artists and fans.[1]

These works by Okada, Kiyotani, Barral, and Kinsella make up a battery of studies that explores the roles *manga* devotees play in the creation and development of the fan cult. They demonstrate how *manga* devotees, with their industrious mindset, have developed social relationships as a way of sharing their interests, establishing their worldviews, and institutionalizing their hobbies. These works also show how *manga otaku*, like the members of religious cults, are often considered "psychotic" by other members of their society. The use of *manga otaku* as a window into understanding contemporary social problems and collective sentiments is particularly relevant to the current discussion of the idol cult. As Kinsella illustrates in her work, the *manga otaku* phenomenon points out concerns that people, especially intellectuals, have about the human condition of Japan in the post-industrial era: from the decay of a closely knit civil society to the growth of individualism—as can be seen in an increasing number of adolescents who preoccupy themselves with specific personal pastimes (Kinsella 1998: 313, 314). Building on these case studies, and incorporating as much of the lived voices and experiences of enthusiastic consumers that can be considered idol *otaku* as possible, I will examine the power dynamic between those who are identified as idol *otaku* and

---

1. The first of these conventions was held in 1975 and was attended by 32 amateur *manga* circles as well as 600 individuals (quoted in Kinsella 1998: 295).

those who distinguish themselves from these devoted idol fans. In doing so, I will delineate ways in which public discourses on gender and sexuality are conditioned at the level of contemporary Japanese popular culture.

RELIGIOSITY OF

THE IDOL CULT

Before proceeding to an ethnographic case study of the idol cult, I should explain my use of the term "cult." Although the notion of the cult is popularly used in both North America as well as Japan, where *karuto* is adopted from the English "cult," it generally connotes religious groups that appear strange, even scary. Over the years, this use of the term has enveloped the more cautious reference to the idiosyncratic religious practices and experiences of mystics and other relatively informal groups. Critics such as Richardson suggest that the term should now be severely limited in scholarly writings about religious groups. To do otherwise is to promote the agenda of those who deliberately use the term as a social weapon against new and apparently exotic religious groups, even if those using the term do so in ways innocent of such intentions. Richardson recommends the term "new religious movements" in place of "religious cults" (Richardson 1996: 30, 37; see also Richardson and Anthony 1982).

To equate idol *otaku* with new religious movements would be misleading because idol *otaku* are not trying to create clientele to be governed under some spiritual inspiration that is consciously derived from outside the predominant religious cultures such as *Shintō*. Yet I consider the mystic orientation of those who worship young, media-promoted personalities as their charismatic role models to be *analogous to* the pattern of idolatry found in new religious movements and the way these movements are differentiated from the rest of society. Thus I propose a working definition of "idol cult" in reference to Ellwood's (1986) concept of the cultic attributes of emergent religion, which include:[2]

---

2. See Ellwood 1986: 218–22; quoted in Richardson 1996: 34, 35.

1. A group that presents a distinct alternative to dominant patterns within the society in fundamental areas of religious life.

2. A group that possesses strong authoritarian and charismatic leadership.

3. A group that is oriented toward inducing powerful subjective experiences and meeting personal needs.

4. A group that operates as separatist in the sense that it strives to maintain distinct boundaries between it and what it considers the outside.

5. A group requiring a high degree of commitment toward its members.

6. A group with a tendency to see itself as legitimated by a long tradition of wisdom or practice of which it is the current manifestation.

Attributes of an idol cult (my working definition):

1. A group that presents a distinct alternative to the majority of audiences within the society in the area of popular culture.

2. A group whose members demonstrate exclusive interest in, and voluntary devotion to, the charismatic quality of an idol.

3. A group that is oriented toward inducing powerful subjective experiences and satisfying personal desires through the worshipping of an idol.

4. A group that operates as separatist in the sense that it strives to maintain distinct boundaries between it and what it considers outsiders.

5. A group whose members expect a high degree of shared interest and sentiment, even though their participation is largely voluntary.

6. A group with a tendency to see itself as legitimated by an extensive knowledge about its idol and the practice of support by virtue of which it is currently manifested.

This definition allows the observer to capture the distinct quality of the idol cult, which encompasses both the tendency of idol fans to distinguish themselves from the rest of their society and the tendency for these aficionados to be distinguished as separate or different by those who consider themselves as part of Japan's cultural mainstream.

As a point of entry into the ethnographic study of the idol cult, the following section examines how fanatic idol fans are characterized in contemporary Japanese society. I will expose positive and negative characterizations of *otaku* that appear in the media-guided discourse. Both of these characterizations contribute to the public perception of fanatic idol fans as eccentric individuals. In the section that follows, I will analyze in reference to my own ethnographic accounts the ritualistic practices of idol *otaku* and the rationale that these enthusiastic idol fans hold for their idol worship.

FANTASIZING "OTAKU"

Otaku is a slang expression that originally meant "you," "your home," or "home" (Kinsella 2000: 128). In the early 1980s, amateur comic artists and fans used this word to address each other in conversation. In 1983, the subculture critic Akio Nakamori highlighted the term in a series of articles he wrote called "*Otaku* studies" ("Otaku no kenkyū"), which appeared in Takarajimasha's low-circulation comic magazine *Manga burikko* (Comic childlike). Nakamori used *otaku* to stand for comic mania and for a peculiar attachment that comic fanatics express toward characters and episodes that appear in comic books.

Comics, better known as *manga*, make up one of the most pervasive forms of popular culture in postwar Japan. The business of weekly and monthly comic magazines has been booming since the 1950s, attracting a large number of readers—young and old, men and women alike. Against this backdrop, those who could be classified as *manga otaku* developed their own sphere of amateur production, making portable offset prints of their own work, organizing conventions, and creating circulation outlets called *komiketto* (an abbreviation of the English "comic market"). These activities attracted the interest of large publishers before long, and the mainstream industry began to hire talented amateur *manga* artists (Kinsella 2000).

Alongside this popular practice, the media characterized the *otaku-zoku*, or the "*otaku* tribe," as consisting of extraordinary individuals who are behaviorally eccentric but culturally creative. In this setting, a curious university student, also a *manga* fan, was turned into a media representative of the *otaku* tribe, Hachirō Taku's family name hinted at an abbreviated form of the word *otaku*. He appeared on a wide variety of television shows throughout the latter half of the 1980s. Then, a sequence of events that occurred in 1989 (the "Miyazaki incident," *Miyazaki jiken*) decisively shattered the positive image of *otaku* as a group of productive individuals. Tsutomu Miyazaki, a 26-year-old worker in a small publishing company, murdered and mutilated four infant girls before being arrested by the police. Wide media coverage followed Miyazaki's arrest, and reports commonly underscored Miyazaki's bizarre lifestyle: his dark small room was packed with comic magazines and animation videos, many of which had pornographic content. Reporters depicted Miyazaki as an *otaku* fan of *Lolicom manga* (Lolita comics), which had become a well-known genre of Japanese *manga* that objectified young female characters—most typically as the victims of rape. According to news reports, Miyazaki was a comic market devotee and a writer of reviews in comic *dōjinshi*, or low-circulation pamphlets that were produced by and for amateur *manga* fans.

The media also focused on a comment Miyazaki made at the opening of his first trial. When the judge asked Miyazaki whether he had anything to say about his crimes, Miyazaki replied that he wanted a video machine in exchange for his car. This reply inflamed a public debate that, in effect, condemned *otaku* as rapists and killers, the psychopathic characters that appeared in *Lolicom manga*. Echoing this media projection, the journalist Azusa Nakajima wrote that *otaku* persons like Miyazaki are incapable of adjusting to the social realities of the contemporary urban lifeworld, which consists of social realities premised on intense interactions between individuals that constantly erode personal territories. So impotent in the context of social communication and so enmeshed in their "fantasy shell" are *otaku* individuals that, according to Nakajima, they can no longer distinguish what is real from what is fantasized, and by extension what is right from what is wrong (Nakajima 1995: 53). These series of events popularized *otaku* as a derogatory term that signified "weirdoes" (*henjin*) who could turn into killers.

Putting media-promoted *otaku* personalities aside, whether someone is an *otaku* or not is, in my observation, a judgment based more on impression than identity. None of my informants identified himself as an *otaku*, while comments such as "That is an *otaku*-like person" (*are wa otakkii na hito da*) were often heard during my fieldwork among idol fans. Even more interesting were situations in which my informants called someone else an *otaku* while putting themselves on a pedestal. Whenever I pointed out that these commentators were themselves enthusiastic idol fans who could be identified as *otaku*, they almost always denied this. Such a denial commonly accompanied a justification that they were worshipping superior personalities—that is, idols who were somehow "incomparably talented," "more elegant," "trendier," "more widely acknowledged" and so on. With this reflection in mind, I placed my ethnographic focus on the behavioral aspects of idol devotees that evoked the image of *otaku* in the minds of others.

THE CULT OF IDOL-"OTAKU": EXCHANGES WITH IDOLS ON THE INTERNET

I spent much of my time in the latter half of 1995 visiting a media agency that offered an internet communication program called the Idol Net, which consisted of on-line correspondences between idol fans and their idols. Female idols were regularly invited to the agency to sit before a computer and have chats with their fans. An interested idol fan paid 3,000 yen to obtain semi-annual membership. This offered me a point of entry into the world of the idol cult.

Each correspondence provided by the Idol Net took place for about 90 minutes. About a dozen eager idol fans logged on to the program simultaneously; the task of the organizers was to make sure that chat time was evenly distributed among participating fans. Staff members were ready to interrupt the chat whenever one fan went beyond his share of time, but fans were generally considerate enough not to dominate cyberspace with what they wanted to express.

Fig. 6.2 An idol, Miyuki Asano, smiles into the author's camera as she gets ready to finish up her chat with fans on line. On her side is a clear sheet on which her autograph is written. This was prepared as a gift for one of her fans who won a competition game played during the chat (photo by the author, October 1995).

The chat naturally highlighted the charm of the participating idol and activities in which she was involved. Fans commented on specific moments they encountered their idol, and they expressed how happy they were being together with her (Fig. 6.2). Fans also inquired of their idol about upcoming events and promised that they would show up to cheer her. Many questions revolved around the type of man their idol liked, but questions and comments about actual love affairs in which the idol was engaged were avoided. Some fans occasionally commented about their idol's mistakes and slip-ups in public events, which they considered amusing. After a bit of teasing, at which the idol expressed how ashamed she was, these fans comforted her by mentioning how these little mistakes made her look even more lovable.

Descriptive details that fans provided throughout my observations were striking. These demonstrated how sensitively fans approached their idol. Whether they focused on the idol's features, behavior, or events related to her, fans took joy in knowing every detail about their idol. Programs such as the Idol Net provided these fans with an opportunity to examine and reinforce their knowledge about their idol, as well as a privileged moment to demonstrate this knowledge before her. Each chat concluded with the idol quizzing her fans about herself. The winner of the game was rewarded with autographs and other memorabilia. These activities in particular demonstrate how media institutions such as the Idol Net keep customers interested in their programs.

"OTAKU" AND THE
INDUSTRIAL APPRENTICESHIP

On one occasion, the Idol Net director introduced me to one of his assistants, Atsushi Tokuyama (a pseudonym). Tokuyama was a college student in his mid-twenties and an idol enthusiast for nearly seven years. Tokuyama met the director through one of his friends at an idol convention several years earlier. All three were dedicated fans of an idol group that was active in the late 1980s, the Onyanko Club (Kitten club).

The ambivalent position Tokuyama held in the Idol Net attracted me all the more: he was neither a customer nor an officially listed member of the staff, but someone who stood between the two as a freelance mediator. Tokuyama was a personal adviser to the director, who provided the director with useful data about the customers' needs and wants from a customer's point of view. Tokuyama's interest in idol production and his connection with other idol enthusiasts won him the position in Idol Net. Through this position, Tokuyama cultivated skills in idol production.

It did not take me long to find out that Tokuyama was following in the very footsteps of the Idol Net director. Promising idol enthusiasts are sometimes adopted by producers as apprentices. In this way, they acquire the know-how to establish themselves in the industry as idol promoters. The industry was always looking for amateur connoisseurs who could provide useful information. On the basis of this experience, I began to notice how the connection between fans and producers shaped the system of idol production—especially in the way that fans functioned as "prompters" for idol producers.

As much as Tokuyama was interested in my role as an idol researcher, his stance as a semi-professional idol producer interested me. I asked Tokuyama to help me learn more about the world of idol enthusiasts. Tokuyama said he could introduce me to people he knew—people who could be considered active idol fans. Taking advantage of this offer, I requested that these potential guests bring with them materials that represented who they were and what they did. The following weekend, Tokuyama and his male friend, Yoshio Yanagawa (a pseudonym), came to my house with bags full of idol autographs, videotapes, scrapbooks, and other idol products that they collected over the years. Both were in the same age group and had known each other for approximately four years. They became acquainted with each other through idol conventions and concerts.

"OTAKU" AS
IDOL CONNOISSEURS

Yanagawa brought with him notepads that were filled with idol autographs, which told me that this aficionado had been chasing different idols rather than being faithful to one particular idol. When I pointed this out, Yanagawa claimed that he was supporting idols as a whole rather than following any particular idol. Yanagawa added that he distinguished himself from the "idol chasers" (*aidoru okkake*), who, because of their affection toward one particular idol, show no interest in nurturing a social environment in which new idols can continuously emerge, perform, and develop their careers. Yanagawa looked down on idol chasers as uncritical consumers who cared only about someone they liked. He contrasted himself with these chasers, indicating his more serious participation in idol production—even though, according to Yanagawa's subsequent confession, he was once a one-track-minded chaser of the Onyanko Club in his early, inexperienced days.

Throughout the time that Yanagawa was telling me about himself, Tokuyama had a cynical look on his face. When Yanagawa made a negative comment about idol chasers, Tokuyama disagreed and said that some idol fans can be knowledgeable about, and respectful toward, idol-pop as a genre at the same time as being a wholehearted devotee of one particular idol. He considered himself as one such fan: he remained faithful to the Onyanko Club several years after the group's dissolution, even though he likes to learn about other idols as well as idol groups and dedicate himself to the development of an environment in which idols can continuously grow. Tokuyama professed his dislike of fans who easily shift from one idol to another in the name of supporting idol-pop as a whole. After these statements, a tension between my two informants filled the air. Yanagawa made a desperate effort to justify himself against the unexpected accusation that was directed toward him, albeit indirectly. He basically argued that he was open to different ways in which people supported idols, but he simply disliked those who, from his point of view, were not meaningfully involved in idol promotion. Tokuyama took Yanagawa's point well. He nodded, looked at me, and said that such a controversy represents their serious involvement in idol promotion. This interaction between my two informants told me that idol fans can come together to form a group without necessarily sharing the same motive. It appeared that occasional conflicts between idol fans contributed to the development of an idol cult as an active arena, and idol enthusiasts enjoyed these competitions and conflicts as parts of their way of life.

Yanagawa's collection of idol autographs included multiple autographs by one idol, but with different dates. Yanagawa argued that each of these autographs commemorated the moment an idol fan came in direct contact with one of his adored idols. Differently dated autographs were accompanied by different stories of the encounter. These stories elaborated on difficulties Yanagawa experienced during his approach, and the sense of satisfaction he felt in overcoming these difficulties. Idols were either quickly moving from one workplace to another or being surrounded by bodyguards who prevented people from getting too close. For Yanagawa, the moment he came into contact with one of these idols was a moment of accomplishment, and each autograph signified such a moment.

Yanagawa's narratives also revealed in striking detail his idols' expressions and movements at the moment of their encounter. These helped him in highlighting the sense of satisfaction he felt when his efforts to obtain the autographs were rewarded. Elsewhere, Yanagawa pointed out idols that were no longer performing as he flipped through some of the autographs in his collection with a nostalgic look on his face. For this informant who can be called an idol fanatic, autographs functioned as symbolic instruments for the personal adoration of idols.

Yanagawa brought videotapes of a wide variety of programs that featured his favorite idols. He kept track of his recordings in minute detail. As he presented me with some of his samples, he provided me with elaborate profiles of the featured idols, their promotion agencies, and sponsoring corporations. He even offered me demographic data, such as total commercial airtime, statistics such as percentage increase in the sales of advertised products in the cases of television commercials, and backstage stories. When I asked how he gathered these data, he replied that he knew people in the industry who passed the information on to him. Yanagawa looked proud of his knowledge of the idol industry, and he apparently took his connection with the insiders of the industry as a privilege. Tokuyama said that people like Yanagawa who proudly identify themselves as connoisseurs of idols can be referred to as "idolians" (*aidorian*).

THE "OTAKU" MISSION
AND THE "OTAKU" AMBITION

Tokuyama and Yanagawa's presentation of themselves as well-informed amateurs of idols seemed in my eyes a way of justifying their childish involvement in the commoditized images of adolescent femininity. I pointed out that they should be old enough to know better: that they ought to graduate from media-directed make-believe in order to work on their real-life affairs. Tokuyama and Yanagawa reacted with disappointment, stressing the meaning of their emotional attachment (*kodawari*) to the nurturing of young talent that embodied their ideal type of Japanese adolescent femininity. Yanagawa claimed that in real life he sees more and more egocentric and untrustworthy women, as represented by *kogal*-type girls. He explained:

I don't know what is happening to young Japanese women these days. More and more young women look increasingly shameless. They are carefree, self-centered. . . .They just can't be communicated with anymore. . . .They look increasingly frustrated with the world around them. They may all be influenced by American feminism, or, I don't know. . . . But this is why we are concerned about pure-looking idols that try to maintain the good old image of young girls. They look healthy to us. We know that these cute idols are not for real. We know that they are made-up images, but we don't care because we are working hard in our own way to cherish classic femininity.

Yanagawa considered his idol fetishism to be a mission to preserve the traditional adolescent femaleness that was becoming lost to the increased influence of American-style sexual liberation, which tended to transform young women in real life into self-centered beings. Tokuyama added to this when he said:

I think that there are many instances in which media-constructed images influence the lifestyle of real people. So, if we can continue to adore pure-looking girls, I am sure that we can remind the world about the kind of personality that should not be forgotten. Where there is an effort to preserve pure idols, there will always be a chance that these idols and what they stand for will revive. We don't want people to look down upon us as a bunch of strange and backward people. We want them to understand that we care about the future of Japanese womanhood.

In this way, Tokuyama normalized his seven-year preoccupation with cute-looking idols and his corresponding lack of interest in many real-life women—young and not so young alike. Like Yanagawa, Tokuyama signified his idol fetishism culturally as an effort to preserve traditional Japanese femaleness.

For Tokuyama and Yanagawa, their idol was lovable because she idealized a submissive female personality that appeared to be un-threatening. Yanagawa argued: "She allows men to love her and cheer her with a great sense of comfort. As a man, I wouldn't have to worry about being criticized, rejected, or betrayed, as could be the case with a real-life girlfriend or sister." This statement reflected a view that cute idols can offer their male fans what real-life women cannot, given the desire of these male fans to romanticize their partnerships with forever accepting, obedient female personalities.

A more elaborate question I had for Tokuyama and Yanagawa concerned their sense of sexuality: whether their attraction toward a young, cute, and innocent personality had any erotic motive. There has been a trend in Japanese popular culture and mass media to place great value on young girls, depicting them as dependent, sexy, and encouraging to adult men (Suzuki 1995: 79). Anchored in this trend is an emergent genre of sexual literature in the 1980s called "Lolita porn," which includes comic books and adult videos featuring sex with young girls and boys. Many sadistic scenes are portrayed in which these subjects are bound, stripped, raped, and beaten. Scenes in which these subjects appear in swimwear, semi-nude, or fully nude, striking various poses that are intended for visual rape, are also present (Funabashi 1995: 257). I found many similar poses assumed by cute idols in magazines and promotion videos, although in principle cute idols as distinguished from young porn stars and animated Lolita figures did not typically appear naked. Some popular magazines for men combined idol photos and articles with erotic themes and stories. In the end, I could not see a noteworthy difference between cute-idol performances and child pornography.[3]

My interest in probing the sexuality of idol *otaku* was partly due to my observation that the chasers of young, innocent-looking female idols tended to avoid socializing with real-life female partners. Tokuyama and Yanagawa were no exceptions to this tendency. Like many other *otaku* idol fans, these two informants had never experienced female partners in their lives, and neither were they interested in having real-life female partners. When I asked them the reason, Yanagawa explained that cheering his favorite idols in concert, or buying their CDs, videos, and photo albums, was a real-life experience that provided him with enough sense of comfort. Tokuyama agreed and said that his current interests in idolatry left no room in his mind to think seriously about any woman other than his idol. He added that he could not engage in anything about which he could not be serious. I then wondered if these individuals sought their "salvation" (so to speak) in innocent, sexu-

---

3. Not surprisingly, some idols become porn stars when they cannot market themselves well enough. One can also find cute porn stars being advertised in idol-like ways, or as pure, honest, and pretty, advocating the fantasized female sexual role: young, innocent, and vulnerable personalities who take pleasure in being raped by men. This also made the observer wonder as to how pure and honest these personalities really were.

ally obedient images of cute idols and preferred to remain in the unattainable relationship between themselves and their female objects because they gave up the possibility of a real-life female partner.[4] Not wanting anyone to see him this way, Tokuyama stressed that his idol could provide him with a peace of mind with which no other female person could provide.

Tokuyama and Yanagawa rejected any direct connection I tried to establish between their attraction toward a virginal figure and Lolita pornography. In response to my question "Do you ever become erotically motivated by your idol?" Tokuyama replied that he did not deny this aspect as a heterosexual man, but his affection toward his favorite cute idol was different from eroticism per se.

Loving a porn star is simply physical, and there isn't much human sentiment involved. The sex drive is animal-like. Adoring your idol is much more romantic than that. You care about her a lot. . . . Having sex with your idol is only one, and the last, reason for your engagement. I enjoy a greater sense of empathy, and I feel happy simply by imagining her next to me.

This confirmed that the motives of idol *otaku* were typically more romantic than sexual: these fans were seeing in their idols the images of their ideal girlfriends. Building on this find, I said to Tokuyama, "So, it is not necessarily about visually raping a Lolita, is it?" Tokuyama replied:

No way! It's nothing that violent, although some maniacs may fantasize that. You enjoy your pursuit of an adorable personality who will always be there for you, though you know you will not be able to reach her completely. You enjoy this sense of distance, and the fact that you can interact with your idol while maintaining this comfortable distance. If it's all about having sex, you don't need such a personality.

On the one hand, such a statement demonstrated that words I intentionally used in my attempt to expose how *otaku* idol fans felt

---

4. Such a sense of escape from actual relationships between men and women, or performers and their audiences, was questioned by critics that differentiated *otaku* as "lunatics" in comparison to their taste for a more realistic image of adolescent sexuality. Employing the association between cute-idol fans and eroticism, critics of idol *otaku* implied that *otaku* idol fans appeared considerably sexist in the eyes of those who favored more self-controlled adolescent role models.

about their objects of worship, such as "visual rape" and "sexuality," were too violent for idol fans. It indicated that male fantasies of idol fanatics are to be differentiated from visual rape. On the other hand, the statement shed light on concepts of masculinity being generated in the construction of cute and innocent-looking idols: the male desire to emphasize meekness in womanhood, empathize with this signified aspect, and find reasons for self-confident living in cherishing this aspect. Cute idols onto which this desire is projected are conceptualized as the "protectorates" (so to speak) of male idol fans—at the same time as being constructed as the sacred healers of these fans' hearts.

Idol enthusiasts such as Tokuyama were ambitious about turning idol fetishism into a career. Tokuyama's love for his idol led him to study computer programming assiduously and obtain skills that were sufficient to qualify for the position of director's assistant in the Idol Net. Elsewhere in my fieldwork, I came across a freelance cartoonist who worked for publishers that posted his hand-drawn idol portraits in their magazines. I also came to know a graphic designer who produced a wide variety of posters that featured idol talent. These people used to send drawings of their favorite idols to magazine companies that invited amateur cartoonists to demonstrate their artwork. Their drawings were repeatedly published until they caught the attention of editing directors that ended up hiring them.

There were also the cases of Yasushi Akimoto and Testuya Komuro, who became well-known for countless hit songs that they wrote for idol pop singers. Their ambitions led them not only to achieve fame in show business but also to take idol talents as their wives. The success stories of Akimoto and Komuro fueled Tokuyama's enthusiasm for transforming his idol worship into a serious career. This indicated to the researcher that while idols fantasize about becoming the objects of public adoration, some enthusiastic idol fans fantasize about penetrating the industry and, given their chance to do so, making idols their own. For Tokuyama, the opportunity to work next to a young idol debutant as her technical assistant at the Idol Net was a proud accomplishment. Yet he was ambitious enough to stay unsatisfied with the position he had.

He was looking for a chance to become an idol manager who could accompany an idol everywhere she went, or an idol producer who could shape and reshape idols in his own image. Idol fans such as Tokuyama were trying to traverse the spiritual-*qua*-secular pathway that allowed them to unify themselves with their objects of worship and ultimately possess these objects more or less as their own symbolic constructions.

THE SOCIOECONOMIC
PRACTICES OF "OTAKU" IDOLIANS

Two months into our repeated get-togethers, Yanagawa introduced me to a new informant, Yoshiki Imamura (a pseudonym), who invited me to his house where he was working on a publication project with three of his friends. All four of these individuals were university students, and two of them belonged to an idol study circle in their university. They have been working on the publication of a fanzine, the name of which could be written as *Sweet Idols* to use the closest pseudonym, for nearly two years. Imamura rented a small room in an apartment complex that he turned into a publishing studio. All of the walls in Imamura's room were filled with idol posters and autograph sheets. In one corner of the room was a shelf that was decorated with idol shots and miniature plastic dolls, which turned the shelf into an idol shrine.

When I visited, the members of the publishing board were preparing the final draft of their upcoming issue, which was to be sent to a printer company that specializes in the publication of texts that people pay for themselves. Each issue of the magazine had a set price of 700 yen per copy. Imamura and his company wanted to make the content of each issue as rich and joyful in the eyes of their readers as possible. To do so, they went through a painstaking process of selecting idols to be featured, contacting these idols' promotion agencies, conducting interviews, summarizing what they gathered from these interviews, and writing featured articles together with monthly hit charts and short essays of their own.

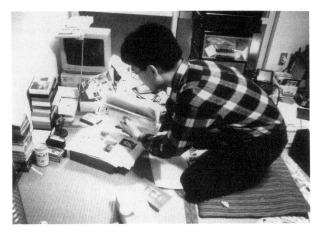

Fig. 6.3   An editor in chief of a mini-communication magazine
organizes the layout of an upcoming issue (photo by the
author, January 1996).

I observed Imamura and his colleagues look through a pile of photographs during their interviews, and scan copies of idol CDs and magazine covers, as well as their own drawings of their favorite idols. They were engaged in a heated discussion regarding which of these items were to be included in their upcoming issue and which ones were to be omitted. Once decisions were reached, they started to work on galley sheets, cutting and pasting chosen items on clean sheets of paper. Imamura said that the deadline for the draft to be turned in to the publisher was approaching so that they had to work quickly (Fig. 6.3).

Toward the end of the day I made my visit, around midnight, the four members of the *Sweet Idols* editorial board continued to put their craftsmanship into the near-complete blueprint of their booklet. The 80–page draft consisted of four front pages of idol photos, followed by a nine-page featured article on a fourteen-year-old idol, monthly hit charts of idols and their songs, and two essays on newcomers. The featured article provided a profile of the interviewed idol at the outset, and it incorporated parts of the interview in which the idol revealed her thoughts about her life and her work, her fans, as well as ideal types of men. The editors developed hit charts on the basis of their surveys among idol fans.

Essays by two members of Imamura's editorial board discussed the charms of two low-teen debutantes that they wanted to highlight.

Imamura told me that there were approximately three dozen readers for each issue, which he considered to be average for a mini-communication magazine. When I pointed out that the number of readers did not seem all that much for the kind of effort Imamura and his company made to produce their publication, Imamura argued that they were doing it for their own pleasure rather than for monetary profit. He also indicated that there were greater rewards he and his company could obtain from their publications, which included enriching their knowledge of idols, brushing up their skills in publishing, and being acknowledged by some of the people in the idol industry. Imamura offered success stories of three of his senior friends who managed to develop their career in the idol industry as professional writers. All of them started out as amateur writers, and they kept publishing their own magazines and newsletters until they captured the attention of idol producers. One of them was a former head of his publishing group. Imamura added that good idol critics were always in demand by the idol promotion agencies and media associates.

I saw Imamura and his company at an idol concert three weeks after this initial visit to Imamura's studio. They brought two hundred copies of their new issue of *Sweet Idols* to the concert. The fact that they preferred to keep parts of their business information confidential prevented me from knowing how much money they spent to produce that and other issues of their magazine, or how much they gained from their sales. Imamura simply revealed that their expense was generally much greater than their gain. He said that all of the members of his publishing group had to put much of their money and their time into publishing their magazine, but they were happy to do so because their magazines were the fruits of their commitment. Imamura and his group very proudly thought that they were making a difference by leaving a visible stamp on the world of idol production through their publications.

RITES OF FETISHISM AS
OBSERVED IN AN IDOL CONCERT

Thirty minutes before the opening of the concert, Imamura and his company joined Tokuyama and his circle of friends in front of the concert hall. Over two hundred fans attended this particular concert. The area was already filled with many of them, who had gathered into groups here and there. After a bit of talking, Imamura and his friends separated from Tokuyama and his group. They began selling the freshly produced copies of their magazine. Walking around the area, they shouted, "Here is our latest issue! It has featured articles about Aika Mizusawa, does anybody want a copy?" Several fans reacted to their calls, and nearly half the copies were sold by the time they prepared to enter the concert hall. I counted three other groups selling their self-produced periodicals that day.

Five minutes before the opening of the concert, fans noisily milled about the hall. Some of these fans were chatting with other fans, while others were putting up hand-made banners bedecked with phrases that cheered their idol, such as "Go for it, Terumi! Lighten up our evening sky!" and "Together, we will burn up with Terumi tonight!" Some fans brought colorful fluorescent tubes, while others had in their hands round fans on which the images of the idol were printed. Other fans carried curious objects such as flags, panels, and large glove-like objects that they themselves created. They used these objects as instruments to cheer on their idol during the concert. All the members of the audience seemed to recognize each other in one way or another—perhaps from repeated encounters at concerts and other idol-related events. Ignoring security guards that stood in their positions motionlessly, fans were all frolicking about in and around their seats. By this time, Tokuyama, Imamura, and their friends were all part of the enthused crowd.

Once the stage show began, the crowd shouted with joy. Some were simply shouting "Yeah!" while others were calling the idol's

Fig. 6.4 Enthusiastic fans cheer their idol in a concert. A handmade banner bedecked with a cheering phrase appears on the side wall of the concert hall (photo by the author, July 1995).

name. As the idol appeared on stage and started to sing, the crowd jumped up and down rhythmically with their arms swinging up in the air. Nobody in the crowd told others what to do, but everyone seemed to know exactly how to synchronize their rhythm with the others. Although seats were lined up in the hall, everyone stood up throughout the show. There was ad-lib talk about the idol between songs, during which some fans in the crowd held up their cheering instruments in order to capture their idol's attention. One fan had colorful electric bulbs coiled onto his head. In effect, his head was lit up like a Christmas tree. The idol could not ignore this, and she mentioned it at one point in her talk. The fan shook his body, looking very pleased, and other fans hissed at him. Elsewhere, half a dozen fans that appeared to be in their early twenties held teddy bears in their hands. When the idol sang, they demonstrated their choreographed cheer, waving the stuffed toys up and down and right to left. Other groups in the crowd danced along with the idol, copying her choreographed movements down to their smallest details (Fig. 6.4).

Many fans brought flowers and presents with them. Most of these offerings were handed over to people in charge of the concert prior to the opening of the stage performance. I noticed an area backstage where these offerings were piled up. Several lucky fans ran up to the stage and handed their gifts directly to their idol at the closing, when the idol stepped forward to express her appreciation. Other fans waited for their idol to come out from backstage after the concert. When she did, they approached the idol, surrounded her, and presented their gifts to her one by one. All of them seemed agitated by their close encounter with their idol. The idol calmly greeted each of them, received the gift, shook the fan's stretched-out hand and said, "Thank you so much for coming today. I will continue to do my best, so please support me well." Some fans replied: "Please do your best" (*Ganbatte kudasai*)! Others had longer comments to make about their will to support her.

One of the last fans the idol greeted started to speak to her persistently about how much he appreciated the concert. After throwing out all sorts of supportive comments, he expressed how much more often he wished to see her. This fan began to speak in a soft voice, but he became increasingly loud and aggressive. The idol's manager, who stood beside the idol throughout the whole time, got worried. He signaled the idol to move on. The idol nodded to the fan and greeted the next fan in line before this fan finished talking. Then, she walked away quickly with her manager and got into a car that was parked right outside the back door of the concert hall. Approximately forty fans waited in the area with cameras in their hands. No camera was allowed in the concert hall, so this was the chance to take photos. Many of these fans had large expensive lenses attached to their cameras in order to make sure that they could capture the images of their idol well. Amidst a volley of flashes, I was reminded of a scene from my earlier conversations with Yanagawa at my place, in which he was elaborating on his close encounter with one of his idols in reference to a photo. The valued photo of an idol smiling commemorated a moment during which Yanagawa captured what he considered to be one of the most lovable expressions of his idol. I could imagine how these fans felt as they zealously clicked the shutters of their cameras.

The fan that turned increasingly assertive before his idol followed her until he was stopped by a security guard at the door. Seeing the idol and her manager take off, he joined his acquaintances to leave the hall. He looked very satisfied. My attempt to approach him for interviews failed. When I introduced myself to him and asked him if I could speak to him about his involvement in idolatry, he glared at me without saying anything and walked away. Other fans that remained in the concert hall loudly celebrated their close encounter with the idol.

In one of my discussions with Tokuyama after the concert, I expressed how strangely childish these fans appeared to me. I described my impression that the concert looked like a playground in which these naïve-looking young adults freely expressed their emotions with one another and to their idol without having to worry about being constricted by the norms of the adult world. Tokuyama indicated that my analysis was not bad: he could use it to explain why many of his acquaintances kept sacrificing so much of their income from part- and full-time jobs, if not their allowances, each month for idol concerts that mostly repeated an identical content. According to the analysis offered by Tokuyama, there was an intricate tie between idol worship and the worshipper's childlike benevolence. He explained:

Haven't you ever noticed idol fans being so lively in front of their idols and their friends, and, in contrast, so lifelessly silent elsewhere? Well, this is because the community of idol fans is antithetical to the rest of their society, where so much of people's attention is placed on how to look good in front of other people. When people preoccupy themselves with good appearances, they tend to turn dishonest. Social life is full of dishonest people competing against one another as they try to use and abuse each other. This can be stressful, especially for those who are not good in covering up their feelings in order to socialize well. Idol fans want to take a good break from the social life. They are looking for places where they can be honest about their feelings. If fans appear like a bunch of kids, this is probably because they are being truthful to their emotions. This is not to say that idol fans don't care about their appearance: we care about the way we look, especially before our idols, and we sure want to look as good as we can in the presence of our idols. Yet we can at least genuinely enjoy ourselves in doing so. It's a pure mind that counts for us—even though occasions in which we can manifest the pure mind may not last

forever. . . . Yes, idols are made-up images, and the idol industry is built
on a bunch of fanciful representations. But these fancies are different
from ill-intended lies, and they do more good to the hearts of idol fans
than harm. Around idols, fans can be truthful to their hearts. In places
such as idol concerts, fans can heal the distress that comes from their social interactions elsewhere. We fans pay our money to acquire the privilege offered by the industry to honestly enjoy what we see, feel and do—
however politically the industry itself may be set up in reality.

This elaborate statement offered by Tokuyama revealed the liminal
function of idol concerts. Idol concerts offer a ritualized space for
fans to isolate themselves from the rest of their society, which is
perceived to be an arena full of stress, and regain their sense of self
through the power of idols to heal their broken hearts and anxious
feelings. Idol fans find their salvation in places such as concert halls
because they can recuperate their senses, which are too often
eroded by the alienating forces of their society.

THE FETISHISM OF COMMODITIZED PERSONALITIES AND THE SECRET THEREOF

These ethnographic observations of idol fans reveal their worldviews and the behaviors that characterize idol fetishism as a cultural practice that can be compared to religious cults. Some groups
of idol enthusiasts set themselves apart from the rest of their society, and they are considered different by the people who think that
they are part of Japan's cultural mainstream.

As in the cases of *manga* fanatics, whose characterization as ec-
centrics was thoroughly investigated by Kinsella and other researchers, idol fanatics are meaningfully constructed by the other
members of Japanese society as those who are not good at socializing with others, especially with those of the opposite sex. What is
seen as the abnormal attraction of male idol fanatics toward young
and cute-looking female celebrities is often explained in terms of
emotional disease arising from these fanatics' unsociable personal
qualities. According to such a perspective, idol fanatics are trying
to recover their sense of selfhood through the worshipping of the
idealized, harmless images of meek, sweet adolescent femininity
that young pop idols embody as part of their career-building strat-

egy. The ethnographic investigations presented in this chapter have confirmed that there is a grain of truth to this sort of popular psychological explanation for the cultlike quality of idol enthusiasts—to the extent that those who consider themselves enthusiastic idol fans use it to explain why they behave in the way they do.

Idol cults as practiced by idol fanatics consist of idolizing adolescent personalities as symbolic figures that can heal distressed hearts, and ritualizing encounters with idols. Enthusiastic idol fans treat idol goods as symbolic objects and use them to create their versions of a shrine for the worship of their idols. These fans visit idol concerts in order to purify their hearts, considered polluted by the politics of everyday life in contemporary urban Japan. Fans presented their idols with gifts, which were regarded as offerings. Internet programs, conventions, and mini-communication magazines provided these idol enthusiasts with opportunities to impress their loyalty on their idols and other members of their communities. As a part of their business strategy, the organizers of idol-related events contextualized these events as sacred spaces where fans could intoxicate themselves with the charismatic power of idolized adolescent personalities.

Religious cults and idol cults are different with respect to the degree of loyalty expressed by their members, the causes and goals of the organization, as well as tasks assigned to their leaders. In maintaining their integration, religious cults tend to demand that members demonstrate their commitment to charismatic leaders. In contrast, idol cults tend to rely on voluntary commitments of fans to their idols. Any idol fan can freely worship two or more different idols without being pressured all that much. Religious cults tend to hold social change as their mission, although idol cults do not necessarily have any revolutionary goals as their mission. When asked, some idol fanatics did say that certain causes drive their dedication to their idols: to preserve their ideal images of Japanese femininity. No idol considered spiritual revolution to be the task, even though she might be happy to see certain values of Japanese society (fashion, for example) change as the result of her performance.

The network of idol producers, media agencies, and some idol fanatics appeared surprisingly connected. The researcher found enthusiastic idol fans operating in this network as mediators between trendsetters and trend-buyers, two typically separated sectors of the popular cultural economy. In its constant search for information, the idol industry has developed ways to recruit idol fans selectively into its system of production and turn these fans into connoisseurs.

7

The Spread of Idol Performances in New Industrial Economies

Japanese-style idol performances are no longer limited to Japan's national boundaries. By the mid-1980s, numerous idols in the Japanese style became popular in some of the explosively developing Asian countries otherwise known as New Industrial Economies (NIEs). Just as in Japan, idols in these countries merchandise the process of maturation in ways that reflect lifestyles for young people. In my view, the spread of idol performances in NIEs is an outcome of the commercial advancement of the Japanese idol industry in these countries, the acquisition of Japanese idol-marketing techniques by local producers, and the popular acceptance of Japanese-style idols by local consumers (Fig. 7.1).

The discussion in this chapter elaborates on the factors that contribute to the transnational process of idol production, particularly on how the themes of Japanese idol marketing are implanted in NIEs as a part of the combined effort of Japanese and local idol producers to encourage Asia's open regionalism. The political implications of this development are important: apparent partnerships between Japanese and local idol promoters conceal conflicts between Japanese idol-promotion agencies. Such agencies operate in NIEs as hegemonic forces; on the other hand, they become emergent local agencies that function as counterhegemonic constituents of local identities.

Fig. 7.1 The cover of the 1996 issue of Japan's *Asian Travellers Journal*. This issue includes a feature article on the emergent popularity of idol pop-stars in Asian countries outside Japan (Travel Journal Sha).

Of specific interest here is the meaningful juxtaposition that is set at the heart of this power dynamic: that is, the double standard of prestige assigned to Japanese products as emblems of socioeconomic achievement and the negative status assigned to Japanese industries as the potential colonizers of Asian economies. In effect, Japanese commodities represent a national power that the local people of NIEs wish to overcome. In this transnational setting, Japanese-style idols act as the symbols of transcendence—the transcendence of local communities from their current socioeconomic state to a rich consumer society, such as Japan, the first nation to achieve this status in postwar Asia. The local idol promoters in NIEs use the know-how of Japanese idol production to transform the consciousness of local consumers, while the local idol consumers in NIEs adore Japanese and homegrown idols (or competition between these two types of idols) with national pride and collective self-empowerment.

The subsequent discussion of Asian idol performances will first follow the activities of Japanese idol productions in NIEs, and next illuminate local reactions to the advancement of Japanese idols and their promotion agencies. Eventually I will look at the perceptions of idol consumers in Hong Kong, which I found important because of their political-economic implications. They demonstrate how Chinese idol fans use Japanese and Japanese-style idols as points of reference for constructing their lifeworld as situated in a moment of historical transition—that is, at the time Hong Kong was about to go from being a British colony to a special economic district of the People's Republic of China.

Through these discussions, I hope to highlight the way in which Japanese idols and their promotion agencies operate as vehicles of cultural transformation for the locals of NIEs in this era of "open regionalism." Studying the popularity of Japanese idols and the activities of the Japanese entertainment industry in other Asian countries will facilitate an understanding of how popular cultural performances contribute to the signification of middle-class lifestyles in the Asia-Pacific region at a time when more and more people in this region are becoming socially, economically, and politically interactive.

IDOL PERFORMANCES AS AN "ASIAN" PHENOMENON

In many Asian countries, forms of Japanese popular culture such as fashion, television drama, popular music, and animation have become as well known as Japanese cars and electronic products. Representing a modern, urban lifestyle, these items have become points of cultural dissemination for students, young working people, and tourists in Asia's upward-moving economic areas. The popularity of Japanese-style idols is one of the most interesting recent examples of Japan's cultural dissemination in this area of the Asian region.

For example, a popular Japanese idol duo, Puffy, burst onto Japan's pop music scene in 1996, using their debut song, *Asian Purity*, as the theme song in a widely shown Kirin Beer television commercial. When the duo did this, they not only joined a long list of Japanese idols and idol groups but also became a prototype on which young performers who have a prestigious presence in NIEs are modeled. The celebration of Puffy in Taiwan and Hong Kong led the duo to release one of their smash hits, *Kore ga watashi no ikiru michi* (This is the way I live), in Chinese. Popular magazines and television programs from China, South Korea, Taiwan, Singapore, Malaysia, Thailand, the Philippines, and Vietnam feature a plethora of images representing young movie, television, and pop music stars who are called "idols." As in the case of Japan, these adolescent personalities attract large numbers of devoted followers, and their images are massively consumed.[1] Japanese idols are also popular in these Asian countries, as evidenced by featured magazine articles and countless internet home pages which are locally produced.

In *Asian Purity* (*Ajia no junshin*), Puffy sings: "Open the door, flow out now and there is Asia. . . . Pure hearts twinkle in the night sky as if they are about to burst open like a spark!" This speaks not only of the growing interest in Japanese and Japanese-style idols in many Asian countries outside Japan but also of Japan's deepening cultural engagement with the rest of Asia in recent years. "Pure hearts," which signify Japanese adolescents as represented by young, cute, and innocent Japanese girls, are willing to explore other Asian countries, or what they might regard as new frontiers that are full of wonder. In Japan, interest in other Asian countries boomed in the 1990s, an era in which Asia as a region

---

1. Among the earliest homegrown big-name idols produced by indigenous promotion agencies following Japanese manufacturing methods are Rao Dai and Jie Liu of China: Soteji Wa Idol and Susie Kang of South Korea; Andy Lau, Vivian Chow, and Sammy Chen of Hong Kong; Emile Chow, Tarcy So, S.O.S., and Vivian Hsu of Taiwan; Christina of Thailand; Itje Trisnawaty and Mellyana of Indonesia; Sheila Majid of Malaysia; Smokey Mountain of the Philippines; and Hong Nhung of Vietnam.

was considered energetic with high expectations for economic growth. This was evidenced by a growing public interest in ethnic foods, increasing travel to Asian destinations, the popularity of studying Chinese or Korean in place of the previously dominant European languages such as English and French, and a growing familiarity with lifestyles of different Asian countries.

In the domain of political economy, the expectation for Asia's regional development is realized in such intergovernmental organizations as APEC, or Asia-Pacific Economic Cooperation.[2] The present goal of APEC is to enhance open regionalism in the Pacific Rim, which has been seen to be evolving as a subglobal system, drawing countries in the area closer together through increased trade, communication, investment, and population movement (e.g., McGee and Watters 1997: 4). At the 1993 APEC summit held in Seattle, Washington (U.S.A.), Japanese Prime Minister Tomiichi Murayama called on APEC participants to develop "partnerships for progress" and thereby "encourage regional institution building to avert sub-regional trade wars and protectionism and to stimulate trade creation" (Hadi 1995: 85). American President Bill Clinton, in agreement with this view, proposed his vision to create what he called the "Asia-Pacific Community." However, critics such as Malaysian Prime Minister Mohammad Mahatir and his ASEAN (Association of Southeast Asian Nations) colleagues perceived such a vision as an ideological cloak serving primarily the interests of Japan and the United States (the two superpowers in the Pacific) to dominate Asia's regional economy.[3]

Aside from this debate rooted in politico-economic cooperation and conflict, there is another trend in the Asian region, one that belongs to the realm of mass culture. This trend coincides with the vision of subglobal development implied by APEC, but is con-

---

2. APEC was founded in 1989. Its original members were Australia, Brunei, Canada, Indonesia, Japan, Malaysia, New Zealand, Singapore, South Korea, Thailand, the Philippines, and the United States. The People's Republic of China, Hong Kong, and Taiwan joined in 1991, followed by Mexico and Papua New Guinea in 1993, and Chile in 1995.

3. ASEAN's members include Indonesia, Malaysia, the Philippines, Singapore, Thailand, and Brunei. Laos, Cambodia, and Myanmar were proposing to join the membership at the time I was conducting my fieldwork in 1996.

ceived of as a popular vision of socioeconomic progress. This view is symbolically embodied in the everyday practices of individuals and groups of NIEs as a part of their efforts to realize an enriched lifestyle. This is where the cultural apparatus, such as the entertainment industry, develops its own themes and events that facilitate the formation of local identities. In this setting, Japanese and Japanese-style idols play evocative roles.

While documenting activities related to the industry's production of idols in various parts of Asia is undoubtedly pivotal, the ethnographic analysis in this chapter focuses on the way local consumers use idols to empower their sense of socioeconomic well-being. How do these consumers develop a web of meaning around their favorite Japanese and Japanese-style idols? After Friedman (1990: 312), the act of consumption is considered in this chapter as a cultural strategy that specifies the structure of desire. Consumption defines the contours of a specific identity space, or a sum of products configured into an arrangement that expresses "what I am." Friedman elaborates: "Consumption within the bounds of the world system is always a consumption of identity, canalized by a negotiation between self-definition and the array of possibilities offered by the capitalist market. . . . [Consumption is] the libidinous half of social reproduction [that] is a significant part of the differential definition of social groups and individuals" (1990: 314). This aspect of consumption is useful in understanding how people of different nationalities develop their local identities in an era in which the world is becoming increasingly interconnected. It also suggests how the difference between local cultures and artifacts are made predictable, surprisingly uniform, and therefore shared on a cross-cultural scale (Wilk 1990, 1995). Through the act of consuming, the local consumers are absorbed into a global arena of contest in which they can evaluate their own culture vis-à-vis other cultures from which the shared art form was originally borrowed. This arena of cultural comparison is also a domain in which power is reinscribed. It is where contradicting identities are asserted as economic power, cultural authority, world recognition, and place in a world order—at a historical moment when boundaries among nations are highly charged (Kondo 1992: 177).

THE DEVELOPMENT OF IDOL
PERFORMANCES IN NIES

Young popular entertainers existed in China, Hong Kong, Taiwan, and South Korea long before Japanese idols appeared on the scene. Yet by the mid-1980s, many of Asia's new homegrown pop stars bore the unmistakable stamp of the Japanese idol. These home-grown personalities have been featured as cute, pure, righteous, or pretty. Their songs have included exact copies of Japanese idol songs or have contained themes borrowed from them. Promotion networks and fan clubs have been developed around them in the same way as the Japanese idol promotion system. These cases imply that many indigenous idol promoters are facilitating a knowledge transfer of Japanese-style idol-marketing techniques.

From the standpoint of Japanese idol promoters, other developing Asian countries represent opportunities for business growth. In August 1993, the Hori Agency of Japan and the Beijing City Department of Culture held a live television broadcast audition that attracted as many as 400,000 Chinese applicants. In spring 1995, the Hori Agency held another audition in cooperation with the Vietnamese government, drawing 1,800 local applicants. Another large-scale audition—the television program Asia Bagus, based in Singapore and involving multinational corporate sponsorship—attracts applicants from all over Asia. In a 1996 collaboration, Japan's Yoshimoto Kōgyō Productions, the Sony Music Entertainment Corporation, and a Japan-based international supermarket chain operator, Yaohan, recruited four young women from the Shanghai region to form an idol group, Shanghai Performance Doll. This was a Chinese version of Japan's Tokyo Performance Doll (debut 1990).[4]

Many Japanese idols have become celebrities in other Asian countries as well. A typical pattern, followed, for example, by Noriko Sakai and Mika Chiba, is for a Japanese singer to start out in Taiwan and then to move into markets such as Hong Kong,

---

4. By 1992, Yaohan had a total of 26 overseas stores in Brunei, China, Costa Rica, Hong Kong, Malaysia, Taiwan, Thailand, and the United States (Kōdansha 1993: 1739). A Canadian branch was established in 1991.

China, and Singapore using Chinese connections. Home-language magazine articles and internet home pages feed the demands of Asian fans for information about Japanese and local idols.

In South Korea, Japanese television programs, magazines, music, animation, and other forms of popular culture have been officially banned until very recently. This is due to Japan's annexation of Korea from 1910 to the end of World War II, which included an attempt to replace the Korean language and culture with those of Japan. The prewar Japanese imperial government issued the Act of Annexation in 1910 and practiced economic deprivation and political suppression in Korea as well as Taiwan. Under the colonial administration, Koreans were denied the rights of full citizenship, were forced to accept a subordinate identity and to serve the interests of metropolitan Japan. Many migrated to Japan against their will as low-wage colonial labor (Weiner 1997: 84). The Korean government's boycott of Japanese items was deeply rooted in this historical past. But even before the boycott ended, many young Koreans looked to Japan for trendy fashions and lifestyle. They obtained information about idols and other forms of Japanese popular culture through underground sources.[5]

One notices that the areas in which Japanese idols and their manufacturing agencies are particularly active are places undergoing rapid economic growth. After Japan, the countries in the Asia-Pacific region with the largest gross national product since 1980 are, in order, China, South Korea, Taiwan, and Hong Kong. As of 1992, China, Hong Kong, South Korea, and Taiwan overtook Japan in their rates of economic growth (PHP Research Center 1995: 52). Although Vietnam has not yet reached these levels, its strong national drive toward economic development is manifested in its recent participation in ASEAN as well as its willingness to open up trade. These cases confirm that the promotion of Asian idols is part of a broader public movement toward what is perceived as regional progress.[6]

---

5. For further details regarding the activities of Asian entertainment companies, see Kawakami (1995).

6. Interestingly, some Japanese producers who were acquainted with overseas Asian markets commented that the idol fad and popular-culture boom in Asian

THE SYMBOL OF

SOCIOECONOMIC AFFLUENCE

Hideyoshi Aizawa, the president of the Sun Music Corporation, pointed out that Noriko Sakai's success in Asia was due not only to Sakai's own achievement but also to the wealth she represented. This representation had an appeal to people in other Asian countries. In fact, Sakai was first acknowledged by consumers in Hong Kong, Taiwan, and China through a Panasonic television commercial, which contributed to the explosion of her popularity as well as the increased market sales of the co-advertised product. Taking advantage of this opportunity, Sun Music debuted Sakai as a singer, produced albums in Chinese, and held frequent concerts in places like Taiwan. In Aizawa's observation, both Sakai and the product offered dreams about a rich and happy world—like Japan, as it was imagined by the people in these countries. The dream manufactured by the idol industry, in this case, is a dream that signifies the nation's socioeconomic well-being.

The successful promotion of Japanese and Japanese-style idols throughout rapidly developing countries in Asia would have been unlikely had there not been a tendency for young people in these countries to look at Japanese popular culture as a source of new trends—in the way the United States, for example, once was for Japan. In my preliminary interviews with informants from China, Hong Kong, South Korea, and Taiwan, I tried to understand how Japanese-style idols are perceived in developing Asian countries. These informants were university students, but they were also identified as being idol fans back in their teenage years. I asked about their thoughts on the meaning of Japanese idols in their home countries, and the relationship between these idols and socioeconomic development in the Asian region. Their responses revealed that these informants saw Japanese-style idols as a point of reference in terms of stylistic trends.

---

countries other than Japan, along with the standards of technology, reminded them of Japan back in the 1960s and early 1970s when it was still economically developing.

For example, one informant indicated that Japanese idols represent a positively imagined way of life for many of her people. She said, "People such as Momoe Yamaguchi and Seiko Matsuda from Japan are extremely popular in my country. . . . I think that they are famous because we admire their way of life. They showed us how to work hard and establish oneself in contemporary society through the messages of their songs and performances" (Female, age 24, from China). This statement confirms the fact that some established Japanese idols provide young Chinese with lifestyle models—just as they do for young Japanese followers. Establishing oneself through hard work is a theme that is typically encouraged by Japanese idols in Japan. The comment demonstrates the significance of this theme as applied to the young idol consumers of NIEs who strive to attain affluence.

Other informants also suggested that Japanese-style idols represent Japan's socioeconomic affluence, to which many people in their countries are drawn.

There are many idols and idol magazines in Taiwan that imitate Japanese idols and Japanese idol magazines. Some of them adopt identical titles, or titles that are so similar that we immediately know which Japanese counterparts they have imitated. I have an impression that Japanese idols are generally like romantic dolls that represent happiness and dreams of a developed country. I think that is why we like them so much. We also want to be fanciful.   (Female, age 22, from Taiwan)

I think that idols dramatize economic dreams and pack them in their songs, which are three to four, or five minutes long. They unite us, for example, like us Chinese all over the world, in Chinatowns in America or Great Britain or Canada. They bring us together spiritually, you know. I think that this kind of spiritual unity is important for Chinese and everybody who listens to the songs of Hong Kong idols, Japanese idols, or Taiwanese idols, or wherever they are from, for regional economic development.   (Male, age 26, from Hong Kong)

These statements show that economic dreams and spiritual affluence are linked in the minds of these informants. What underlies the socioeconomic dream is the desire to realize economic affluence through social progress, as it is especially evident in the second informant's comments. In his view, all people of developing Asian countries can explore their local identities in a prosperous age, when affluence is no longer associated with North America and developed European nation-states. In such a setting, idols act as a lubricant in the formation of local identity for adolescents in Asia.

One other informant explicated the leadership role of Japanese-style idols.

If idols can contribute to the modernization of Asia, that would be because they can direct many people to one and the same economic or social issue. It is like leadership, but an entertaining one—not as serious and boring as political statements made by politicians, and not so lighthearted or ironic as jokes made by comedians. I'd rather listen to idols sing than go to a political speech, and hear about our cross-cultural friendship, or unity, or development.   (Female, age 26, from South Korea)

This informant compared idol leadership with political leadership and saw a greater advantage in the former over the latter due to its entertaining function. This recalls my own observation of political campaigns in which idols were used allegorically, to attract people. Politicians relied on idols' fame as well as their cheerful images to turn their campaigns into public spectacles. Even so, some young people in the audience rejected political messages and "just wanted to have fun" with idols.

Two other comments clarify the role played by Japanese-style idols in constructing Asian identity.

Japanese idols keep inspiring young performers from Hong Kong by offering the messages of love, dreams, and hopes, although whether they are valuable or not depends on the person's evaluation. These messages can at least unite the feelings of many Asians and construct some kind of identity that is different from Americans or Europeans.   (Male, age 26, from Taiwan)

Idols are simply entertainers, and I do not think they have any essential significance. But that is why I think they are necessary. People everywhere cannot live without some kind of entertainment, right? We all have to take a break and run away from the real world. That is, I think, what entertainment, including idol performances, is all about. The reason that idols are so popular these days in Asia is, I think, because people in Asia are working hard now and they need to take a break sometimes. Hollywood movie stars and other exotic-looking actors are okay, too, but I think as an Asian I prefer to see people who look like me . . . with black hair, black pupils, yellow skin. . . . I feel like I can relax more when I see idols. Then, I can refresh myself and get to work for Asia's economic development the next day.   (Male, age 24, from Taiwan)

Both of these informants used Japanese-style idols to identify Asia's socioeconomic potential against Europeans and North Americans. Asian idols, represented by the Japanese prototype, emerged as popular icons under which all Asian people can unite, work hard, and overcome what they perceive as the Occidental economic superpowers, represented by glamorous Hollywood actors. In these views, Japanese-style idols constitute a brand not simply of singers or actors but of a modern lifestyle.

Takumi Hayashi, a Japanese columnist and culture critic, observes in a 1990 survey conducted in Taiwan that Japanese idols provide their Taiwanese audiences with various fictions about Japanese culture. The people of Taiwan use these fictions to expand their knowledge of other aspects of Japan: entertainment, arts, subcultures, fashion, comics, music, and so on (Hayashi 1994). This indicates that Japan, for many stylistic trends, has become the place to watch for other Asians—in the way Europe and the United States once were for Japanese during the era of postwar economic development.

My preliminary interview data also revealed that Japanese-style idols provide a point of reference for making sense of the changing social conditions that accompany economic growth. Most interview respondents were skeptical about any direct impact of idols upon regional economic development. Yet it was generally acknowledged that idols are symbolically significant for enhancing a developmental atmosphere in a region where people are trying to catch up and surpass what they see as the Japanese level of economic and technological development. Japanese-style idols propel the desire among the people of developing Asian countries to have the rest of the world perceive them on equal terms with the Japanese in economy and lifestyle.

In a separate interview, Eric Suen (debut 1993), an idol-pop singer from Hong Kong, indicated his intention to contribute to the cross-cultural communication and exchange in Asia "It would be my greatest pleasure to unify the hearts of many people all around Asia, encouraging them with my music and acting. I would certainly like to help us cope together with a variety of social problems that might occur in many parts of Asia, and support the development of the region in any way I can." Suen's attempt to join the list of famous Japanese-style idols includes his frequent business trips to Japan, where he was adopted by Sun Music to be debuted in Japan. In the spring of 1995 he released a duet single with Noriko Sakai that symbolized the partnership between Hong Kong and Japan, and he participated in the 1996 Asia Music Festival, held in Fukuoka, Japan. These not only provided Suen with opportunities for being recognized in Japan but also for being acknowledged back home by earning a place in the Japanese entertainment industry. In an increasingly cosmopolitan world, the recognition of idols reinforces performers' national identity (the country from which they come, or the area that they represent), just as athletes in the Olympic Games would impart a sense of national pride.

Given the connection made above between Japanese-style idol performances and the growing ethos in NIEs for socioeconomic development, what are the factors that contribute to the use of Japanese-style idols as tools in formulating local social identities? In the next section I will delve into consumer consciousness and show that Japanese-style idols serve as a symbolic guide in the expansion of local knowledge and imagination.

IDOL CONSUMPTION
IN HONG KONG

For the people of developing countries, particularly those with a colonial past, the influx of products from what they acknowledge as developed countries tends to generate a feeling that jumbles admiration for the national power that enabled the production of these commodities, fear that their local lifeworld may be absorbed into the socioeconomic order of the countries from which the products are being imported, and hope that they will be able to reconstruct their local lifeworld into one that is strong enough to compete against the developed source of importation. As for idol performances, the importation of Japanese idols into NIEs as objects of public adoration is made possible by the popular acceptance of these commoditized personalities as models of a Japanese lifestyle that local consumers admire. The acceptance of Japanese idols by such consumers corresponds to the efforts of local promoters to develop homegrown idols that can act as vehicles for transforming the local lifestyle into one that appears to be as rich as the Japanese counterpart.

With this point in mind, let us look into how particular informants from certain NIEs perceive Asian idols as a way of claiming their identities for themselves within what they conceive to be an increasingly modernizing world. Idols can be seen as one example of a historic discourse in which the future is realized in new ways— ways that reference such notions as socioeconomic progress.

The Consumer

Gregory Lin (a pseudonym) was a 24-year-old university student (a business major) who lived in Hong Kong. He was the son of an upper-middle-class family; his father owned a business, and his mother worked as a secretary in a large company. Upon graduating from high school, Lin was given an apartment in the Kowloon district by his parents, where he lived alone. They gave him all the money he needed, including a monthly allowance of 12,000 Hong Kong dollars, which enabled Lin to buy most of the things he wanted. His room was well equipped with furniture and electronic appliances, including a 16-inch color television, radio cassette, CD player, and a high-powered computer.

I spent three weeks living with Lin in the spring of 1996 to examine his activities. A longtime acquaintance of mine, Lin was disturbed neither by my presence nor by my intention to analyze him. He treated me just as he would have any of his other friends under normal circumstances. I have known Lin to be a big fan of Japanese idols. His ability to read, speak, and write in Japanese, though limited, helped him to decode lyrics of idol songs and Japanese magazine articles related to idols. Taking advantage of my presence, he frequently asked me to translate parts of these songs, articles, and Japanese television dramas that he could not comprehend.

The Environment

Hong Kong, where Lin was born and raised, developed as a center of commercial exchange between the British and the Chinese when it became a colony of the British empire in the nineteenth century. Over the years, the city prospered as a paragon of capitalism because of its *laissez-faire* economy (market competition, free enterprise, and free trade). Hong Kong's hard-working labor force has been mobilized into textile manufacturing, financial institutions, insurance companies, telecommunication agencies, tourism, and retail corporations. In concurrence with the terms indicated in the 1898 Second Convention of Beijing, which authorized the British rule of Hong Kong for 99 years, Hong Kong was returned to China on July 1, 1997. The city became part of the People's Republic of China. Under the 1994 Sino-British Joint Declaration, however, the Chinese government promised to retain Hong Kong's economic autonomy for at least 50 years by making it a Special Administrative Region. Today, Hong Kong's six million people—most of whom have a Cantonese background—live in an area of only 1,070 square kilometers.

My fieldwork took place when Hong Kong's return to China was approaching, and people as well as the mass media were becoming more outspoken about their local identity than ever before. As for Lin, he was certain that Hong Kong would maintain its autonomy as a city with advanced industry, sophisticated service systems, and many educated workers. Hong Kong was expected to grow continuously as China's gateway to Western capitalism. Lin believed that Hong Kong would continue to prosper as a center of cosmopolitan fashion and lifestyle. He said that Hong Kong citizens held the key to China's future socioeconomic development.

The Development of Idol
Performances in Hong Kong

Until the early 1970s, the pop-music scene in Hong Kong was dominated by a style inspired by traditional Chinese operas: a form of musical theater in which actors appear on stage with elaborate makeup and costumes to perform mythical tales, classical love stories, and military legends as they sing in high-pitched voices and dance with a mainly percussive orchestra. Many young people of the time who were less interested in this rather classical form of performance turned their attention to Taiwanese pop music, which consisted of Western-inspired, Mandarin-language ballads.

The first locally produced pop music in Hong Kong emerged when a major television network, TVB, began hiring songwriters who composed theme songs in the local Cantonese dialect for television dramas. Outstripping the shows in popularity, these songs constituted a new genre of popular music, known as Canton-pop. This genre featured singers such as Samuel Hui, Alan Tam, and George Lam. Hui, considered to be the pioneer of Hong Kong's pop music, wrote and sang songs that spoke of everyday matters, the hardship of life and tragicomedies of romance, which were set to Western-style melodies and instrumentation. Other singers imitated his successful formula.

This original style of pop music gave way to a new wave of Japanese idol-pop at the end of the 1970s, inspiring the reorganization of Cantonese pop music into a more elaborate style of musical performance in terms of melodies, ornate fashions, and complicated choreography. Like Japanese idols, many young singers in Hong Kong began acting in movies and television dramas. Long-term planning was incorporated into their promotion system, enabling the successful performers to develop their careers as they matured from novices to experienced actors. I could not find any source that accurately describes how Japanese idols became popular in Hong Kong. I did find that many popular magazines of this period dedicated a page or section to information related to Japanese idols, discussing anything from their styles to private affairs.

Later reports, on the other hand, confirm the emergent popularity of Japanese idol pop, as the following example shows:

At the end of the [19]70s, the Canto[n-]pop boom hit unexpected resistance, as Hong Kong teenagers turned their attention to Japanese idols, whose peppy, electronic music was more fun and easier to dance to than the melodramatic love songs of the local Canto[n]-minstrels. The J[apanese]-pop fad ultimately faded, but only because the Hong Kong music industry had learned to assimilate and adapt to this new challenge: The [19]80s saw the emergence of a crop of artists who combined the teen-idol appeal and . . . dance groove of Japanese pop-stars with a feel for traditional romantic ballads. (Yang et al. 1997: 255, brackets mine)

This short passage indicates how Canton-pop burgeoned through the borrowing of Japanese idol styles. It also shows that the Cantonese audience in Hong Kong enmeshed themselves into Japanese idol performances until homegrown artists employed similar techniques. As greater numbers of local artists appeared on the scene, the popularity of Japanese idols began to drop in Hong Kong.

A Pattern of Idol Consumption in Hong Kong

Lin's interest in Japanese idols began when he became aware of their popularity in high school.

Everyone around me talked about Noriko [Sakai], Rie Miyazawa, and other Japanese idols. Both boys and girls competed over how much they knew about these personalities, and the most recent and the trendiest Japanese fashion they represented. The more you demonstrated how much you knew, the more you felt privileged—like showing off the most recent famous model of Japanese car you acquired and telling your close friends what you know about its mechanism, you know. I thought I needed to brush up my knowledge about Japanese idols, too, and here I am now.

Lin's sense of empathy toward his idol intensified as he developed knowledge about that idol and her cultural background. This knowledge was also a status marker that helped Lin establish position in his high school.

Sakai for Lin was not only an adorable personality but also a "guiding angel" (as he called her) that provided him with a chance to expand his knowledge about Japanese-style science, technology, and modern culture.

Originally, I was only interested in Noriko [Sakai], I mean only her attractive personality. Then, I got interested in her activities, the way she performed, how she was being produced, and so on. I started to pay attention to her surroundings. Suddenly, I realized that I was becoming interested in Japanese idol-production technology. I noticed that I was fascinated not only by Noriko, but by the way she was being produced, and how her promotion agencies operated. Then I realized I was becoming interested in something much more general—about Japanese popular culture, then contemporary Japan at large. I never thought I would come this far, or that I would associate Noriko with what I already knew and admired about Japanese hardware technology—you know, like how they make cars and electronic equipment. It was somewhat exciting to see all of these [specific and general] bits of information about Japanese culture and technology coming together through Noriko.

This discussion of Sakai as a symbol of innovative style for which Japan is currently a dissemination point reminds the researcher of the role American pop stars once had for the Japanese audience, when Japan was trying to mimic the United States in the 1950s and 1960s. For example, a middle-aged Japanese female informant recalled how she was crazy about many American actors such as Clark Gable, James Dean, and Marlon Brando during her youth, and that hundreds of young people rushed to movie theatres every time their performances were featured on screen. In her view, these Hollywood actors and movies brought with them a desirable vision of a bright future (*akarui mirai*) where poverty and shortages (common in Japan during and immediately after World War II), was no longer an issue. In such a future world, greater emphasis was placed on personal happiness through luxurious lifestyles.

As American political and economic influence dominated the international scene in the postwar period, American material and popular culture began to permeate Japanese society. The early postwar period in Japan brought with it a craze for American-made movies (e.g., Creighton 1995: 143, 144). In a similar way, Japanese and Japanese-style idols now offer the desirable image of an affluent modern nation for adolescents in those countries wanting to be equally modernized.

Lin struggled to keep his knowledge about Japanese idols and their manufacturing agencies updated by purchasing magazines and newspapers regularly and paying special attention to sections on Japanese entertainment. One of his most intense hobbies was to collect CDs of Japanese and Cantonese idols and listen to them comparatively. He had hundreds of these CDs, which he had collected over the years, piled up on his shelf. Lin sang most of the songs on these CDs, including Japanese songs in Japanese whether or not he understood what the lyrics meant exactly. His apartment was covered with idol posters, many of which featured Sakai, which he said created an encouraging atmosphere. Lin also sat in front of his computer for two to three hours every evening browsing through idol-related sources on internet home pages.

For Lin, all these activities were part of learning about Japanese science, technology, and culture through entertainment sources. In school, Lin's interest in Japan led him to take courses in Japanese language, business, history, and culture. His interest in Japanese idols and their environs expedited his studies in Japan-related subjects. Lin also thought that all the knowledge he was gaining about Japan, revolving around Japanese idols, would encourage him to become an informed businessman in the near future, someone who could communicate with and even impress the Japanese.

The Worldview of an Idol Consumer in Hong Kong

My interview with Lin was conducted as part of an effort to delve into the meaning assigned to Japanese idol performances by a member of the Cantonese audience in Hong Kong—particularly this individual's perception regarding the cause of the development of Japanese-style idol pop in Hong Kong. The following interview excerpts substantiate the role played by Japanese idols as motifs of modernity in Asia—the state of socioeconomic well-being to be achieved by the citizens of Hong Kong.

For Lin, Japan's contemporary culture, represented by a series of Japanese trendy goods, was a great source of inspiration. These Japanese products offered criteria with which to evaluate Hong Kong's economic power. As Lin commented:

Japanese products were always admired in Hong Kong. But especially since the early 1980s, many people here in Hong Kong looked up to Japanese popular culture, too, when a whole new set of consumer goods started to come into Hong Kong—mostly software products. These added an entirely new dimension to the existing market of Japanese hardware products, and they fascinated us with futuristic images and digitized audiovisual effects. We just fell in love with them.

This suggests that the people of Hong Kong looked to Japan as a trend source. Yet Lin also indicated that Japanese culture is not altogether attractive for people in Hong Kong. He distinguished between more traditional and more modern aspects of Japanese culture: "Our image of traditional Japanese is not a good one—you know, like those represented by Shintō shrines, serious-looking samurai swinging their swords, *kamikaze* fighters, and subordinate women. These things evoke bad memories of War, you know . . . Japan's invasion of China during the Second World War." This reflected an interesting idea about Japan's image construction in a global context: that Japan, as an image statement, is being constructed differently by Asia and by North Americans and Western Europeans. The latter two tend to emphasize images of traditional Japan, or a more Asian Japan, in their symbolic processing: images of samurai, sushi, geisha, and so forth. In North American politics, business, and consumerism, this is manifested in the representation of traditional motifs in architecture, furniture, and tourist campaigns, as well as ads and articles about various made-in-Japan products.[7] In contrast, the Japan that other Asian countries look at, in terms of the motif-dissemination point, is in fact the aspect of modernity found in Japan.

In a subsequent interview, I asked Lin about the way Japanese popular culture items, as motifs of modernity, entered Hong Kong and earned their recognition by people there. He replied:

In the beginning, many idol-pop singers from Japan like Akina Nakamori and Hideki Saijō came to Hong Kong to sing, and young people went crazy over Japanese pop music. People listened to Japanese pop music

---

7. Images of *samurai*, *geisha*, *sumō* wrestlers, and Mt. Fuji are considered to be symbols of traditional Japan. These appear on the front covers of popular magazines that discuss Japan (see, for example, *International Business Week*, Sept. 7, 1987; *New York Times*, Sept. 26, 1987; *Fortune International*, Feb. 26, 1990). Logos featuring *samurai* and *geisha* figures on the side of Japan studies articles in recent issues of *Ethnology* are academic examples of the traditional characterization of Japan.

more than British and American pop music put together, and many Canton-pop singers covered Japanese songs in Cantonese or assimilated their style to the Japanese-pop style. That's when young Hong Kong singers like Alan Tam, Sandy Lam, and Anita Mui became big stars, too. Singers like Alan [Tam] went to Japan to get good training in J-pop, did you know? . . . People thought Japanese pop-songs were more upbeat and livelier. Japanese animation like *Gandam, Macros*—was it?—and *Doraemon*, and soap operas followed this J-pop boom and ignited the Japan boom. When they were imported and broadcast in Hong Kong, almost everyone that I knew was nailed to the television every day. Hong Kong television, magazines, and newspapers started to talk about Japan, too. My favorite program to watch was *Enjoy Yourself Tonight* or *Fun Lok Gam Siu* in Cantonese, which introduced where to travel and what to buy in Japan.

This confirmed how the importation of Japanese idol pop served as a gateway for people in Hong Kong to learn about other popular cultural forms from Japan. I then wanted to know why people tended to look up to Japanese trends so much, to which Lin replied:

I think we admire Japanese science and technology a lot. Japan is the first world, and it's the most advanced country in Asia. We have a lot to learn from it. . . . Japanese pop music, fashion, lifestyles, and all the hardware and software products that they produce are outcomes of Japan's technological development and economic prosperity. People here in Hong Kong want to show that they are as capable as the contemporary Japanese in that sense. . . . American consumer products are becoming increasingly trendy in Hong Kong, especially since the early 1990s when many American companies started to invest in China and Hong Kong. Many of us eat at McDonald's, wear Hard Rock Cafe T-shirts, and put on jeans. Yet, there are two good reasons that Hong Kong people prefer Japanese products. First, Japanese products are more suitable for Hong Kong people in size and style. They are Asian, you know. In clothing for example, American and European produces are often too big, wide, or colorful to wear, whereas Japanese clothing fits better. . . . Another reason is that Americans and Europeans often use Hong Kong as a dumpsite. I mean, they bring things that didn't sell well back home, so we feel that we are discriminated—not only economically but also racially. . . . When it comes to Japan, things imported from there may be more expensive, but they are as high quality as they are in Japan, and we'd love to consume them.

The question of fair trade aside, this comment illustrates how modern Japanese products are popularized around the idea of ethnic fitness. The gist of Japan's modernization has been to master cultures and technologies of industrialized Western countries according to the nation's domestic needs. Innovative customs and products that support indigenous lifestyles have been enthusiastically incorporated into the existing system, strengthening the idea that Japan has risen to the level of the Western superpowers.[8] Lin offered a similar explanation for the situation in Hong Kong—that modern Japanese fashions and products were more suitable to Hong Kong people in terms of their body size, stylistic familiarity, and perhaps the scarcity of space in Hong Kong.[9]

Lin revealed how Japanese-style idols joined other popular arts in the creation of what he saw as a contemporary atmosphere in which other Asians are looking to Japan as a preferred choice for Hong Kong people in terms of innovative lifestyles.

Japanese idols are our role models. They bring us fashion, music, and dramas about our closest first-world nation. It's the leading Asian country in the world, too. Japanese idols allow us to visualize the lifestyle of the developed nation that we look up to. . . . They symbolize Japan's economic well-being as a dream for Hong Kong people.

Lin elucidated the role of Japanese idols as providers of dreams for Hong Kong people. Homegrown idols in Hong Kong, through their images of becoming, represented the local effort to realize the Japanese dream:

---

8. In her interview-based article, Creighton (1995: 143) shows that Japan copies Western fashion while seeing it as based on a different body type. The Japanese sense of mastering Western technology in the Japanese way was also observed in a talk I attended in Seattle at the height of economic conflict between Japan and the United States. In this talk a Japanese ambassador suggested that Japanese are good at refining American products in such a way that they become smaller, more portable, more energy efficient, and therefore better suited to less space.

9. One of the well-known characteristics of Japanese manufacturing technology is miniaturization. Various companies emphasize the production of small products with maximum utility in order to accommodate an environment in which space has always been scarce. The development of a pocket-size transistor radio in the 1950s, led by Tokyo Telecommunications Engineering Company (now Sony), is a typical example (e.g., Schiffer 1991). Hong Kong faces a problem similar to Japan in terms of the availability of space. It would not be surprising that the people of Hong Kong prefer Japanese products over relatively larger imports from elsewhere for this reason.

There is more to this. Hong Kong idols are our own Chinese role models. Japanese are Japanese, as we all know, who will never be culturally Chinese. Our idols bring the Japanese dream even closer to us. They make us believe that we can actually be like Japanese as Chinese, you know. . . . And I think the level of Hong Kong idols—and Hong Kong pop culture for that matter—improved greatly over the last few years. We are indeed catching up well with the Japanese! . . . I hope that in the near future, we'll be able to come up with leading Cantonese pop stars on an international stage or have a world-renowned Canton pop! Why not!?

Lin saw Hong Kong idols as embodiments of local striving for a desired standard of living that has not yet been obtained. While Japanese idols in Hong Kong function as fantasy depictions that assist the people's sense of cultural development by portraying modern personal ideal types, home-grown idols in Hong Kong reify these ideal types as a series of dream-come-true native celebrities. Clearly, Lin saw Japanese-style idols as a vehicle to enhance Hong Kong's current economic status and future progress in Asia.

Lin's case demonstrates how everyday adoration of Japanese-style idols can facilitate the formation of cultural identity. Japanese idols and their Chinese versions provided Lin with a way of assessing his local identity, in the context of Asia as a region, in terms of the level of socioeconomic development. The process in which Lin crafted his local identity in light of Japanese-style role models was also the process whereby he was socialized into an evermore global consumer culture, grounded in capitalist-class values and manifested in the historical discourse on the Asia-Pacific economic development. The political, economic, cultural, and historical meaning of idols is read, understood, and developed by consumers like Gregory Lin who are conscious of their own national well-being.

ASIAN IDOLS AS INDICES
OF SOCIOECONOMIC DEVELOPMENT

The development of Japanese-style idols in Hong Kong, as a communicative response of the local industry to cultural exposure, is analogous to the general process of language change in contact situations. The assimilation of Canton pop into Japanese idol pop is reflected in stylistic development, the changes in the performers' roles, as well as the performers' extended life expectancy in the industry. These salient features of change to the form and function of Cantonese idol performances are recognized by the audience (such as Gregory Lin) as prestigious markers representing favorable aspects of Hong Kong's technological and social development.

In discussing the growing presence of Japanese industries in Taiwan, a local intellectual and a cultural critic, Shu-yu Chuang, contends that the Japanese are once more colonizing Taiwan. She writes that the Taiwanese market is becoming a fortress as well as a testing ground for the Japanese merchants' invasion of the overseas Chinese communities in the world (Chuang 1989). Drawing on the analogy between Japan's colonial aggression in the first half of the twentieth century and its postwar economic expansion, Chuang warns local Taiwanese to be aware of well-calculated Japanese corporate strategies. These strategies, according to Chuang, include long-term investment in what producers see as a launching pad to the world's 11.5 billion Chinese market, and customer servicing that is founded on a combination of corporate ideology and cultural imperialism. This view is similar to the general attitude of South Korean officials, who have been rejecting Japanese culture throughout the postwar decades.

In his response to these views, a Taiwanese cultural analyst, Leo Ching (1984), contends that although the growing influence of Japanese industries in other Asian countries since the mid-1980s can be attributed to Japan's ascendancy as the world's prominent economic power and to local changes, the economic power of Japanese industries does not necessarily entail cultural dominance. He calls for thorough studies concerning attitudes of those who produce and consume Japanese products in local contexts. Ching stresses the need to examine the extent to which these local producers and consumers accept, apply, or resist Japanese culture through local distribution and consumption of Japanese trendy goods (Ching 1994: 219).

Taking on where Ching left off, this chapter has provided a preliminary ethnographic case study of the local manifestation of Japanese corporate hegemony, using Japanese-style idols as a window. It is clear that idols are thought to be more than venerable personalities in one culture. In other developing Asian countries, specifically NIEs, Japanese-style idols are being marketed by their manufacturing agencies and consumed by their audiences as a vehicle for identifying their positions in an increasingly modernizing world. Using Friedman's theory that consumption in an increasingly global world serves as a means for people to constitute an identity space as a point of departure, we have seen that the expanding capitalization of Japanese-style idols in the Asian market today is an attribute of the emergent ethos in the Asian region that emphasizes the idea of socioeconomic progress.

The growing popularity of idol performances in developing Asian countries testifies to the fact that such youth-oriented personalities are becoming widely celebrated in these places as symbols of national wealth. Japanese-style idols are produced and used by their manufacturing agencies as a set of commodities that arouse, channel, and domesticate a fantasy of a materially developed world, as represented by Japanese consumer culture. The current popularity of idols in various parts of Asia indicates the reception this informed purpose has among observers who are inclined to interpret themselves and their local cultures in an increasingly global world through iconic representations.

The discussion in this chapter has tried to draw on ethnographic examples of idol performances and to show how the cultivating function of popular culture performances is applicable not only within the domain of one culture or society but also across different cultures and societies. A sense of historical coherence—the feeling that Asia is currently catching up with the West in terms of fashion, lifestyle, and consumer culture—is cumulatively created and increasingly shared among Asian people through the consumption of personified symbolic commodities. At the same time, this symbol consumption contributes to the realization of the difference in Asian people's cultural backgrounds and identities.

The consumption of idols tends to be prominent in places such as China, Hong Kong, South Korea, Taiwan, and Vietnam—countries that are currently undergoing rapid socioeconomic transition. Japanese idol styles provide a point of motif dissemination for the producers in these countries. On one hand, this motivates some Japanese promotion agencies to collaborate with local agencies from other Asian countries and create cross-cultural ties and networks. On the other hand, it demonstrates the effort of many Asians outside Japan to master the technologies of Japanese-style popular culture production.

Pop-culture forms can inscribe ideological themes that nevertheless allow audiences to generate meanings that meet the needs of their own local identities. That is, potentially variable meaningful articulations of a specific cultural form must be understood in terms of their dialogic relationship with ideological themes, rather than anarchistic or pluralistic constructions as such (Mukerji and Schudson 1991: 41). To borrow from Hall (1980), popular art forms that are produced at any given moment in history can simultaneously include their preferred and alternative, or even opposing, readings of the time. The emerging genre of Asian idol pop can inscribe the "partnerships for progress" (the ideological theme of APEC in the early 1990s) in the form of a dialogue between political and symbolic forces. While the political side of this dialogue emphasizes the modernizing process led by governmental leadership, its symbolic counterpart focuses on the idealized outcomes of modernization as represented by a rich consumer society such as Japan.

We live in a world where the increasingly global impact of capitalism stimulates more people in more areas to adopt comparable lifestyles and share similar values through the consumption of widely distributed commodities. The study of popular culture in this context entails the understanding of the dialogue between capitalism and its local or regional manifestations. This requires analyzing the various international links through an examination of their consequences within a particular site (Miller 1997: 12) or investigating the impact of deterritorialization on the imaginative resources of lived, local experiences (Appadurai 1991: 196). The overall aim of this chapter has been to contribute to such a study by emphasizing the role played by idols and their image-making institutions as a mediating apparatus that bridges the gap between global flows and local articulations.

CONCLUSION

Capitalizing Adolescence

The public role of idols is made possible within a culture that regards adolescence as a life stage in which individuals are expected to explore themselves as they socialize with peers. Idols represent this life stage through their images and narratives. They develop social ties with their generation of fans by emphasizing their roles as adolescent companions. To use a religious analogy, idols, operating as charismatic forces, can be said to generate communities of young worshippers seeking to heal their hearts, which are stressed by the requirements and expectations of the adult lifeworld into which they are being integrated. Eventually, idols transform their images from those of an innocent novice to an experienced actor in the process of winning public recognition. Adolescents can grow up together with their favorite personalities through the act of consumption for which the very process of self-transformation is merchandized.

To become a socially competent adult is to accommodate oneself to culturally defined roles, and by extension establish one's position properly with respect to gender, class (or status), and nationality (or ethnicity). For female idols in particular, becoming a professional meant molding oneself into a personality that could act out the ideological role of "good wife, wise mother" in media spaces, if not in real life as well. To this end, many idols in the past have embodied a cute style—a meek, weak, and benevolent style of femininity. This formerly predominant image of subservient femaleness has given way to a more self-assertive, sexually vibrant image of adolescent femaleness along with a trend toward women's public advancement since the late 1980s. As the cultural definition of what is appropriate changed, so did the image of idols.

However, the self-assertive image of new idols, or "post-idols," could not be taken at face value because it was questionable as to whether this movement advocating a powerful image of adolescent femaleness truly empowered its actors and imitators. These new images of adolescent femaleness were designed under the supervision of male producers who dominated the industry, acting according to the principles of masculinity. In the end, the empowering female imagery was shown to be appropriated by the industry and retooled to suit the masculine mode of production. As an encompassing cultural matrix, the idol system generated a repertoire of gender ideals over time from which consumers could choose and develop their own gender identities.

As Seiko Matsuda's life history has shown, the career of one particular idol can symbolize the change in the image of women. Matsuda, represented originally as a cute and innocent novice, was eventually projected as an independent, self-reliant, and self-creative personality who rejected her earlier socially subservient role. Part of this metamorphosis, which enlightened the lifestyle of many young female fans, is expressed in the form of Matsuda's convergence with urban American lifestyles. Her frequent trips to New York in combination with her adoption of various American fashions, values, and techniques in stage performances provided her Japanese audience with a playful excursion into an exotic world of fantasies. What made this all the more interesting was the fact that, at a certain point, Matsuda took control of her own image. That is, she managed to take control of the means of production as she encountered various challenges in her life as a maturing performer.

While Matsuda's incorporation of exotic Western images into her style signified her popular role as a bearer of innovative style and value, it also imposed a moral threat upon many of her viewers. Since Western culture is often considered to carry negative values of egoism that go against the traditional emphasis on collectivities, the Americanized Matsuda has been seen as an alien figure who espouses individual self-indulgence and sensuality. A series of articles about Matsuda in the Japanese mass media attempted to criticize her and suggested that Matsuda's innovative activities posed a moral threat to the public.

Against this, Matsuda projected herself as a clever cultural strategist who absorbed media-created scandals into her self-promotion process; her public accepted this characterization. Matsuda appealed to the idea of accomplishment, an important concept in Japanese culture. One who accomplishes her or his goals in life through hard work and the overcoming of various obstacles deserves public recognition in Japan, and Japanese popular literature is filled with idealized personalities who sacrifice themselves for a greater social achievement. This is the value that Matsuda came to represent. The idea of accomplishment is not unique to Matsuda, however, and it runs through the mediation process—between self and society, childhood and adulthood, and traditional values and modern lifestyles—that characterizes idol performances in general.

Successful idols not only market dreams that can feed the minds of thousands of people, but also facilitate a belief that one can make these dreams come true with passion and effort. Largely, this process of accomplishment is dramatized by the mass media, which sets the idol subject in a recurrent agonistic situation. Thus, idol performances become a showcase in which the management of personal trajectory is publicly demonstrated. Personal trajectories of successful idols such as Matsuda constitute folklore, which is narrated and transmitted by the story-telling mass media and shared by the audience in contemporary urban Japan.

The "images of becoming" that idol performances merchandize are not limited to the representation of adolescents' personal quest for accomplishment in the period of their maturation. Idol performances can also represent the youth of a nation. This point is suggested by the expanding popularity of idols outside Japan and in particular developing Asian countries. Japanese idols in these places signify Japan as a model of modern consumer society. Subsequently, homegrown idols emerge in these areas as "facilitators" (so to speak) of socioeconomic progress. Idol performances can be characterized as rites of modernization in this regard (Peacock 1968). What might be for adolescent individuals a field in which adult social values are playfully acquired through a series of cultural role models may also be a domain in which the people of developing Asian nations construct modern fashions and lifestyles. In such a way, Japanese idol performances provide a point of dissemination for the producers and consumers of trends in these Asian countries.

IDOL PERFORMANCES AND WHITE-COLLAR IDENTITY

The question of identity and that of cultural boundary are deeply implicated in each other. To identify oneself with certain cultural forms is to distinguish oneself meaningfully from those who do not identify themselves with that form. In the Japanese entertainment industry, this distinction is manifested in terms of different genres of popular cultural performances. In popular music, for example, there are *enka* for elders and working-class people, rock and roll for youngsters who are *kōha* or "on the solid side," folk and new music for *nanpa* or the "moderate," and idol pop for younger adolescents and lovestruck audiences of all ages.

Within the field of idol performances, this distinction is further demonstrated by the differentiation of styles between idols and idol groups, as well as by fans and fan groups who support different idols and idol groups. Audience members establish different degrees of involvement in idol performances: while some are enthusiastic fans who fall into (*hamatteiru*) the trap of idol attraction, others simply enjoy seeing likable personalities. Different layers of boundaries can be seen among idol fans themselves. There were even those, less serious about their engagement, who tended to ridicule those who take great joy and pride in chasing and cheering on their idols. Enthusiastic fans are considered abnormal (*ijō*) because of their heavy involvement in what other people think is *karui goraku*, or "light entertainment."

These distinctions in popular cultural performances coexist with distinctions based on commodity tastes in other spheres, together constituting the social environment of contemporary Japan, which can be characterized as a consumer society (Bourdieu 1984, 1993). In this sense, idol performances socialize young people into the capitalist system, where differentiation through acts of consumption and consumption-driven production become the primary means of locating oneself. As Clammer points out, such a tendency in consumption decisions concentrates around a middle-class identity, which implies the recognition of reality based on the large but nevertheless surprisingly structured range of consumption choices. This range of choices is linked to similar incomes as well as the desire for homogeneity, which operates as a powerful element in Japanese psychology (Clammer 1997: 102). This emphasis on homogeneity in Japan does not eliminate difference, but defines it within, and assigns it to, particular categories in such a way that those who express themselves accordingly must conform to the norms and expectations regarding the categorical definitions of who they are. In addition, the cultural ideal relevant to this process is the idea of classificatory status, expressed in Japanese as *bun*, or "one's part" (Lebra 1976).

Oriented toward cooperative aspects of relationship, Japanese gain a strong sense of self by approximating ideal role types, joining groups, and situating themselves in relation to others (Smith 1983, quoted in Rosenberger 1992: 10). Although Japanese can engage in keen competition, Japanese-style competition, due to the cultural emphasis on group conformity, focuses on keeping up with others rather than on standing out. Thus, Japanese frame personal differences on the basis of a scheme of interpersonal similarity or the idea of group harmony (Kumon 1982: 26, 27; see also Creighton 1990: 294, 295). Present-day Japanese consumer society can be perceived in terms of such a prominent cultural framework—as a manifestation of social ties in the structured range of consumption choices (Clammer 1997: 102).

The pop-idol industry certainly embodies this framework as it develops a system that promotes convergence on the very unity of identity, the parameters of which are set both by conventions about age (or generation), gender, or sexuality and by the objective consumption possibilities—personal motifs that are made available in the market. The stylistic promotion and symbolic competition that occur in idol performances signify the nature of social interaction enacted by those who identify themselves with Japan's middle class: that is, competition over symbolic details within a homogeneous social category. This competition simultaneously plays down the disruptive and overtly competitive consequences of such rivalry.

IDOL PERFORMANCES AND THE
LOGIC OF LATE CAPITALISM

The study of idol performances further demonstrates the cultural logic of late capitalism. Above all, this logic emphasizes the multiplicity of meanings that are manifested in the ongoing, dynamic interplay among different views, values, and interpretations—none of which predominates (Jameson 1984; Kaplan 1988; Hutcheon 1989).

The aesthetic of the present-day consumer society marks a social life that is characterized by planned obsolescence; an ever more rapid rhythm of fashion and styling changes; and the penetration of advertising, television, and the media throughout society to a hitherto unparalleled degree. The replacement of the old tension between city and country, center and province, is paralleled by the growth of the great networks of superhighways and the arrival of the automobile culture. In such a social setting, the boundaries between illusions and realities are blurred as people invest socially, economically, and physically in the fantasies with which they represent their social realities and use to escape them (Allison 1996: 18). This is where industries that rely on trends step in, with their idea of marketing "dreams." In Japan, *yume*, or "dreams," and *fantajii* from the English "fantasies" have been an important marketing concept used to drive the public, especially young people who are sensitive to trends, toward the act of consumption.

The idol system is precisely a system that has been built on this middle-class logic of late capitalism. It facilitates the symbolic exchange of commodities that borrow from and produce sensual illusions. Not only do idols contribute to this form of capitalized symbolism by wearing fancy costumes, singing romantic songs, emphasizing dreams in their narratives, and appearing on stage with stage effects illuminating exotic wonderlands, but also by continuously driving love-struck audiences to participate in the re-production of a fantasy world that allows them repeatedly to escape from the realities in which they are usually situated.

It is no wonder that a youth-oriented movement like the idol boom reached its peak when it did in Japan during the 1980s—at the height of the nation's economic bubble, which followed years of rapid economic growth. The ideology of hard work geared toward the modernization of the country gave birth to a new cultural atmosphere, fed by rising incomes and inhabited by a new generation intent on differentiating themselves from their elders by enjoying the fruits of socioeconomic and technological developments. This is also the time when the idea of Japan as a middle-class society became popular, and terms such as "postmodern" and "avant garde" became key words that appeared and were discussed in academic as well as popular texts (e.g., Miyoshi and Harootunian 1989). In this respect, idols, like television and other consumer products, function as objects that signify class identity. The study of idol performances provides the understanding of the relationship between popular art forms and class differentiation.

IMPLICATIONS FOR
FUTURE STUDIES IN IDOLOGY

Several aspects of idol performances offer themselves for further investigations. For example, my research focused mainly on female idols and their promotion agencies. This is because I was able to contact a large number of people who were related to female idols in the realms of both production and consumption. In contrast, I was not able to develop enough quality contacts among the small number of agencies that control male idols. A comparison of the production of masculinity in male idols with the femininity of female idols, therefore, would be an important component of future research.

Likewise, a cross-cultural comparison between Japanese, Asian, and non-Asian idol performances needs further examination in our era of increased transnationalism. In the scope of my ethnographic fieldwork, I examined some aspects of Asian idols and their local production techniques in comparison to their Japanese counter-parts. However, Asian idols, as much as the categorical concept "Asia" itself, must be deconstructed further in relation to different ethnic identities, ideologies, religious beliefs, socioeconomic trends, and other cultural values that exist and interact within this vast region in the Pacific. Such a point has been elaborated recently by Iwabuchi (2002) from the perspective of media analysis, but a more extensive investigation of the growing impact of Asian transna-tionalism on the lifestyles of local residents using ethnographic ap-proach is called for. Such an investigation involves the thick de-scription of correlations between cultural hybridization and consuming activities, and the integrating role played by idolized personalities. A similar task applies to the examination of similari-ties and differences between Japanese idols and their Euro-American counterparts—especially in reference to such recently popular idols as Britney Spears or Christina Aguilera, or groups such as the Backstreet Boys and the Spice Girls, attracting millions of teenagers all around the world. Whether these specific cases have any tie with Japanese idol-production technology or not may re-veal some important information regarding the global spread of public culture.

In spite of its limitations, this study of Japanese idol perform-ances works to contribute to the anthropological understanding of symbolism in a contemporary social context. Using "idol" as a guiding concept, I have tried to show how cultural institutions manipulate the very arbitrary nature of symbols. Francis Bacon in the quote in Chapter 1 that introduced this work's thesis describes idols as a "faulty and unskillful abstraction." In my analysis, I have examined the skills used to craft these embodiments of cultural ideas. Idols are used by commercial institutions to saturate the pub-lic consciousness, substantiate meanings that can become part of cultural competence, and organize social events, practices, and experiences within their power structure. This study of idols has shown in part how individuals within this institutional power structure lead their lives through the ongoing dialectic between self and society.

Reference Matter

Works Cited

Adshead, Samuel. 1997. *Material Culture in Europe and China, 1400–1800: The Rise of Consumerism*. Houndsmills, Eng.: St. Martin's Press.

Akiyama, Masami. 1992. *Shōjo-tachi no Shōwashi* (The girls' history of the Shōwa era). Tokyo: Shinchōsha.

Allison, Anne. 1996. *Permitted and Prohibited Desires: Mothers, Comics, and Censorship in Japan*. Boulder, Colo.: Westview Press.

Aoyagi, Hiroshi. 2000. "Pop Idols and the Asian Identity." In Timothy Craig, ed., *Japan Pop!: Inside the World of Japanese Popular Culture*. Armonk, N.Y.: M. E. Sharpe, pp. 309–26.

Appadurai, Arjun. 1991. "Global Ethnoscapes: Notes and Queries for a Transitional Anthropology." In Richard Fox, ed., *Recapturing Anthropology: Working in the Present*. Santa Fe, N.M.: School of American Research Press, pp. 191–210.

Auer, Peter, ed. 1998. *Code-Switching in Conversation: Language, Interaction, and Identity*. London: Routledge.

Babcock, Barbara. 1986. "Modeled Selves: Helen Cordero's 'Little People.'" In Victor W. Turner and Edward M. Bruner, eds., *The Anthropology of Experience*. Urbana: University of Illinois Press, pp. 316–43.

Bachnik, Jane. 1994. "*Uchi/soto*: Challenging Our Conceptualizations of Self, Social Order, and Language." In Jane M. Bachnik and Charles J. Quinn, Jr., eds., *Situated Meaning: Inside and Outside in Japanese Self, Society, and Language*. Princeton: Princeton University Press, pp. 3–37.

Bacon, Francis. 1985 [1625]. "Idols of the Mind." In John Pitcher, ed., *Francis Bacon: The Essays*. Middlesex, Eng.: Penguin Books, pp. 277–85.

Barnouw, Erik, and Catherine Kirkland. 1992. "Entertainment." In Richard Bauman, ed., *Folklore, Cultural Performances and Popular Entertainments*. Oxford: Oxford University Press.

Barral, Étiene. 1999. *Otaku: les enfants du virtuel*. Paris: Editions Denoël.

Bartky, Sandra. 1990. *Femininity and Domination: Studies in the Phenomenology of Oppression*. London: Routledge.

Battaglia, Debbora. 1995. "Problematizing the Self: A Thematic Introduction." In Debbora Battaglia, ed., *Rhetorics of Self-Making*. Berkeley: University of California Press, pp. 1–15.

Baudrillard, Jean. 1981. *For a Critique of the Political Economy of the Sign*. St. Louis: Telos Press.

———. 1988 [1968]. "The System of Objects." In Mark Poster, ed., *Jean Baudrillard: Selected Essays*. Stanford: Stanford University Press, pp. 10–28.

Bauman, Richard. 1986. *Story, Performance, and Event: Contextual Studies or Oral Narrative*. Cambridge: Cambridge University Press.

———. 1992. "Folklore." In Richard Bauman, ed., *Folklore, Cultural Performances, and Popular Entertainments: A Communications-Centered Handbook*. New York: Oxford University Press, pp. 29–40.

Beasley, William G. 1972. *Meiji Restoration*. Stanford: Stanford University Press.

Befu, Harumi. 1986. "An Ethnography of Dinner Entertainment in Japan." In Takie S. Lebra and William P. Lebra, eds., *Japanese Culture and Behavior*. Honolulu: University of Hawai'i Press, pp. 108–20.

Bell, Catherine. 1997. *Ritual: Perspectives and Dimensions*. New York: Oxford University Press.

Ben-Amos, Ilana. 1994. *Adolescence and Youth in Early Modern England*. New Haven: Yale University Press.

Benedict, Ruth. 1946. *The Chrysanthemum and the Sword: Patterns of Japanese Culture*. Boston: Houghton Mifflin.

Bethe, Monica, and Karen Brazell. 1990. "The Practice of Noh Theatre." In Richard Schechner and Willa Appel, eds., *By Means of Performance: Intercultural Studies of Theatre and Ritual*. Cambridge: Cambridge University Press, pp. 167–93.

Bettelheim, Bruno. 1976. *The Uses of Enchantment: The Meaning and Importance of Fairy Tales*. New York: Alfred A. Knopf.

Bocknek, Gene. 1980. *The Young Adult: Development After Adolescence*. Monterey: Brooks/Cole.

Bolitho, Harold. 1977. *Meiji Japan*. Cambridge: Cambridge University Press.

Bourdieu, Pierre. 1984. *Distinction: A Social Critique of the Judgment of Taste*. Cambridge: Harvard University Press.

———. 1993. *The Field of Cultural Production: Essays on Art and Literature*. New York: Columbia University Press.

Brake, Mike. 1980. *The Sociology of Youth Culture and Youth Subcultures: Sex and Drugs and Rock'n'Roll?* London: Routledge and Kegan Paul.

Brannen, Mary. 1992. "Bawana Mickey: Constructing Cultural Consumption at Tokyo Disneyland." In Joseph Tobin, ed., *Re-made in Japan:*

Everyday Life and Consumer Taste in a Changing Society. New Haven: Yale University Press.

Bruner, Stuart. 1984. *Text, Play, and Story: The Construction and Reconstruction of Self and Society. 1983 Proceedings of the American Anthropological Association.* Washington, D.C.: American Ethnological Society.

Buruma, Ian. 1984. *A Japanese Mirror: Heroes and Villains of Japanese Culture.* London: Penguin Books.

Butler, Judith. 1990. *Gender Trouble: Feminism and the Subversion of Identity.* New York: Routledge.

Certeau, Michel de. 1984. *The Practice of Everyday Life.* Berkeley: University of California Press.

Ching, Leo. 1994. "Imagings in the Empire of the Sun: Japanese Mass Culture in Asia." In Rob Wilson and Alif Dirik, eds., *Boundary 2.* Durham, N.C.: Duke University Press, pp. 198–219.

Chuang, Shu-yu. 1989. "Speed, Infiltration and Occupation." *Commonwealth* 1: 12–21.

Clammer, John. 1995. "Consuming Bodies: Constructing and Representing the Female Body in Contemporary Japanese Print Media." In Lise Skov and Brian Moeran, eds., *Women, Media and Consumption in Japan.* Honolulu: University of Hawai'i Press, pp. 197–219.

———. 1997. *Contemporary Urban Japan: A Sociology of Consumption.* Oxford: Blackwell Publishers.

Cohen, Abner. 1990 [1979]. "Political Symbolism." In Frank E. Manning and Jean-Marc Philbert, eds., *Customs in Conflict: The Anthology of a Changing World.* Peterborough, Ont.: Broadview Press, pp. 28–57.

Coleman, John. 1980. *The Nature of Adolescence.* London: Methuen.

Collier, Jane, Michelle Rosaldo, and Sylvia Yanagisako. 1997. "Is There a Family?: New Anthropological Views." In Roger Lancaster and Micaela di Leonardo, eds., *The Gender Sexuality Reader: Culture, Economy, and Political Economy.* New York: Routledge, pp. 72–81.

Condon, Richard. 1987. *Inuit Youths: Growth and Change in the Canadian Arctic.* New Brunswick, N.J.: Rutgers University Press.

Creighton, Millie. 1990. "Revisiting Shame and Guilt Cultures: A Forty-Year Pilgrimage." *Ethos* 18, 3: 279–305.

———. 1994. "'Edutaining' children: Consumer and Gender Socialization in Japanese Marketing." *Ethnology* 33, 1: 35–52.

———. 1995. "Imaging the Other in Japanese Advertising Campaigns." In James G. Carrier, ed., *Occidentalism: Images of the West.* Oxford: Clarendon Press, pp. 135–60.

———. 1996. "Marriage, Motherhood, and Career Management in a Japanese 'Counter Culture.'" In Anne E. Imamura, ed., *Re-Imaging*

Japanese Women. Berkeley: University of California Press, pp. 192–220.

Dalby, Liza. 1983. *Geisha.* New York: Vintage Books.

Damon, William, and Daniel Hart. 1988. *Self-Understanding in Childhood and Adolescence.* New York: Cambridge University Press.

Davis, Susan, and Douglas Davis. 1989. *Adolescence in a Moroccan Town: Making Social Sense.* New Brunswick, N.J.: Rutgers University Press.

Doi, Takeo. 1973. *The Anatomy of Dependence.* Tokyo: Kōdansha.

Dore, Ronald, and Mari Sako. 1989. *How the Japanese Learn to Work.* London: Routledge.

Eckert, Charles. 1991. "Shirley Temple and the Construction of Authenticity." In Christine Gledhill, ed., *Stardom: Industry of Desire.* London: Routledge, pp. 132–40.

Ellwood, Robert. 1986. "The Several Meanings of Cult." *Thought* 61, 241: 212–24.

Endō, Orie. 1995. "Aspects of Sexism in Language." In Kumiko Fujimura-Fanselow and Atsuko Kameda, eds. *Japanese Women: New Feminist Perspectives on the Past, Present, and Future.* New York: Feminist Press, pp. 29–42.

———. 1997. *Onna no kotoba no bunkashi* (The cultural history of women's language). Tokyo: Gakuyō shobō.

Epstein, Steven. 1987. "Gay Politics, Ethnic Identity: The Limits of Social Construction." *Socialist Review* 93/94: 9–54.

Erikson, Eric. 1968. *Identity: Youth and Crisis.* New York: Norton.

Ewen, Stuart. 1988. *All Consuming Images: The Politics of Style in Contemporary Culture.* New York: Basic Books.

Fiske, John. 1992. "The Cultural Economy of Fandom." In Lisa Lewis, ed., *The Adoring Audience: Fan Culture and Popular Media.* London: Routledge, pp. 30–49.

Frank, Lisa, and Paul Smith, eds. 1993. *Madonnarama: Essays on Sex and Popular Culture.* Pittsburgh: Cleis Press.

Freeman, Derek. 1983. *Margaret Mead and Samoa: The Making and Unmaking of an Anthropological Myth.* Cambridge: Harvard University Press.

Friedman, Jonathan. 1990. "Being in the World: Globalization and Localization." In Mike Featherstone, ed., *Global Culture: Nationalism, Globalization and Modernity.* London: SAGE, pp. 311–28.

Frith, Simon. 1981. *Sound Effects: Youth, Leisure, and the Politics of Rock and Roll.* New York: Pantheon Books.

Fujimura-Fanselow, Kumiko. 1985. "Women's Participation in Japanese Higher Education." *Comparative Education Review* 29, 4: 471–90.

Funabashi, Kuniko. 1995. "Pornographic Culture and Sexual Violence." In Kumiko Fujimura-Fanselow and Atsuko Kameda, eds., *Japanese*

Women: New Feminist Perspectives on the Past, Present, and Future. New York: Feminist Press, pp. 255–63.

Fuss, Diana, ed. 1991. *Inside/Out: Lesbian Theories, Gay Theories.* New York: Routledge.

Geertz, Clifford. 1973. *The Interpretation of Cultures.* New York: Basic Books.

Goffman, Erving. 1959. *Presentation of Self in Everyday Life.* Garden City, N.Y.: Doubleday.

———. 1974. *Frame Analysis: An Essay on the Organization of Experience.* Boston: Northeastern University Press.

Goulding, Jay. 2001. "Tokugawa Japan in 21st Century Japan: Culture and Language in Flux." In Masao Nakamura, ed., *Japan in the Global Age: Cultural, Historical and Political Issues on Asia, Environment, Households, and International Communication.* Vancouver: Center for Japanese Research, University of British Columbia, pp. 159–73.

Gumperz, John. 1976. *The Sociolinguistic Significance of Conversational Code-Switching.* Berkeley: University of California Press.

Hadi, Soesastro. 1995. "Pacific Economic Cooperation: The History of an Idea." In Ross Garnaut and Peter Drysdale, eds., *Asia Pacific Regionalism.* Sydney: Harpers Educational, pp. 77–88.

Hall, Stanley. 1904. *Adolescence: Its Psychology and Its Relation to Physiology, Anthropology, Sex, Crime, Religion and Education.* New York: Appleton.

Hall, Stuart. 1980. "Encoding and Decoding." In Stuart Hall and Dorothy Hobson, eds., *Culture, Media, and Language.* London: Hutchinson, pp. 128–38.

Hall, Stuart, and Tony Jefferson, eds. 1976. *Resistance Through Rituals: Youth Subcultures in Post-War Britain.* London: Hutchinson.

Hamaguchi Eshun. 1977. *Nihonrashisa no saihakken* (The rediscovery of Japaneseness). Tokyo: Nihon keizai shinbunsha.

Hara, Kimi. 1995. "Challenges to Education for Girls and Women in Modern Japan: Past and Present." In Kumiko Fujimura-Fanselow and Atsuko Kameda, eds., *Japanese Women: New Feminist Perspectives on the Past, Present, and Future.* New York: Feminist Press, pp. 93–106.

Haraway, Donna. 1991. *Simians, Cyborgs, and Women: The Reinvention of Nature.* New York: Routledge.

Hardacre, Helen. 1997. *Marketing the Menacing Fetus in Japan.* Berkeley: University of California Press.

Harvey, David. 1985. *Consciousness and the Urban Experience: Studies in the History and Theory of Capitalist Urbanization.* Baltimore: John Hopkins University Press.

Hatley, Barbara. 1990. "Theatrical Imagery and Gender Ideology in Java." In Monnig Atkinson and Shelly Errington, eds., *Power and Difference: Gender in Island Southeast Asia*. Stanford: Stanford University Press, pp. 177–207.

Haug, Wolfgang. 1986. *Critique of Commodity Aesthetics: Appearance, Sexuality and Advertising in Capitalist Society*. Minneapolis: University of Minnesota Press.

Hayashi, Makiko. 1998. "Alternative Images of Young Japanese Women in a Changing Society." Unpublished research paper.

Hayashi Takumi. 1994. "Ajia no otaku genshō: Higashi Shinakai no mu-kō" (Lunatic phenomena in Asia: beyond the East China Sea). In *Warera no jidai* (Our era). Tokyo: Takarajimasha, pp. 154–67.

Hebdige, Dick. 1979. *Subculture: The Meaning of Style*. London: Methuen.

Hendry, Joy. 1993. *Wrapping Culture: Politeness, Presentation and Power in Japan and Other Societies*. Oxford: Clarendon Press.

———. 1995. *Understanding Japanese Society*. London. Routledge.

Herd, Judith. 1984. "Trends and Taste in Japanese Popular Music: A Case-Study of the 1984 Yamaha World Popular Music Festival." *Popular Music* 4: 75–96.

Higgins, Edward. 1987. "Self-discrepancy: A Theory Relating Self and Affect." *Psychological Review* 94: 319–40.

Hollos, Marida, and Philip Leis. 1989. *Becoming Nigerian in Ijo Society*. New Brunswick, N.J.: Rutgers University Press.

Hooks, Bell. 1992. "Madonna: Plantation Mistress or Soul Sister?" In Bell Hooks, ed., *Black Looks: Race and Representation*. Boston: South End Press, pp. 157–64.

Hsu, Francis. 1953. *American and Chinese*. New York: Schuman.

Hutcheon, Linda. 1989. *The Politics of Postmodernism*. London: Routledge.

Inamasu Tatsuo. 1989. *Aidoru kōgaku* (Idol engineering). Tokyo: Chikuma shobō.

Inoue Kōzō. 1996. *Kagami no naka no Seiko* (Seiko in the mirror). Tokyo: Asuka shinsha.

Ito, Takatoshi. 1992. *The Japanese Economy*. Cambridge: The MIT Press.

Ivy, Marilyn. 1988. "Tradition and Difference in the Japanese Mass Media." *Public Culture Bulletin* 1, 1: 21–29.

Iwabuchi, Koichi. 2002. *Recentering Globalization: Popular Culture and Japanese Transnationalism*. Durham, N.C.: Duke University Press.

Jameson, Frederic. 1984. "Postmodernism, or the Cultural Logic of Late Capitalism." *New Left Review* 146: 53–92.

Jansen, Marius. 1980. *Japan and Its World: Two Centuries of Change*. Princeton: Princeton University Press.

Jenkins, Henry. 1992. *Textual Poachers: Television Fans and Participatory Culture.* New York: Routledge.

Joseigaku kenkyūkai, ed. 1987. *Onna no me de miru: kōza kyōiku 4* (Seeing through women's eyes: lectures on women's studies 4). Tokyo.

Jourdan, Christine. 1995. "Masta Liu." In Vered Amit-Talai and Helena Wulff, eds., *Youth Culture: A Cross-Cultural Perspective.* London: Routledge, pp. 202–22.

Kameda, Atsuko. 1995. "Sexism and Gender Stereotyping in Schools." In Kumiko Fujimura-Fanselow and Atsuko Kameda, eds., *Japanese Women: New Feminist Perspectives on the Past, Present, and Future.* New York: Feminist Press, pp. 107–24.

Kanda Noriko. 1986. *Seiko.* Tokyo: Shōgakkan.

Kaneko, Sachiko. 1995. "The Struggle for Legal Rights and Reforms: A Historical View." In Kumiko Fujimura-Fanselow and Atsuko Kameda, eds., *Japanese Women: New Feminist Perspectives on the Past, Present, and Future.* New York: Feminist Press, pp. 3–14.

Kaplan, E. Ann. 1988. *Postmodernism and Its Discontents: Theories, Practices.* London: Verso.

Karasawa Shun'ichi. 1995. *Bishōjo no gyakushū: yomigaere!! kokoro kiyoi, yogore naki, kedakaki shōjo-tachi yo* (The counterattack of girls: revive!! pure-hearted, clean, and noble girls). Tokyo: Nesuko.

Kawai Hayao. 1994. *Seishun no yume to asobi* (Adolescent's dreams and plays). Tokyo: Iwanami shoten.

Kawakami Hideo. 1995. *Gekidō-suru Asia ongakushijō* (Upheaval in the Asian music market). Tokyo: Cinema House.

Kawanobe Shizuki and Seiko Matsuda Special Team. 1994. *Matsuda Seiko onna kakumei* (Seiko Matsuda: a woman's liberation). Tokyo: Wani magajinsha.

Kawashima, Yūko. 1995. "Female Workers: An Overview of Past and Current Trends." In Kumiko Fujimura-Fanselow and Atsuko Kameda, eds., *Japanese Women: New Feminist Perspectives on the Past, Present, and Future.* New York: Feminist Press, pp. 271–93.

Kaya, Emiko. 1995. "Mitsui Mariko: An Avowed Feminist Assemblywoman." In Kumiko Fujimura-Fanselow and Atsuko Kameda, eds., *Japanese Women: New Feminist Perspectives on the Past, Present, and Future.* New York: Feminist Press, pp. 384–92.

Kelsky, Karen. 1996. "The Gender Politics of Women's Internationalism in Japan." *International Journal of Politics, Culture, and Society* 10, 1: 29–50.

Kinsella, Sharon. 1995. "Cuties in Japan." In Lise Skov and Brian Moeran, eds., *Women, Media and Consumption in Japan.* Honolulu: University of Hawai'i Press, pp. 220–54.

———. 1998. "Japanese Subculture in the 1990s: *Otaku* and the Amateur *Manga* Movement." *Journal of Japanese Studies* 24, 2: 289–316.

———. 2000. *Adult Manga: Culture and Power in Contemporary Japanese Society.* Honolulu: University of Hawai'i Press.

Kiyotani Shin'ichi. 1998. *Le Otaku: France otaku-jijō* (*Le Otaku*: the condition of *otaku* in France). Tokyo: Best Sellers.

Kōdansha. 1993. *Japan: An Illustrated Encyclopedia.* Tokyo.

Koga Sei'ichi. 1996. *The Best Mook Series-61: The Best Super Photo: Oscar Promotion.* Tokyo: K.K. Best Sellers.

Kondo, Dorinne. 1990. *Crafting Selves: Power, Gender, and Discourses of Identity in a Japanese Workplace.* Chicago: University of Chicago Press.

———. 1992. "The Aesthetics and Politics of Japanese Identity." In Joseph Tobin, ed., *Remade in Japan: Everyday Life and Consumer Taste in a Changing Society.* New Haven: Yale University Press, pp. 176–203.

Konoshi Takamitsu. 1994. "Nihon shinwa nyūmon: kuniumi / kunizukuri" (Introduction to Japanese myths: giving birth to the land/ creating the land). *Kokubungaku* 39, 6: 115–37.

Kumon, Shunpei. 1982. "Some Thoughts Concerning the Behavior of Japanists Contextualists." *Journal of Japanese Studies* 8: 5–28.

Lanham, Betty. 1979. "Ethics and Moral Precepts Taught in Schools of Japan and the United States." *Ethos* 7, 1: 1–18.

Leahy, Robert. 1985. *The Development of the Self.* Orlando, Fla.: Academic Press.

Lebra, Takie. 1976. *Japanese Patterns of Behavior.* Honolulu: University of Hawai'i Press.

Leemon, Thomas. 1972. *The Rites of Passage in a Student Culture.* New York: Teachers College Press.

Lewis, David. 1993. "Religious Rites in a Japanese factory." In Mark Mullins, Susumu Shimazono, and Paul Swanson, eds., *Religion and Society in Modern Japan: Selected Readings.* Berkeley: Asian Humanities Press, pp. 157–70.

Lewis, Lisa. 1990. *Gender Politics and MTV: Voicing the Difference.* Philadelphia: Temple University Press.

Lindholm, Charles. 1995. "Love as an Experience of Transcendence." In William Jankowiak, ed., *Romantic Passion: A Universal Experience?* New York: Columbia University Press, pp. 57–71.

MacKinnon, Catherine. 1989. *Towards a Feminist Theory of the State.* Cambridge: Harvard University Press.

Malinowski, Bronislaw. 1922. *Argonauts of the Western Pacific.* New York: Dutton.

Marica, James. 1966. "Development and Validation of Ego-Identity Status." *Journal of Personality and Social Psychology* 3: 551–59.

——. 1967. "Ego-Identity Status: Relationship to Change in Self-esteem, 'General Maladjustment,' and 'Authoritarianism.'" *Journal of Personality* 35: 118–33.

Maslow, Abraham. 1962. *Towards a Psychology of Being.* Princeton: Van Nostrand.

Matsuda Seiko. 1980. *Ryōte de Seiko* (Seiko in both arms). Tokyo: Shūeisha.

——. 1981. *Mō ichido anata* (You once again). Tokyo: Wani Books.

——. 1982. *Seiko 20-sai: ai to uta no seishunfu* (Seiko 20 year-old: a youthful chronicle on love and music). Tokyo: Shōnen gahōsha.

McGee, Terry, and Raymond Watters. 1997. "Introduction." In McGee and Watters, eds., *Asia-Pacific: New Geographies of the Pacific Rim.* Vancouver: University of British Columbia Press, pp. 1–12.

McNay, Lois. 1992. *Foucault and Feminism.* Boston: Northeastern University Press.

McRobbie, Angela. 1984. "Dance and Social Fantasy." In Angela McRobbie and Mica Nava, eds., *Gender and Generation.* London: Macmillan, pp. 130–61.

Mead, George. 1962 [1934]. *Mind, Self, and Society from the Standpoint of a Social Behaviorist.* Chicago: University of Chicago Press.

Mead, Margaret. 1928. *Coming of Age in Samoa.* New York: William Morris.

Merleau-Ponty, Maurice. 1960. *Signes.* Paris: Gallimard.

Miller, Daniel. 1997. *Capitalism: An Ethnographic Approach.* Oxford: Berg.

Mills, C. Wright. 1956. *The Power Elite.* London: Oxford University Press.

Miyadai Shinji. 1994. *Seifuku shōjo-tachi no sentaku* (The selection for girls in uniform). Tokyo: Kōdansha.

Miyoshi, Masao, and Harry Harootunian. 1989. *Postmodernism and Japan.* Durham, N.C.: Duke University Press.

Moeran, Brian. 1986. "Individual, Group and *Seishin*: Japan's Internal Cultural Debate." In Takie E. Lebra and William P. Lebra, eds., *Japanese Culture and Behavior.* Honolulu: University of Hawai'i Press, pp. 62–79.

Mouer, Ross, and Yoshio Sugimoto. 1986. *Images of Japanese Society: A Study in the Social Construction of Reality.* London: Kegan Paul International.

Mukerji, Chandra, and Michael Schudson. 1991. "Rethinking Popular Culture." In Chandra Mukerji and Michael Schudson, eds., *Rethinking Popular Culture: Contemporary Perspectives in Cultural Studies.* Berkeley: University of California Press, pp. 1–61.

Murakami, Yasusuke, and Thomas Rohlen. 1992. "Social Exchange Aspects of the Japanese Policitcal Economy: Culture, Efficiency and Change." In Shumpei Kumon and Henry Rosovsky, eds., *The Political*

Economy of Japan, vol. 3, *Cultural and Social Dynamics*. Stanford: Stanford University Press, pp. 63–105.

Naitō Masanobu and the Pop-Idol Evaluation Committee. 1994. "Zoku tarento no senzaiteki shōhin-nōryoku ha'aku no kokoromi" (An attempt to grasp the latent commodity power of talents, continued). Unpublished manuscript. Tokyo: Dentsū.

Nakajima Azusa. 1995. *Komyunikeeshon funen shōkōgun* (The imperfect combustion syndrome in communication). Tokyo: Chikuma shobō.

Nelson, John. 1996. *A Year in the Life of a Shinto Shrine*. Seattle: University of Washington Press.

Noonan, William. 1996. "Western Hospitalization for Surgery as 'Rite of Passage.'" In Michael Aune and Valerie DeMartinis, eds., *Religious and Social Ritual*. New York: State University of New York Press, pp. 293–313.

Ochiai Emiko. 1989. *Kindai kazoku to feminizumu* (The modern family and feminism). Tokyo: Keisō shobō.

———. 1997. *The Japanese Family System in Transition*. Tokyo: LTCB International Library.

Ogawa Hiroshi. 1988. *Ongaku-suru shakai* (A musical society). Tokyo: Keisō shobō.

Ogura Chikako. 1988. "Feminizumu kara mita Momoe to Seiko no kigō-ron" (The semiotics of Momoe and Seiko from the perspective of feminism). *Nenkan Asahi Journal, 1988*: 1284–87.

———. 1989. *Matsuda Seiko ron* (A treatise on Seiko Matsuda). Tokyo: Asuka shinsha.

———. 1990. *Aidoru jidai no shinwa* (Myths in the age of idols). Tokyo: Asahi shinbunsha.

Ohinata, Masami. 1995. "The Mystique of Motherhood: A Key to Understanding Social Change and Family Problems in Japan." In Kumiko Fujimura-Fanselow and Atsuko Kameda, eds., *Japanese Women: New Feminist Perspectives on the Past, Present, and Future*. New York: Feminist Press, pp. 199–211.

Ohnuki-Tierney, Emiko. 1990. "The Ambivalent Self of the Contemporary Japanese." *Cultural Anthropology* 5, 2: 197–216.

Okada Toshio. 1996. *Otakugaku nyūmon* (Introduction to otakuology). Tokyo: Ōta shuppan.

———. 1997. *Tōdai otakugaku kōza* (A Tokyo University course on otakuology). Tokyo: Kōdansha.

Okonogi Keigo. 1981. *Moratorium ningen no jidai* (The age of moratorium). Tokyo: Chūkō bunko.

———. 1985. *Moratorium ningen o kangaeru* (Some thoughts concerning moratorium people). Tokyo: Chūkō bunko.

Ōtsuka Eiji. 1989. *Shōjo minzokugaku: seikimatsu no shinwa o tsumugu miko no matsuei* (The folklore of girls: descendants of maidens who spin the wheel of legend at the end of the century). Tokyo: Kōbunsha.

———. 1990. "Bikkuriman to ten'nōsei" (Bikkuriman and the imperial system). *Chūō kōron* 104, 6: 310–18.

Ōuchi, William. 1981. *Theory Z: How American Business Can Meet the Japanese Challenge*. Addison-Wesley.

Paige, Karen, and Jeffrey Paige. 1981. *The Politics of Reproductive Ritual*. Berkeley: University of California Press.

Peacock, James. 1968. *Rites of Modernization: Symbolic and Social Aspects of Indonesian Proletarian Drama*. Chicago: University of Chicago Press.

PHP Research Center, ed. 1995. *Sūji de miru sengo gojūnen no ayumi: seiji, keizai, sangyō, seikatsu* (Looking at the course of Japan during the fifty postwar years through numbers: politics, economy, industry, and living). Tokyo.

Portelli, Alessandro. 1991. *The Death of Luigi Trastulli and Other Stories: Form and Meaning in Oral History*. Albany: State University of New York Press.

Rappaport, Roy. 1999. *Ritual and Religion in the Making of Humanity*. Cambridge: Cambridge University Press.

Richardson, James. 1996. "Definitions of Cult: From Sociological-Technical to Popular-Negative." In Lorne Dawson, ed., *Cults in Context: Readings in the Study of New Religious Movements*. Toronto: Canadian Scholars' Press, pp. 29–38.

Richardson, James, and Dick Anthony. 1982. "Deprogramming, Brainwashing and the Medicalization of Deviant Religious Groups." *Social Problems* 29: 283–97.

Robertson, Jennifer. 1998. *Takarazuka: Sexual Politics and Popular Culture in Modern Japan*. Berkeley: University of California Press.

Robins-Mowry, Dorothy. 1983. *The Hidden Sun: Women of Modern Japan*. Boulder, Colo.: Westview Press.

Rohlen, Thomas. 1974. *For Harmony and Strength: Japanese White-Collar Organization in Anthropological Perspective*. Berkeley: University of California Press.

———. 1986. "'Spiritual Education' in a Japanese Bank." In Takie S. Lebra and William P. Lebra, eds., *Japanese Culture and Behavior*. Honolulu: University of Hawai'i Press, pp. 307–35.

———. 1988. "Education System in Japan." In Daniel I. Okimito and Thomas P. Rohlen, eds., *Inside the Japanese System: Readings on Contemporary Society and Political Economy*. Stanford: Stanford University Press, pp. 137–57.

Rosenberger, Nancy. 1992. "Introduction." In Nancy R. Rosenberger, ed., *Japanese Sense of Self*. Cambridge: Cambridge University Press, pp. 1–20.

———. 1995. "Antiphonal Performances?: Japanese Women's Magazines and Women's Voices." In Lise Skov and Brian Moeran, eds., *Women, Media and Consumption in Japan*. Honolulu: University of Hawai'i Press, pp. 143–69.

———. 1996. "Fragile Resistance, Signs of Status: Women Between State and Media in Japan." In Anne E. Imamura, ed., *Re-Imaging Japanese Women*. Berkeley: University of California Press, pp. 12–45.

Sasakura Naoko and Satomi Nakajima. 1990. *Onna ga seiji o kaeru* (Women change the politics). Tokyo: Gakuyō shobō.

Satō Atsuhiro. 1991. *Shōnen* (Young boy). Tokyo: Shūeisha.

Satō, Ikuya. 1991. *Kamikaze Biker: Parody and Anomy in Affluent Japan*. Chicago: University of Chicago Press.

Satō, Yōko. 1995. "From the Home to the Political Arena." In Kumiko Fujimura-Fanselow and Atsuko Kameda, eds., *Japanese Women: New Feminist Perspectives on the Past, Present, and Future*. New York: Feminist Press, pp. 365–72.

Schiffer, Michael B. 1991. *The Portable Radio in American Life*. Tucson: University of Arizona Press.

Schlegel, Alice. 1973. "The Adolescent Socialization of the Hopi Girl." *Ethnology* 4: 449–62.

Schlegel, Alice, and Herbert Barry III. 1991. *Adolescence: An Anthropological Inquiry*. New York: Free Press.

Schwichtenberg, Cathy, ed. 1993. *The Madonna Connection: Representational Politics, Subcultural Identities, and Cultural Theory*. Boulder, Colo.: Westview Press.

Scott, Adolph. 1955. *The Kabuki Theatre of Japan*. London: George Allen & Unwin.

Seigle, Cecilia. 1993. *Yoshiwara: The Glittering World of the Japanese Courtesan*. Honolulu: University of Hawai'i Press.

Seymour, Christopher. 1996. *Yakuza Diary: Doing Time in the Japanese Underworld*. New York: Atlantic Monthly Press.

Shibamoto, Janet. 1985. *Japanese Women's Language*. San Diego: Academic Press.

Shils, Edward. 1965. "Charisma, Order and Status." *American Sociological Review* 30: 199–213.

Sievers, Sharon. 1983. *Flowers in Salt: The Beginnings of Feminist Consciousness in Meiji Japan*. Stanford: Stanford University Press.

Silverberg, Miriam. 1991. "The Modern Girl as Militant." In Gail L. Bernstein, ed., *Recreating Japanese Women, 1600–1945*. Berkeley: University of California Press, pp. 239–66.

Simpson, Amelia. 1993. *Xuxa: The Mega Marketing of Gender, Race, and Modernity.* Philadelphia: Temple University Press.

Singleton, John. 1989. "Japanese Folkcraft Pottery Apprenticeship: Cultural Patterns of an Educational Institution." In Michael Coy, ed., *Apprenticeship: From Theory to Method and Back Again.* Albany: State University of New York Press, pp. 13–30.

Smith, Robert. 1983. *Japanese Society: Tradition, Self, and the Social Order.* Cambridge: Cambridge University Press.

Sofue, Takao. 1965. "Childhood Ceremonies in Japan." *Ethnology* 4: 148–64.

Strathern, Marilyn. 1981. "Self-Interest and the Social Good: Some Implications of Hagen Gender Imagery." In Sherry Ortner and Harriet Whitehead, eds., *Sexual Meanings: The Cultural Construction of Gender and Sexuality.* Cambridge: Cambridge University Press, pp. 166–91.

Suzuki, Hikaru. 2000. *The Price of Death: The Funeral Industry in Contemporary Japan.* Stanford: Stanford University Press.

Suzuki, Midori. 1995. "Women and Television: Portrayal of Women in the Mass Media." In Kumiko Fujimura-Fanselow and Atsuko Kameda, eds., *Japanese Women: New Feminist Perspectives on the Past, Present, and Future.* New York: Feminist Press, pp. 75–91.

Suzuki, Takao. 1976. "Language and Behavior in Japan: The Conceptualization of Personal Relations." *Japan Quarterly* 23, 3: 255–66.

Takayanagi, Nariko. 1995. "A Cross-Cultural Comparison of Women's Magazines in Japan and North America." Unpublished master's thesis, University of British Columbia.

Tanaka Sumiko, ed. 1975. *Josei kaihō no shisō to kōdō: sengo hen* (The thoughts and activities of women's liberation: the postwar edition). Tokyo: Jiji tsūshinsha.

Tanaka, Yukiko. 1995. *Contemporary Portraits of Japanese Women.* Westport, Conn.: Praeger Publishers.

Tanioka, Ichirō, and Daniel Glaser. 1991. "School Uniforms, Routine Activities, and the Social Control of Delinquency in Japan." *Youth and Society* 23, 1: 50–75.

Taussig, Michael. 1980. *Devil and Commodity Fetishism in South America.* Chapel Hill: University of North Carolina Press.

Tobin, Joseph, ed. 1992. *Re-made in Japan: Everyday Life and Consumer Taste in a Changing Society.* New Haven: Yale University Press.

Tomosaka Rie. 1997. "Tomosaka wa futsū desu yo, futsū no hito yori jimi kamo shiremasen" (Tomosaka is ordinary, perhaps much more plain than the ordinary people). In Masahiro Kitagawa and T. P. Ranking, eds., *Nippon aidoru tanteidan '97* (*Japan Idol Detectives '97*). Tokyo: Takarajimasha, pp. 118–19.

Turner, Victor. 1982. *From Ritual to Theatre: The Human Seriousness of Play*. New York: PAJ Publications.

Ueno, Chizuko. 1987. "The Position of Japanese Women Reconsidered." *Current Anthropology* 28, 4: 75–84.

Umezawa Nobuyoshi. 1984. *Shōhisha niizu o hitto shōhin ni shiageru hō* (How to turn consumer needs into hit-products). Tokyo: Daiamond sha.

Uno, Kathleen. 1993. "Death of 'Good Wife, Wise Mother'?" In Andrew Gordon, ed., *Postwar Japan as History*. Berkeley: University of California Press, pp. 293–322.

Van der Linden, Frans. 1991. *Adolescent Lifeworld: Theoretical and Empirical Orientations in Socialization Processes of Dutch Youth*. Amsterdam: Swets and Zeitlinger.

Watsuji Tetsuro. 1935. *Rinrigaku* (Ethics). Tokyo: Iwanami shoten.

Weber, Max. 1958. *The Protestant Ethic and the Spirit of Capitalism*. New York: Charles Scribner's Sons.

———. 1968. *On Charisma and Institution Building: Selected Papers*. Ed. S. N. Eisenstadt. Chicago: University of Chicago Press.

Weiner, Michael. 1997. "The Representation of Absence and the Absence of Representation: Korean Victims of the Atomic Bomb." In Michael Weiner, ed., *Japan's Minority: The Illusion of Homogeneity*. London: Routledge, pp. 79–107.

White, Merry. 1993. *The Material Child: Coming of Age in Japan and America*. New York: Free Press.

———. 1995. "The Marketing of Adolescence in Japan: Buying and Dreaming." In Lise Skov and Brian Moeran, eds., *Women, Media and Consumption in Japan*. Honolulu: University of Hawai'i Press, pp. 225–73.

Whittaker, Elvi. 1992. "The Birth of the Anthropological Self and Its Career." *Ethos* 20: 191–219.

Wilk, Richard. 1990. "Consumer Goods as Dialogue About Development: Research in Progress in Belize." *Culture and History* 7: 79–100.

———. 1995. "Learning to Be Local in Belize: Global Systems of Common Difference." In Daniel Miller, ed., *Worlds Apart: Modernity Through the Prism of the Local*. London: Routledge, pp. 110–33.

Willis, Paul. 1977. *Learning to Labor: How Working Class Kids Get Working Class Jobs*. Farnborough, Eng.: Saxon House.

Wulff, Helena. 1995. "Introducing Youth Culture in Its Own Right: The State of the Art and New Possibilities." In Vered Amit-Talai and Helena Wulff, eds., *Youth Culture: A Cross-Cultural Perspective*. London: Routledge, pp. 1–18.

Yamada, Haru. 1990. "Topic Shifts in American and Japanese Conversations." *Georgetown Journal of Languages and Linguistics* 1, 2: 249–56.

Yamane Kazuma. 1986. *Hentai shōjo moji no kenkyū* (An anomalous research of teenage handwriting). Tokyo: Kōdansha.

————. 1990. *Gyaru no kōzō* (The structure of gals). Tokyo: Sekai bunka-sha.

Yang, Jeff; Dina Gan; and Terry Hong. 1997. *Eastern Standard Time: A Guide to Asian Influence on American Culture from Astroboy to Zen Buddhism.* New York: Houghton Mifflin.

Yano, Christine. 1997. "Charisma's Realm: Fandom in Japan." *Ethnology* 36, 4: 335–49.

Yasuda Takeshi. 1984. *Kata no Nihonbunka* (The Japanese culture of forms). Tokyo: Asahi shinbunsha.

Yoshida Yutaka. 1984. "Seijukuki ni haitta kodomo-shijō" (Junior market that entered the period of maturity). *Shōgyōkai,* no. 2190: 115–20.

Yoshino, Kosaku. 1998. "Culturalism, Racism, and Internationalism in the Discourse on Japanese Identity." In Dru C. Gladney, ed., *Making Majorities: Constituting the Nation in Japan, Korea, China, Malaysia, Fiji, Turkey, and the United States.* Stanford: Stanford University Press, pp. 13–30.

Yoshizumi, Kyōko. 1995. "Marriage and Family: Past and Present." In Kumiko Fujimura-Fanselow and Atsuko Kameda, eds., *Japanese Women: New Feminist Perspectives on the Past, Present, and Future.* New York: Feminist Press, pp. 183–97.

Young, Frank. 1965. *Initiation Ceremonies: A Cross-Cultural Study of Status Dramatization.* Indianapolis: Bobbs-Merrill.

Zarrilli, Phillip. 1990. "What Does It Mean to 'Become the Character': Power, Presence, and Transcendence in Asian In-body Disciplines of Practice." In Richard Schechner and Willa Appel, eds., *By Means of Performance: Intercultural Studies of Theatre and Ritual.* Cambridge: Cambridge University Press, pp. 131–48.

Index

Abortion, 13–14, 92

Adolescence, 56–66 *passim*, 192; agency, 57; Euro-American analyses, 58, 61–62; femaleness, 107, 109, 112, 120, 260; Japan, 59–66 *passim*; *seishun-jidai*, 62; and sexuality, 65–66n5

Adult, *see Seijin*

Affluence, 241

Aidagara (interpersonal relationships), 25

Aidoru, see Idol

Aidoru o sagase, 5

Aidoru tanteidan (Idol detectives), 54

Aizawa, Hideyoshi, 67, 139–44 *passim*, 240

Akogare (longing), 202

Allison, Anne, 124n17, 172

Amae, 26, 187

Amuraa (followers of Namie Amuro), 101

Amuro, Namie, 101, 113, 118–20, 122, 163

Androgyny, 16

Aoyagi, Hiroshi, 145–58 *passim*. See *also* Fieldwork

APEC (Asian-Pacific Economic Cooperation), 236, 236n2, 236n3, 257

Asahi shinbun, 41, 83, 97

ASEAN (Association of Southeast Asian Nations), 236, 236n3, 239

Asia, 262, 266; idols, 265–66. *See also* Hong Kong; Idols

Back Street Boys, 4, 266

Bacon, Francis, 31, 266

Barnouw, Francis, 84

Barral, Etienne, 206

Bauman, Richard, 167–68

Beauty, 132

Benedict, Ruth, 178

Bethe, Monica, 28–29

Bi (beauty), 132; *shūdan-bi*, 160. See *also* Oscar Promotion, Inc.

Bikkuriman Chocolate, 128–29. *See also* Ōtsuka, Eiji

Bodikon fashion, 140

Bomb! (magazine), 69, 72, 180, 181

Bōsōzoku (speed tribes), 100

Bourdieu, Pierre, 18, 126–27

Brazell, Karen, 28–29

Butler, Judith, 27

Burriko, 74, 98; *buri-buri ishō* (fake child costumes), 76; *manga*, 210

Canada, 145, 149

Canton-pop, 247–48, 254

Capitalism, 12, 13, 16, 193, 246, 264

Certeau, Michel de, 46n8
Chants, *see* "cheering" *under* Idol
Charisma, 25, 30, 34, 35n7
Cherchez L'idole, 4
Chiba, Mika, 238
Childlike, 82, 181–82, 184. *See also* Cute; Matsuda, Seiko
China, 234–35, 238–41, 246, 251
Ching, Leo, 255
Chūsonji, Yukko, 100. *See also* Oyajigyaru
Clammer, John, 125, 263
Coleman, John, 61
Commodity, 44; advertised, 137; fetishism, 11–15, 43, 46
Consumer, 3, 11; consciousness, 244; consumer culture, 44, 254; *manga*, 207; society, 3, 12, 31, 37, 43, 45, 257, 261–62
Consumerism, 15
Consumption, 16, 44, 45, 46 *passim*, 127, 237, 263, 265; idol, 17, 127, 205–31, 255–56; NIEs, 256. *See also* Otaku
Cool, *see* "style" *under* Idol
Corporate institutions, 48–49
Creighton, Millie, 145–46, 160n5, 253n8
Cute, 73–78, 81–82, 88, 121, 140–42, 235; handwriting, 140; idol training 111–13; speech, 140; versus sexuality, 120–21. *See also* Kawaii; Sakai, Noriko
Cute style, *see* Cute
Cutesy, *see* Cute
Cyberspace, *see* Internet

Dance, 115–20
Dentsū, 136
Disney, 74, 82, *See also* Funiciello, Annette

DoCoMo, 1
Dream (song), see Hikaru Genji

Eckert, Charles, 36
Education, Ministry of, 60, 91, 93, 151
Enjo-kōsai, 102
Enka, 37, 262
Epstein, Steven, 27
Equal Employment Opportunity Law (EEOL), 93, 140
Eugenic Protection Law (1948), 92
Ewen, Stuart, 127n1
Exotic Japan, 146. *See also* Ivy, Marilyn

Fans, 41, 72, 161–62, 204–5, 219–20; identity, 262; *ijō* (abnormal), 262; internet interactions, 212–14; publishing, 222–25 *passim*; surrogate, 159. *See also* Otaku; "fans" *under* Idol
Fantajii (fantasies), 264
Fear of Flying, see Jong, Erica
Fieldwork, 20, 38–41 *passim*, 50, 64–65, 70; access, 50–55; among fans, 130–31, 161–64; production project, 144–58 *passim*; Hong Kong, 246
Financially aided affairs, *see Enjo-kōsai*
Fiske, John, 207
Freeman, Derek, 57n1
Friedman, Jonathan, 237, 256
Funiciello, Annette, 74
Furin (extramarital affairs), 195
Fūzoku (sex trade), 151

Gankuro, 99, 102–3
Geertz, Clifford, 37
Geinōkai (entertainment world), 46

Gender, 86–88; identity, 27; ideology, 17, 90–95; language, 104; mass media, 94–95
Genji monogatari (The tale of Genji), 133
Giri/on, 187
Goffman, Irving, 27
Good wife, wise mother, *see Ryōsai kenbo*
Gossip, 178–79
Gyaru, 89, 98

Hall, Stewart, 204, 257
Harada, Toshihiko, 78–79
Hardacre, Helen, 10n2, 13–14
Harvey, David, 9
Haug, Wolfgang, 44
Health, Ministry of, 73
Hendry, Joy, 60
Herd, Judith, 37, 67
Hikaru Genji, 80
Hirosue, Ryōko, 1–2
Hong Kong, 96, 234, 238–39, 244–54 *passim*, 253n9
Honne/tatemae, 26, 62
Hori Agency, 238

Identity, 27
Idol, 3–11, 30–31, 265–66; advertisement, 49, 136; autographs, 70, 216–17; boom, 49, 82; cheering, 72, 198–200; chasers (*aidoru okkake*), 72; concerts, 225–29; companion, 67–68; competition, 49, 150, 159, 164–65; cult, 206–10 *passim*, 216, 230; dance, 114–17; etymology, 30–31, 86; fad, 7; fans, 41, 47, 72, 161–64 *passim*, 204–30 *passim*, 262; fanzine, 222–24; fetishism, 217–22 *passim*, 229–31: genealogies, 129–30; gift giving, 227, 230; goods (*aidoru guzzu*), 4; governmental campaigns, 159–64; groupies, 9; headhunting, 47–48; hierarchy, 163; "homegrown," 23, 245, 248; Idol Net, 212–15; intimacy, 68–70; imitation, 126; Japanese-style, 23, 232, 237, 240–44 *passim*, 253–54; magazines, 65, 72, 86; male, 78–79, 89–90, 137–38; manufacture industry, 2; motif dissemination, 251, 255–56, 262; music, 9, 78–81 *passim*, 142; "packaging," 18, 86, 88, 139; performance, 4, 28, 29, 30, 70, 115–20, 264; personifiers, 67; political role, 241–42; post-bubble recession, 83–84; promotion agencies, 21, 34, 46–51 *passim*, 113, 132, 185, 214, 234; recruitment process, 105–7, 145; role models, 3, 87–88, 193; romance, 78–81 *passim*; scouts, 47, 105; sexuality, 78–79, 170; sexual objectification, 77; sexual style, 118–19; sponsorship, 49; status marker, 248; style, 75–76, 111–12, 126, 128–31 *passim*, 159, 166, 262; symbolism, 128; taxonomies, 131–32; training, 107–13 *passim*; transformation of, 168, 192; value, 34, 126. *See also* Cute; *individual ministries by name*; Internet; *Karuto*; Kimura, Takuya; *Kyonyū aidoru;* Matsuda, Seiko; Purity; Sexy; Skinship; SMAP
Idolian, 217. *See also* Fans; *Otaku*
"Idology," 19
Ikigai (meaning of life), 169
Inamasu, Tatsuo, 37
Innocence, 140. *See also* Childlike
Internationalization, 169, 197

Internet, 71, 212–14, 235. *See also* "Idol Net" *under* Idol
Ivy, Marilyn, 146
Iwabuchi, Koichi, 266

Jenkins, Henry, 46n8
Jishukisei, see Self
Johnny's, 6, 133
Jong, Erika, 96

Kamachi, Noriko, *see* Matsuda, Seiko
Kamera kozō (camera kids), 70
Karaoke, 7
Karuto (cult), 208–10. *See also under* Idol
Kata, 28–29, 91, 116, 120
Kawaii, 74, 121. *See also* Cute
Kazoku kokka (family state), 91
Keiretsu, 46
Kelsky, Karen, 197
Kimura, Takuya, 137–38. *See also* SMAP
Kinsella, Sharon, 81–82, 125, 142, 206–7, 229
Kinship, 143–44
Kirkland, Catherine, 84
Kiyotani, Shin'ichi, 206
Kogyaru, 99, 102, 104–5, 217
Kojiki, 128, 129
Kokoro, 131
Komiketto (comic market), 207, 210
Kondo, Dorinne, 200n9
Kuchi-komi (rumors), 178
Kyonyū aidoru (large-breast idols), 133, 134

Lauper, Cyndi, 170n4
LDP (Liberal Democratic Party), 92
Lebra, Takie, 190

Lewis, Lisa, 204
Lolicom manga, 211
Lolita, 150, 219–20

Madonna, 36, 170n4, 196
Magazines, *see under Boom!*; Idol; *Momoco*
Malinowski, Bronislaw, 38
Manga (comics), 206, 229; artists, 210. *See also Otaku*
Marketing, 131, 232. *See also under* Idol
Marx, Karl, 12
Masculinity, 89–90
Mass media, 34, 48, 95, 145, 167–68, 171, 180, 219
Matsuda, Seiko, 21, 34–35, 69–70, 74, 78, 167–203 *passim,* 240, 260–61; Americanization, 260; autobiographical writing, 185–93 *passim;* cute, 74; early career, 172–75; *mamadoru* (mom idol), 174, 177; marriage, 174, 177, 182–86 *passim;* mother, 178–79; New York, 196–98, 200, 202n11; performance, 193–96 *passim,* 198–200; tabloids, 175–80; womanhood, 182–83
Matsuri, 164–65
Mead, Margaret, 56
Middle class, 22, 37, 94, 234, 264–65
Mills, C. Wright, 36
Miyadai, Shinji, 44–45, 105
Miyazaki, Tsutomu, 211
Modernity, 125, 251
Moeran, Brian, 26n2
Moga, 99
Momoco (magazine), 69, 72, 180
Motherhood, 134, 178. *See also Ryōsai kenbo*

Nakajima, Azusa, 211–12

Nakamori, Aiko, 52, 210
National Police Agency, 73
Nelson, John, 32–34, 113
New Industrial Economies (NIEs), 232–34
New Kids on the Block, 173
Nihonjinron, 26
Noda, Yoshiharu, 133–35
Noh, 28
Noonan, William, 10*n*2
Nori-P, *see* Sakai, Noriko
North America, 9, 51, 132, 202
Nostalgia, 82
NTT, 1

Ogawa, Hiroshi, 37
Ogura, Chikako, 37, 169–70, 183–85
Okada, Toshio, 206
Omote/ura, 26
Onna-kotoba, 104. *See also under* Gender
Onna no jidai, 88
Onnarashisa, 99–100, 104
Onyanko Club (Kitten Club), 6, 214–16
Oscar Promotion, Inc., 132–33
Otaku, 7, 22, 205–31 *passim*; *Le Otaku: France otaku-jijō* (book), 206; *manga otaku*, 206–7; *Otaku: les enfants du virtuel* (book), 206; *Otaku nyūmon* (Introduction to otakuology), 206; *otaku-zoku*, 210–11
Ōtsuka, Eiji, 10, 60, 65*n*5, 128–29
Ouen-dan (cheering squads), *see* "cheering" *under* Idol
Oyajigyaru, 99–101

Performance, 27, 29
Popular culture, 18, 31, 45
Pornography, 219–20, 219*n*3
Post-idol, 84, 113, 124, 260

Public opinion, 180
Public Welfare, Ministry of, 159
Puffy, 235
Pure/purity, 3, 76–77, 106, 115–16, 132, 134; *shintō*, 33; *Asian Purity* (song), 235

Rappaport, Roy, 10
Richardson, James, 208
Risutora (restoration), 88
Ritual, 10, 13
Robertson, Jennifer, 18–19, 87
Rosenberger, Nancy, 125
Ryōsai kenbo (good wife, wise mother), 90–91, 95, 96*n*7, 121, 184, 259; against role, 179. *See also* Matsuda, Seiko

Sakai, Noriko, 77, 139–44 *passim*, 240, 244, 248–49; *noropiigo*, 141–42; Nori-P Land, 142; *Nori-P zoku* (Nori-P tribe), 142
Sarariiman (salaryman), 156
School, 93, 104, 117, 162; *gakkō mondai* (school problem), 97; School Uniform Improvement Committee (S.K.I.), 159–62
Schwichtenberg, Cathy, 36
Scott, Adolph, 29*n*4
Seijin, 184
Seishun-jidai, *see* Adolescence
Self, 2–3, 16, 25–28 *passim*, 81, 170–71, 263; *jiko kakuritsu* (establishing the self), 166
Self-framing, 25
Selfhood, *see* Self
Sexy, 89, 105, 132
Shanghai Performance Doll, 238
Shineitai (support squads), *see* Fans; *and under* Idol
Shinjinrui, 61, 64

Shintō, 32–34, 59, 76, 113, 128, 208, 251
Simpson, Amelia, 36
Singleton, John, 28*n*3
Skinship, 69
SMAP, 6, 133, 137
Sony, 187, 238, 253*n*9
South Korea, 235, 239–40, 242, 255–56
Spa!, 2, 52, 145–58 *passim*, 181
Spears, Britney, 4, 266
Spice Girls, 266
Star tanjō (TV program), 6
Subculture, 142. *See also* Youth subculture
Suen, Eric, 243–44
Sukeban, 99–100, 122
Symbolic: capital, 158; competition, 150, 159, 165

Tabloids, 21, 34, 48, 175–80 *passim*
Taishū, 45
Taiwan, 239–40, 255
Takarazuka, 19
Takeuchi, Maria, 2
Taku, Hachirō, 211. *See also* Matsuda, Seiko
Tarento (talents), 2; *keiyaku* (contracts), 47
Tatemae, see Honne/tatemae
Taussig, Michael, 11–12

Teenager, *see* Adolescent
Temple, Shirley, 36, 74
Tokyo, 39–42 *passim*, 102, 183, 185, 189

Uchi/soto, 62
United States, 2, 96, 197, 202, 236, 240
Urban society, 10, 17, 82, 49

Weber, Max, 35
White, Merry, 63–64, 72
White-collar identity, 262–64
Women: employment, 93–95. *See also Ryōsai kenbo*
Womanliness, see *Onnarashisa*

Xuxa, 36

Yamada, Haru, 66*n*7
Yamane, Kazuma, 141
Yano, Christine, 37, 45, 159
Yaohan, 238, 238*n*4
Yellow Cab, 133–34, 133*n*2
Yoshiwara, 127*n*1
Youth: culture, 56–57, 89, 98, 140; market, 30; socialization, 57, 63–65, 87; subculture, 142
Yume (dreams), 264

Zarrili, Phillip, 28–29

Harvard East Asian Monographs
(* out-of-print)

*1. Liang Fang-chung, *The Single-Whip Method of Taxation in China*

*2. Harold C. Hinton, *The Grain Tribute System of China, 1845–1911*

3. Ellsworth C. Carlson, *The Kaiping Mines, 1877–1912*

*4. Chao Kuo-chün, *Agrarian Policies of Mainland China: A Documentary Study, 1949–1956*

*5. Edgar Snow, *Random Notes on Red China, 1936–1945*

*6. Edwin George Beal, Jr., *The Origin of Likin, 1835–1864*

7. Chao Kuo-chün, *Economic Planning and Organization in Mainland China: A Documentary Study, 1949–1957*

*8. John K. Fairbank, *Ch'ing Documents: An Introductory Syllabus*

*9. Helen Yin and Yi-chang Yin, *Economic Statistics of Mainland China, 1949–1957*

*10. Wolfgang Franke, *The Reform and Abolition of the Traditional Chinese Examination System*

11. Albert Feuerwerker and S. Cheng, *Chinese Communist Studies of Modern Chinese History*

12. C. John Stanley, *Late Ch'ing Finance: Hu Kuang-yung as an Innovator*

13. S. M. Meng, *The Tsungli Yamen: Its Organization and Functions*

*14. Ssu-yü Teng, *Historiography of the Taiping Rebellion*

15. Chun-Jo Liu, *Controversies in Modern Chinese Intellectual History: An Analytic Bibliography of Periodical Articles, Mainly of the May Fourth and Post-May Fourth Era*

*16. Edward J. M. Rhoads, *The Chinese Red Army, 1927–1963: An Annotated Bibliography*

17. Andrew J. Nathan, *A History of the China International Famine Relief Commission*

*18. Frank H. H. King (ed.) and Prescott Clarke, *A Research Guide to China-Coast Newspapers, 1822–1911*

19. Ellis Joffe, *Party and Army: Professionalism and Political Control in the Chinese Officer Corps, 1949–1964*

*20. Toshio G. Tsukahira, *Feudal Control in Tokugawa Japan: The Sankin Kōtai System*

21. Kwang-Ching Liu, ed., *American Missionaries in China: Papers from Harvard Seminars*

22. George Moseley, *A Sino-Soviet Cultural Frontier: The Ili Kazakh Autonomous Chou*

23. Carl F. Nathan, *Plague Prevention and Politics in Manchuria, 1910–1931*

*24. Adrian Arthur Bennett, *John Fryer: The Introduction of Western Science and Technology into Nineteenth-Century China*

25. Donald J. Friedman, *The Road from Isolation: The Campaign of the American Committee for Non-Participation in Japanese Aggression, 1938–1941*

*26. Edward LeFevour, *Western Enterprise in Late Ching China: A Selective Survey of Jardine, Matheson and Company's Operations, 1842–1895*

27. Charles Neuhauser, *Third World Politics: China and the Afro-Asian People's Solidarity Organization, 1957–1967*

28. Kungtu C. Sun, assisted by Ralph W. Huenemann, *The Economic Development of Manchuria in the First Half of the Twentieth Century*

*29. Shahid Javed Burki, *A Study of Chinese Communes, 1965*

30. John Carter Vincent, *The Extraterritorial System in China: Final Phase*

31. Madeleine Chi, *China Diplomacy, 1914–1918*

*32. Clifton Jackson Phillips, *Protestant America and the Pagan World: The First Half Century of the American Board of Commissioners for Foreign Missions, 1810–1860*

33. James Pusey, *Wu Han: Attacking the Present Through the Past*

34. Ying-wan Cheng, *Postal Communication in China and Its Modernization, 1860–1896*

35. Tuvia Blumenthal, *Saving in Postwar Japan*

36. Peter Frost, *The Bakumatsu Currency Crisis*

37. Stephen C. Lockwood, *Augustine Heard and Company, 1858–1862*

38. Robert R. Campbell, *James Duncan Campbell: A Memoir by His Son*

39. Jerome Alan Cohen, ed., *The Dynamics of China's Foreign Relations*

40. V. V. Vishnyakova-Akimova, *Two Years in Revolutionary China, 1925–1927*, trans. Steven L. Levine

*41. Meron Medzini, *French Policy in Japan During the Closing Years of the Tokugawa Regime*

42. Ezra Vogel, Margie Sargent, Vivienne B. Shue, Thomas Jay Mathews, and Deborah S. Davis, *The Cultural Revolution in the Provinces*

*43. Sidney A. Forsythe, *An American Missionary Community in China, 1895–1905*

*44. Benjamin I. Schwartz, ed., *Reflections on the May Fourth Movement.: A Symposium*

*45. Ching Young Choe, *The Rule of the Taewŏngun, 1864–1873: Restoration in Yi Korea*

46. W. P. J. Hall, *A Bibliographical Guide to Japanese Research on the Chinese Economy, 1958–1970*

47. Jack J. Gerson, *Horatio Nelson Lay and Sino-British Relations, 1854–1864*

48. Paul Richard Bohr, *Famine and the Missionary: Timothy Richard as Relief Administrator and Advocate of National Reform*

49. Endymion Wilkinson, *The History of Imperial China: A Research Guide*

50. Britten Dean, *China and Great Britain: The Diplomacy of Commercial Relations, 1860–1864*

51. Ellsworth C. Carlson, *The Foochow Missionaries, 1847–1880*

52. Yeh-chien Wang, *An Estimate of the Land-Tax Collection in China, 1753 and 1908*

53. Richard M. Pfeffer, *Understanding Business Contracts in China, 1949–1963*

54. Han-sheng Chuan and Richard Kraus, *Mid-Ching Rice Markets and Trade: An Essay in Price History*

55. Ranbir Vohra, *Lao She and the Chinese Revolution*

56. Liang-lin Hsiao, *China's Foreign Trade Statistics, 1864–1949*

*57. Lee-hsia Hsu Ting, *Government Control of the Press in Modern China, 1900–1949*

58. Edward W. Wagner, *The Literati Purges: Political Conflict in Early Yi Korea*

*59. Joungwon A. Kim, *Divided Korea: The Politics of Development, 1945–1972*

*60. Noriko Kamachi, John K. Fairbank, and Chūzō Ichiko, *Japanese Studies of Modern China Since 1953: A Bibliographical Guide to Historical and Social-Science Research on the Nineteenth and Twentieth Centuries, Supplementary Volume for 1953–1969*

61. Donald A. Gibbs and Yun-chen Li, *A Bibliography of Studies and Translations of Modern Chinese Literature, 1918–1942*

62. Robert H. Silin, *Leadership and Values: The Organization of Large-Scale Taiwanese Enterprises*

63. David Pong, *A Critical Guide to the Kwangtung Provincial Archives Deposited at the Public Record Office of London*

*64. Fred W. Drake, *China Charts the World: Hsu Chi-yü and His Geography of 1848*

*65. William A. Brown and Urgrunge Onon, trans. and annots., *History of the Mongolian People's Republic*

66. Edward L. Farmer, *Early Ming Government: The Evolution of Dual Capitals*

Harvard East Asian Monographs

*67. Ralph C. Croizier, *Koxinga and Chinese Nationalism: History, Myth, and the Hero*

*68. William J. Tyler, trans., *The Psychological World of Natsume Sōseki*, by Doi Takeo

69. Eric Widmer, *The Russian Ecclesiastical Mission in Peking During the Eighteenth Century*

*70. Charlton M. Lewis, *Prologue to the Chinese Revolution: The Transformation of Ideas and Institutions in Hunan Province, 1891–1907*

71. Preston Torbert, *The Ching Imperial Household Department: A Study of Its Organization and Principal Functions, 1662–1796*

72. Paul A. Cohen and John E. Schrecker, eds., *Reform in Nineteenth-Century China*

73. Jon Sigurdson, *Rural Industrialism in China*

74. Kang Chao, *The Development of Cotton Textile Production in China*

75. Valentin Rabe, *The Home Base of American China Missions, 1880–1920*

*76. Sarasin Viraphol, *Tribute and Profit: Sino-Siamese Trade, 1652–1853*

77. Ch'i-ch'ing Hsiao, *The Military Establishment of the Yuan Dynasty*

78. Meishi Tsai, *Contemporary Chinese Novels and Short Stories, 1949–1974: An Annotated Bibliography*

*79. Wellington K. K. Chan, *Merchants, Mandarins and Modern Enterprise in Late Ching China*

80. Endymion Wilkinson, *Landlord and Labor in Late Imperial China: Case Studies from Shandong by Jing Su and Luo Lun*

*81. Barry Keenan, *The Dewey Experiment in China: Educational Reform and Political Power in the Early Republic*

*82. George A. Hayden, *Crime and Punishment in Medieval Chinese Drama: Three Judge Pao Plays*

*83. Sang-Chul Suh, *Growth and Structural Changes in the Korean Economy, 1910–1940*

84. J. W. Dower, *Empire and Aftermath: Yoshida Shigeru and the Japanese Experience, 1878–1954*

85. Martin Collcutt, *Five Mountains: The Rinzai Zen Monastic Institution in Medieval Japan*

86. Kwang Suk Kim and Michael Roemer, *Growth and Structural Transformation*

87. Anne O. Krueger, *The Developmental Role of the Foreign Sector and Aid*

*88. Edwin S. Mills and Byung-Nak Song, *Urbanization and Urban Problems*

89. Sung Hwan Ban, Pal Yong Moon, and Dwight H. Perkins, *Rural Development*

*90. Noel F. McGinn, Donald R. Snodgrass, Yung Bong Kim, Shin-Bok Kim, and Quee-Young Kim, *Education and Development in Korea*

Harvard East Asian Monographs

91. Leroy P. Jones and Il SaKong, *Government, Business, and Entrepreneurship in Economic Development: The Korean Case*

92. Edward S. Mason, Dwight H. Perkins, Kwang Suk Kim, David C. Cole, Mahn Je Kim et al., *The Economic and Social Modernization of the Republic of Korea*

93. Robert Repetto, Tai Hwan Kwon, Son-Ung Kim, Dae Young Kim, John E. Sloboda, and Peter J. Donaldson, *Economic Development, Population Policy, and Demographic Transition in the Republic of Korea*

94. Parks M. Coble, Jr., *The Shanghai Capitalists and the Nationalist Government, 1927–1937*

95. Noriko Kamachi, *Reform in China: Huang Tsun-hsien and the Japanese Model*

96. Richard Wich, *Sino-Soviet Crisis Politics: A Study of Political Change and Communication*

97. Lillian M. Li, *China's Silk Trade: Traditional Industry in the Modern World, 1842–1937*

98. R. David Arkush, *Fei Xiaotong and Sociology in Revolutionary China*

*99. Kenneth Alan Grossberg, *Japan's Renaissance: The Politics of the Muromachi Bakufu*

100. James Reeve Pusey, *China and Charles Darwin*

101. Hoyt Cleveland Tillman, *Utilitarian Confucianism: Chen Liang's Challenge to Chu Hsi*

102. Thomas A. Stanley, *Ōsugi Sakae, Anarchist in Taishō Japan: The Creativity of the Ego*

103. Jonathan K. Ocko, *Bureaucratic Reform in Provincial China: Ting Jih-ch'ang in Restoration Kiangsu, 1867–1870*

104. James Reed, *The Missionary Mind and American East Asia Policy, 1911–1915*

105. Neil L. Waters, *Japan's Local Pragmatists: The Transition from Bakumatsu to Meiji in the Kawasaki Region*

106. David C. Cole and Yung Chul Park, *Financial Development in Korea, 1945–1978*

107. Roy Bahl, Chuk Kyo Kim, and Chong Kee Park, *Public Finances During the Korean Modernization Process*

108. William D. Wray, *Mitsubishi and the N.Y.K, 1870–1914: Business Strategy in the Japanese Shipping Industry*

109. Ralph William Huenemann, *The Dragon and the Iron Horse: The Economics of Railroads in China, 1876–1937*

110. Benjamin A. Elman, *From Philosophy to Philology: Intellectual and Social Aspects of Change in Late Imperial China*

111. Jane Kate Leonard, *Wei Yüan and China's Rediscovery of the Maritime World*

Harvard East Asian Monographs

112. Luke S. K. Kwong, *A Mosaic of the Hundred Days:. Personalities, Politics, and Ideas of 1898*

113. John E. Wills, Jr., *Embassies and Illusions: Dutch and Portuguese Envoys to K'ang-hsi, 1666–1687*

114. Joshua A. Fogel, *Politics and Sinology: The Case of Naitō Konan (1866–1934)*

*115. Jeffrey C. Kinkley, ed., *After Mao: Chinese Literature and Society, 1978–1981*

116. C. Andrew Gerstle, *Circles of Fantasy: Convention in the Plays of Chikamatsu*

117. Andrew Gordon, *The Evolution of Labor Relations in Japan: Heavy Industry, 1853–1955*

*118. Daniel K. Gardner, *Chu Hsi and the "Ta Hsueh": Neo-Confucian Reflection on the Confucian Canon*

119. Christine Guth Kanda, *Shinzō: Hachiman Imagery and Its Development*

*120. Robert Borgen, *Sugawara no Michizane and the Early Heian Court*

121. Chang-tai Hung, *Going to the People: Chinese Intellectual and Folk Literature, 1918–1937*

*122. Michael A. Cusumano, *The Japanese Automobile Industry: Technology and Management at Nissan and Toyota*

123. Richard von Glahn, *The Country of Streams and Grottoes: Expansion, Settlement, and the Civilizing of the Sichuan Frontier in Song Times*

124. Steven D. Carter, *The Road to Komatsubara: A Classical Reading of the Renga Hyakuin*

125. Katherine F. Bruner, John K. Fairbank, and Richard T. Smith, *Entering China's Service: Robert Hart's Journals, 1854–1863*

126. Bob Tadashi Wakabayashi, *Anti-Foreignism and Western Learning in Early-Modern Japan: The "New Theses" of 1825*

127. Atsuko Hirai, *Individualism and Socialism: The Life and Thought of Kawai Eijirō (1891–1944)*

128. Ellen Widmer, *The Margins of Utopia: "Shui-hu hou-chuan" and the Literature of Ming Loyalism*

129. R. Kent Guy, *The Emperor's Four Treasuries: Scholars and the State in the Late Chien-lung Era*

130. Peter C. Perdue, *Exhausting the Earth: State and Peasant in Hunan, 1500–1850*

131. Susan Chan Egan, *A Latterday Confucian: Reminiscences of William Hung (1893–1980)*

132. James T. C. Liu, *China Turning Inward: Intellectual-Political Changes in the Early Twelfth Century*

133. Paul A. Cohen, *Between Tradition and Modernity: Wang T'ao and Reform in Late Ching China*

134. Kate Wildman Nakai, *Shogunal Politics: Arai Hakuseki and the Premises of Tokugawa Rule*

135. Parks M. Coble, *Facing Japan: Chinese Politics and Japanese Imperialism, 1931–1937*

136. Jon L. Saari, *Legacies of Childhood: Growing Up Chinese in a Time of Crisis, 1890–1920*

137. Susan Downing Videen, *Tales of Heichū*

138. Heinz Morioka and Miyoko Sasaki, *Rakugo: The Popular Narrative Art of Japan*

139. Joshua A. Fogel, *Nakae Ushikichi in China: The Mourning of Spirit*

140. Alexander Barton Woodside, *Vietnam and the Chinese Model.: A Comparative Study of Vietnamese and Chinese Government in the First Half of the Nineteenth Century*

141. George Elision, *Deus Destroyed: The Image of Christianity in Early Modern Japan*

142. William D. Wray, ed., *Managing Industrial Enterprise: Cases from Japan's Prewar Experience*

143. T'ung-tsu Ch'ü, *Local Government in China Under the Ching*

144. Marie Anchordoguy, *Computers, Inc.: Japan's Challenge to IBM*

145. Barbara Molony, *Technology and Investment: The Prewar Japanese Chemical Industry*

146. Mary Elizabeth Berry, *Hideyoshi*

147. Laura E. Hein, *Fueling Growth: The Energy Revolution and Economic Policy in Postwar Japan*

148. Wen-hsin Yeh, *The Alienated Academy: Culture and Politics in Republican China, 1919–1937*

149. Dru C. Gladney, *Muslim Chinese: Ethnic Nationalism in the People's Republic*

150. Merle Goldman and Paul A. Cohen, eds., *Ideas Across Cultures: Essays on Chinese Thought in Honor of Benjamin L Schwartz*

151. James M. Polachek, *The Inner Opium War*

152. Gail Lee Bernstein, *Japanese Marxist: A Portrait of Kawakami Hajime, 1879–1946*

153. Lloyd E. Eastman, *The Abortive Revolution: China Under Nationalist Rule, 1927–1937*

154. Mark Mason, *American Multinationals and Japan: The Political Economy of Japanese Capital Controls, 1899–1980*

155. Richard J. Smith, John K. Fairbank, and Katherine F. Bruner, *Robert Hart and China's Early Modernization: His Journals, 1863–1866*

156. George J. Tanabe, Jr., *Myōe the Dreamkeeper: Fantasy and Knowledge in Kamakura Buddhism*

157. William Wayne Farris, *Heavenly Warriors: The Evolution of Japan's Military, 500–1300*

Harvard East Asian Monographs

158. Yu-ming Shaw, *An American Missionary in China: John Leighton Stuart and Chinese-American Relations*

159. James B. Palais, *Politics and Policy in Traditional Korea*

160. Douglas Reynolds, *China, 1898–1912: The Xinzheng Revolution and Japan*

161. Roger R. Thompson, *China's Local Councils in the Age of Constitutional Reform, 1898–1911*

162. William Johnston, *The Modern Epidemic: History of Tuberculosis in Japan*

163. Constantine Nomikos Vaporis, *Breaking Barriers: Travel and the State in Early Modern Japan*

164. Irmela Hijiya-Kirschnereit, *Rituals of Self-Revelation: Shishōsetsu as Literary Genre and Socio-Cultural Phenomenon*

165. James C. Baxter, *The Meiji Unification Through the Lens of Ishikawa Prefecture*

166. Thomas R. H. Havens, *Architects of Affluence: The Tsutsumi Family and the Seibu-Saison Enterprises in Twentieth-Century Japan*

167. Anthony Hood Chambers, *The Secret Window: Ideal Worlds in Tanizaki's Fiction*

168. Steven J. Ericson, *The Sound of the Whistle: Railroads and the State in Meiji Japan*

169. Andrew Edmund Goble, *Kenmu: Go-Daigo's Revolution*

170. Denise Potrzeba Lett, *In Pursuit of Status: The Making of South Korea's "New" Urban Middle Class*

171. Mimi Hall Yiengpruksawan, *Hiraizumi: Buddhist Art and Regional Politics in Twelfth-Century Japan*

172. Charles Shirō Inouye, *The Similitude of Blossoms: A Critical Biography of Izumi Kyōka (1873–1939), Japanese Novelist and Playwright*

173. Aviad E. Raz, *Riding the Black Ship: Japan and Tokyo Disneyland*

174. Deborah J. Milly, *Poverty, Equality, and Growth: The Politics of Economic Need in Postwar Japan*

175. See Heng Teow, *Japan's Cultural Policy Toward China, 1918–1931: A Comparative Perspective*

176. Michael A. Fuller, *An Introduction to Literary Chinese*

177. Frederick R. Dickinson, *War and National Reinvention: Japan in the Great War, 1914–1919*

178. John Solt, *Shredding the Tapestry of Meaning: The Poetry and Poetics of Kitasono Katue (1902–1978)*

179. Edward Pratt, *Japan's Protoindustrial Elite: The Economic Foundations of the Gōnō*

180. Atsuko Sakaki, *Recontextualizing Texts: Narrative Performance in Modern Japanese Fiction*

181. Soon-Won Park, *Colonial Industrialization and Labor in Korea: The Onoda Cement Factory*

182. JaHyun Kim Haboush and Martina Deuchler, *Culture and the State in Late Chosŏn Korea*

183. John W. Chaffee, *Branches of Heaven: A History of the Imperial Clan of Sung China*

184. Gi-Wook Shin and Michael Robinson, eds., *Colonial Modernity in Korea*

185. Nam-lin Hur, *Prayer and Play in Late Tokugawa Japan: Asakusa Sensōji and Edo Society*

186. Kristin Stapleton, *Civilizing Chengdu: Chinese Urban Reform, 1895–1937*

187. Hyung Il Pai, *Constructing "Korean" Origins: A Critical Review of Archaeology, Historiography, and Racial Myth in Korean State-Formation Theories*

188. Brian D. Ruppert, *Jewel in the Ashes: Buddha Relics and Power in Early Medieval Japan*

189. Susan Daruvala, *Zhou Zuoren and an Alternative Chinese Response to Modernity*

190. James Z. Lee, *The Political Economy of a Frontier: Southwest China, 1250–1850*

191. Kerry Smith, *A Time of Crisis: Japan, the Great Depression, and Rural Revitalization*

192. Michael Lewis, *Becoming Apart: National Power and Local Politics in Toyama, 1868–1945*

193. William C. Kirby, Man-houng Lin, James Chin Shih, and David A. Pietz, eds., *State and Economy in Republican China: A Handbook for Scholars*

194. Timothy S. George, *Minamata: Pollution and the Struggle for Democracy in Postwar Japan*

195. Billy K. L. So, *Prosperity, Region, and Institutions in Maritime China: The South Fukien Pattern, 946–1368*

196. Yoshihisa Tak Matsusaka, *The Making of Japanese Manchuria, 1904–1932*

197. Maram Epstein, *Competing Discourses: Orthodoxy, Authenticity, and Engendered Meanings in Late Imperial Chinese Fiction*

198. Curtis J. Milhaupt, J. Mark Ramseyer, and Michael K. Young, eds. and comps., *Japanese Law in Context: Readings in Society, the Economy, and Politics*

199. Haruo Iguchi, *Unfinished Business: Ayukawa Yoshisuke and U.S.-Japan Relations, 1937–1952*

200. Scott Pearce, Audrey Spiro, and Patricia Ebrey, *Culture and Power in the Reconstitution of the Chinese Realm, 200–600*

201. Terry Kawashima, *Writing Margins: The Textual Construction of Gender in Heian and Kamakura Japan*

202. Martin W. Huang, *Desire and Fictional Narrative in Late Imperial China*

203. Robert S. Ross and Jiang Changbin, eds., *Re-examining the Cold War: U.S.-China Diplomacy, 1954–1973*

Harvard East Asian Monographs

204. Guanhua Wang, *In Search of Justice: The 1905–1906 Chinese Anti-American Boycott*

205. David Schaberg, *A Patterned Past: Form and Thought in Early Chinese Historiography*

206. Christine Yano, *Tears of Longing: Nostalgia and the Nation in Japanese Popular Song*

207. Milena Doleželová-Velingerová and Oldřich Král, with Graham Sanders, eds., *The Appropriation of Cultural Capital: China's May Fourth Project*

208. Robert N. Huey, *The Making of 'Shinkokinshū'*

209. Lee Butler, *Emperor and Aristocracy in Japan, 1467–1680: Resilience and Renewal*

210. Suzanne Ogden, *Inklings of Democracy in China*

211. Kenneth J. Ruoff, *The People's Emperor: Democracy and the Japanese Monarchy, 1945–1995*

212. Haun Saussy, *Great Walls of Discourse and Other Adventures in Cultural China*

213. Aviad E. Raz, *Emotions at Work: Normative Control, Organizations, and Culture in Japan and America*

214. Rebecca E. Karl and Peter Zarrow, eds., *Rethinking the 1898 Reform Period: Political and Cultural Change in Late Qing China*

215. Kevin O'Rourke, *The Book of Korean Shijo*

216. Ezra F. Vogel, ed., *The Golden Age of the U.S.-China-Japan Triangle, 1972–1989*

217. Thomas A Wilson, ed., *On Sacred Grounds: Culture, Society, Politics, and the Formation of the Cult of Confucius*

218. Donald S. Sutton, *Steps of Perfection: Exorcistic Performers and Chinese Religion in Twentieth-Century Taiwan*

219. Daqing Yang, *Technology of Empire: Telecommunications and Japanese Expansion, 1895–1945*

220. Qianshen Bai, *Fu Shan's World: The Transformation of Chinese Calligraphy in the Seventeenth Century*

221. Paul Jakov Smith and Richard von Glahn, eds., *The Song-Yuan-Ming Transition in Chinese History*

222. Rania Huntington, *Alien Kind: Foxes and Late Imperial Chinese Narrative*

223. Jordan Sand, *House and Home in Modern Japan: Architecture, Domestic Space, and Bourgeois Culture, 1880–1930*

224. Karl Gerth, *China Made: Consumer Culture and the Creation of the Nation*

225. Xiaoshan Yang, *Metamorphosis of the Private Sphere: Gardens and Objects in Tang-Song Poetry*

226. Barbara Mittler, *A Newspaper for China? Power, Identity, and Change in Shanghai's News Media, 1872–1912*

Harvard East Asian Monographs

227. Joyce A. Madancy, *The Troublesome Legacy of Commissioner Lin: The Opium Trade and Opium Suppression in Fujian Province, 1820s to 1920s*

228. John Makeham, *Transmitters and Creators: Chinese Commentators and Commentaries on the Analects*

229. Elisabeth Köll, *From Cotton Mill to Business Empire: The Emergence of Regional Enterprises in Modern China*

230. Emma Teng, *Taiwan's Imagined Geography: Chinese Colonial Travel Writing and Pictures, 1683–1895*

231. Wilt Idema and Beata Grant, *The Red Brush: Writing Women of Imperial China*

232. Eric C. Rath, *The Ethos of Noh: Actors and Their Art*

233. Elizabeth J. Remick, *Building Local States: China During the Republican and Post-Mao Eras*

234. Lynn Struve, ed., *The Qing Formation in World-Historical Time*

235. D. Max Moerman, *Localizing Paradise: Kumano Pilgrimage and the Religious Landscape of Premodern Japan*

236. Antonia Finnane, *Speaking of Yangzhou: A Chinese City, 1550–1850*

237. Brian Platt, *Burning and Building: Schooling and State Formation in Japan, 1750–1890*

238. Gail Bernstein, Andrew Gordon, and Kate Wildman Nakai, eds., *Public Spheres, Private Lives in Modern Japan, 1600–1950: Essays in Honor of Albert Craig*

239. Wu Hung and Katherine R. Tsiang, *Body and Face in Chinese Visual Culture*

240. Stephen Dodd, *Writing Home: Representations of the Native Place in Modern Japanese Literature*

241. David Anthony Bello, *Opium and the Limits of Empire: Drug Prohibition in the Chinese Interior, 1729–1850*

242. Hosea Hirata, *Discourses of Seduction: History, Evil, Desire, and Modern Japanese Literature*

243. Kyung Moon Hwang, *Beyond Birth: Social Status in the Emergence of Modern Korea*

244. Brian R. Dott, *Identity Reflections: Pilgrimages to Mount Tai in Late Imperial China*

245. Mark McNally, *Proving the Way: Conflict and Practice in the History of Japanese Nativism*

246. Yongping Wu, *A Political Explanation of Economic Growth: State Survival, Bureaucratic Politics, and Private Enterprises in the Making of Taiwan's Economy, 1950-1985*

247. Kyu Hyun Kim, *The Age of Visions and Arguments: Parliamentarianism and the National Public Sphere in Early Meiji Japan*

Harvard East Asian Monographs

248. Zvi Ben-Dor Benite, *The Dao of Muhammad: A Cultural History of Muslims in Late Imperial China*

249. David Der-wei Wang and Shang Wei, eds., *Dynastic Crisis and Cultural Innovation: From the Late Ming to the Late Qing and Beyond*

250. Wilt L. Idema, Wai-yee Li, and Ellen Widmer, eds., *Trauma and Transcendence in Early Qing Literature*

251. Barbara Molony and Kathleen Uno, eds., *Gendering Modern Japanese History*

252. Hiroshi Aoyagi, *Islands of Eight Million Smiles: Idol Performance and Symbolic Production in Contemporary Japan*